# MODERN DECORATIVE ART

*Frontispiece*

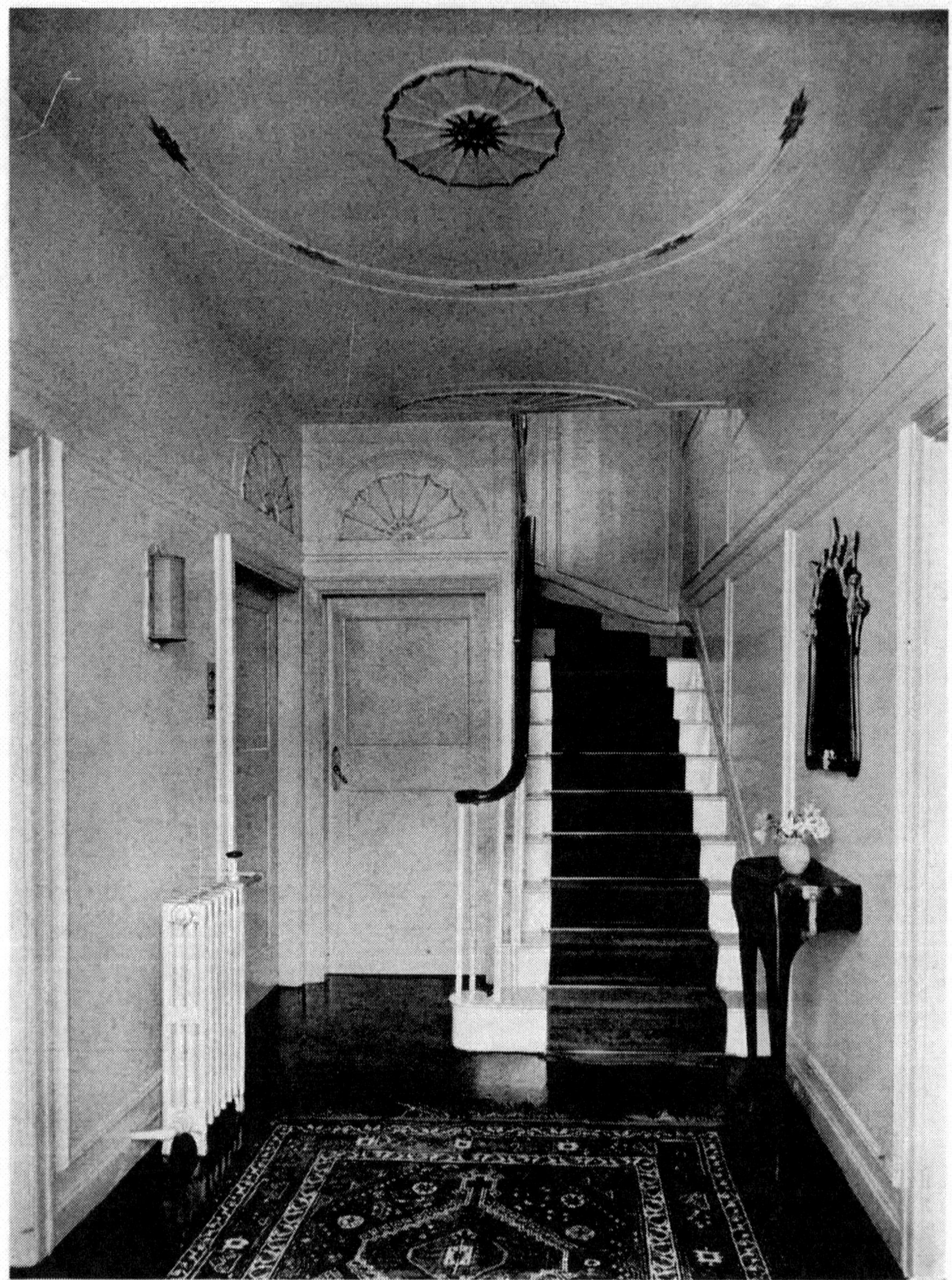

ENTRANCE HALL DESIGNED BY MAURICE ADAMS

# MODERN DECORATIVE ART

A SERIES OF TWO HUNDRED EXAMPLES OF INTERIOR DECORATION, FURNITURE, LIGHTING FITTINGS AND OTHER ORNAMENTAL FEATURES

*By*

MAURICE S. R. ADAMS

*Designer and Craftsman*

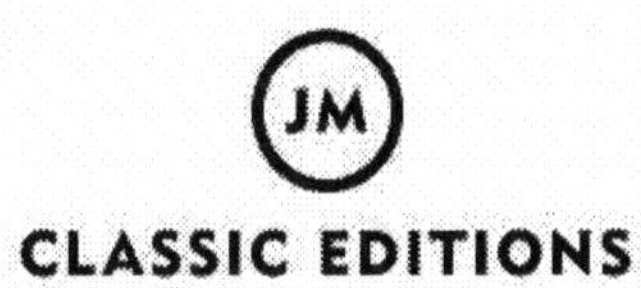

This edition digitally re-mastered and
published by JM Classic Editions © 2007


ISBN 978-1-905217-63-2

# AUTHOR'S FOREWORD

THIS book is the outcome of a quarter-of-a-century's practical study of art and design. The author, as a boy, learnt the rudiments of workshop practice and cabinet-making, while his subsequent architectural training gave him a thorough grounding in the principles and practice of design. Averse to taking anything for granted in these fields, this actual first-hand experience helped to form his later convictions on the reality of artistic and practical limitations.

The chaotic condition of modern art during his student period gave him considerable food for thought. At that time steel frame construction for buildings was being first employed. The nature of this form of construction differs entirely in principle from the older forms upon which all previous types of architecture had been based. For obvious reasons, if only for truth's sake, this difference should find expression in exterior architectural treatment. At that time, however, it was the usual practice of architects to design their building elevations as if no change whatever had taken place in methods of construction. This led to many kinds of absurdities, such as heavy walls of masonry appearing to stand on nothing but sheets of plate glass.

This kind of blunder set him thinking. It seemed obvious that before the subjects of art and design could be mastered, their nature must first be thoroughly understood. It is, therefore, now his invariable rule in preparing designs of any kind to put the subject through a very fine sieve of mental analysis.

As a result of many years' study and experience, he has arrived at mature opinions on art in general and furniture design in particular; and these opinions have been put to a practical test. His definite purpose from the time when he first began designing furniture has been to produce, if possible, a type of furniture definitely an outcome of its own time as well as of contemporary art. The purpose of this book is to place on record these views and ideals of art and furniture design; to illustrate by actual examples how these theories work out in practice, and by these means to arouse a wider and more intelligent interest in the subject of decorative art in general. It is hoped that the book, both in precept and example, will assist in raising the standard of public taste.

*March*, 1930

# CONTENTS

# FIRST CONSIDERATIONS

IN these pages, the precise subject with which we have to deal is home furnishing. The writer has spent the last twenty-five years in the study and practice of his profession and has long made the furnishing of houses as homes his business. Therefore, he speaks from experience with some authority.

In all subjects, however, there should be room for differences of opinion and points of view. Particularly is this the case in all matters relating to questions of art. It will be well, however, straight away to make clear our own point of view and the ideas and ideals upon which this view is formed. We shall endeavour to explain, as clearly as possible, what we understand by artistic furnishing. Otherwise, much that we have to say on the subject may not rightly be understood, and some remarks and suggestions may risk misinterpretation.

We approach our subject with the views, opinions and ideals of an artist. This world of ours we love specially for its beauty. To create in beautiful form is at once our work and joy. To us a thing of beauty is a durable pleasure, an ugly thing always a pain. For us each small detail has its share of importance in any undertaking. In other words, work must be thorough. To give and achieve our best alone will meet our goal. To accomplish is but to realize where we fall short of the ideal; and herein lies the chief incentive to win. We attempt because we must. Ever to strive for perfection, the nearer the approach, the more desirable the aim. No money can buy the reward of even partial success in its achievement.

Therefore, the fundamental basis of our work is to make furnishing really an art. In all respects our work must be the best that is possible.

The underlying purpose of this book is to arouse interest. Actual examples of first-class work, illustrated and described, clearly show what we have done. The richest decorative schemes necessarily cost money, although it by no means follows that large expenditure insures artistic results. People invariably get the furniture they deserve. Without personal cultivated taste or expert guidance large expenditures usually result in work devoid of refinement and perhaps vulgar to boot.

Then there may be those with both money and taste, but lacking sufficient faith in their own judgment, and so avoid acquiring modern furniture. These people buy either antiques or mere reproductions. Personally, I have a great admiration for fine old furniture, but it should be remembered that most of the best old furniture was specially made for some particular room, with a special place assigned to it. In course of time, the old sets of furniture become scattered, so that except for sets of chairs, only odd pieces of old furniture are obtainable. Thus purchasers of antique furniture become "collectors," and rooms so furnished become "collections"—mere assortments of odd pieces of cabinet work. Times and manners have changed since this old work was made and consequently now can scarcely express present requirements or ideas. Historic furniture is frequently purchased, not because of its practical suitability, but on account of its age and old-world charm. Many items essential to present-day needs were not made in former times. Such pieces now required are manufactured and faked to simulate age. To many, the museum atmosphere of old furniture is attractive. No doubt, suitably arranged, old furniture looks extremely well. It must be remembered, however, that genuine historic pieces command very high prices, and by far the larger quantity sold to-day as antique is of modern make. Real antique furniture is suitable for those who have made the subject a special study. Consequently their homes are interesting as the result of this knowledge.

As mentioned above, the best old furniture was specially made as part of a complete scheme. Maurice Adams Ltd. are now doing to-day exactly what the old master craftsmen did in their time. We create rooms in which decoration and furniture form one complete whole. This insures harmony, unity and sense of artistic fitness impossible when furniture is casually purchased without special regard to the particular room for which it is bought. Speaking artistically, satisfactory results are possible only when furniture, carpets, fabrics and decorations are thought relatively to form one complete scheme.

The failure of contemporary furnishing schemes is not due to restricted expenditure, but to want of expert supervision. It is surprising that many people who spend large sums on furnishing and decoration are content to be guided by the chance advice of shop assistants. This duty entails considerable artistic judgment and skill. Men thus gifted are not usually to be met in the ranks of shop-walkers and salesmen.

But the commonest fallacy is to imagine that, without study or experience, one can artistically furnish and decorate without trained help. Many people, whether artistically inclined or not, are too apt to consider themselves good judges in all matters of furnishing and decoration. "I know exactly what I want," too frequently is the prelude to many an excellent room being spoiled and made unsatisfactory.

Even those who have had the advantage of a first-class architect to design their house, take the whole matter of furnishing and decoration into their own hands. We have experienced many instances of being asked to advise in the furnishing, where the owner has carried out his own decorations. It is usually impossible to make the furnishing an artistic success under such conditions. One usually finds the walls covered with impossible papers and flat paintwork devoid of merit or interest. The ordinary local decorator has neither the knowledge nor skill to insure artistic harmony without guidance.

We are not advocating that, having called in the expert, the entire matter of decoration and furnishing should be left to him. The expert's job rather should be to carry out the requirements of his client. His business should be to put those requirements and ideas into artistic and practical shape and create unity out of the several parts of the scheme.

It is a mistake to assume that fine furnishing is easy enough when one is not troubled about expense, whereas the result depends upon intuitive judgment.

It may be accepted at once that a designer who cannot create interest and charm with the very simplest and least expensive materials does not know his job, and certainly is not a capable artist. Rich, luxurious effects in furnishing cannot be obtained without corresponding outlay, but solid comfort and an atmosphere of befitting charm and good taste should be possible even where expenditure is restricted by a minimum. Failure must inevitably result when rich, ambitious effects are attempted without good taste and proper execution. When funds are limited few things are possible, nevertheless each article must be the very best one can afford. If the work be sincere and free from shams and incongruities, artistic success will not be far off.

The question may be asked, "What should be the style of present-day furniture and decorations"?

If the meaning of art were more universally understood, there would be less confusion of thought on this subject than commonly exists. The word "art" is currently misapplied to almost everything from cooking to flying. In fact, any work requiring more than ordinary skill is claimed to be an "art." It has also been commonly understood that the term "artist" implies a man who paints pictures. We must, therefore, make clear our own meaning of the term "art," otherwise our remarks will be misunderstood.

We limit the word "art" to creative work carried out in accord with natural laws. We apply the term "artist" to the man having a flair for beauty in all its forms, whether in poetry, literature, painting, music, architecture, sculpture or dancing as well as acting. An artist is in tune with nature. To him beauty of form, colour and texture is all important, and he will demand that everything made by man be identified with beautiful form and so replete in charm.

Whether it be the lettering on a book cover, the design of a gas fire, the making of a table spoon, an artist will require these things to be beautifully shaped and made pleasing to the eye. Artistic sensibility should not be confused with executive skill. An artist is not less an artist because he can neither paint nor draw. Indeed first-class artists may be found to-day in the ranks of photographers.

Our definition of "art" precludes its use to all reproduction work, designs limited to "period" styles which are really not designs so much as the application of old forms to new requirements. Period furnishing may please us but it is not "art." Copying is not "art." The almost identical reproduction of old-world buildings is not "art" nor "architecture." These things have or should have their own descriptive title, but none are included within our comprehension of the term "Art."

It follows that the art of to-day must be the creation of to-day. To design a room and make it a work of art it cannot be the outcome of yesterday. The art of yesterday does not cease to be art to-day, but it remains the art of the previous and can never be an output of to-day's art. We may be very clever at designing in old styles, but as such we are merely adaptors and copyists. No man devoid of creative gifts can produce a work of contemporary art.

Vitalized art is, therefore, the product of to-day. To-day's style is the expression of contemporary life and circumstances. For the production of art we must embody the requirements of the present, using the methods of to-day by giving available materials natural and artistic expression.

Applying these principles to furniture, we find that in order to be the product of art, furniture must belong to its own day. Copies and replicas are not living works of art. In these productions we miss art itself in a mere reflection of the art of former days. The very essence of art is vitality.

Moreover, we have in use to-day materials and processes of manufacture hitherto unknown and impossible. Our requirements to-day, our manner of living and manner of thinking differ from those of any former age. These circumstances must find expression in current art—otherwise we have no art. Artistic furniture of to-day must be the product and expression of our time, otherwise it so far fails to justify itself.

Maurice Adams Ltd. were first among living furniture designers to further these principles. Consequently our work has had considerable influence on modern design in general. Our later designs are made possible only by modern processes of manufacture. Nevertheless our primary aim was not restricted by originality. This furniture expresses in beautiful form current requirements, manufacturing processes and material.

It is rather difficult to make clear our meaning without going deeply into the whole basis of art, and that would be beyond the scope of this book. We will, however, endeavour to touch upon factors essential in art production. First must be found sincerity of purpose; nothing must appear to be other than what it is. A table, for instance, must look like a table. A cottage chair must not look as if it belonged to a palace. Material must present a natural appearance. Wood furniture must look as if made of wood. The form of any design will be governed by the nature of the material with which it is to be constructed. A design intended for marble, for instance, should not be used for wood. Unity is essential. Each design must have a single idea underlying its conception. The several parts of a design must all be in perfect harmony.

The term "style" relates to unity of expression, Harmony of parts throughout a design produces an effect of marked character which warrants the term "style."

Design, as we have insisted, must accord with the nature of the stuff employed. Natural characteristics of the material utilised should be emphasized in the design. A design adapted to oak is not suitable for walnut.

In former times evolution of design was gradual. Design followed and expressed the slow yet continual change in taste and in the manner of living of its creators and patrons. Furniture style was a matter of tradition. A total absence of modern facilities made this inevitable. Craftsmen worked to the forms and details in which they had been trained. A conservatism natural to those who take pride in fine workmanship produces a marked distaste for novelty. A choice of "style," as now understood, was aforetime a thing unknown.

The quite recent developments in the evolution of the cinema, the radio and the motor-car, etc., have brought to everyone a much wider view of life. The old conceptions of life have changed. Now we live differently, and think differently. Modern man demands more freedom. He likes to think things out for himself and to live his own life in his own way freed from all the many seemingly quite silly restrictions and narrow views of past generations. He intends no sneer at the past, but he does want to take full advantage of the wider life that recent inventions and discoveries have brought to him. This outlook is surely healthy. For ourselves we are in entire agreement with it.

Under these advancing conditions, reproductions of old furniture are obviously out of accord. We want our furniture to express ourselves and our ideas, and not the notions of a past age. We admire tremendously the work of the old designers, but we have no ambition, no creative ability, no artistic feeling if we consent merely to repeating the past instead of creating furniture ourselves as good as, yea better perhaps than, our forefathers. The fact is that thinking people of to-day are fed up with the fake culture incidental to so-called "period" furnishing.

The need to-day, therefore, is for modern furniture, but it must be remembered that most people furnish their home once and for all. Any furniture they buy they will probably have to live with for many years, if not for the rest of their time. Therefore, when buying furniture, remember that novelty in style is pleasing only while it is new. Novelty is its sole attraction. The Continent has during recent years embodied novel ideas in furniture. This type of thing is at the back of all the "modern" furniture that English house furnishers are vainly endeavouring to popularise. Unusual forms carried out in highly decorative materials may at first sight appear up-to-date and so attractive. Whereas, in practically all this work, novelty is the sole appeal. Very little of it is beautiful. Mostly it is definitely ugly; being devoid of any relationship with art in any form. It is the product of impudent incompetence. As an essay or passing fad, some of this work is not devoid of interest. The bare idea is insufferable—to live for any length of time in the restless and semi-exotic atmosphere produced by such exotic furniture.

The first Maurice Adams furniture followed very closely eighteenth century models. These were not copies but new productions imbued with the old atmosphere. Gradually, as we began to think things out personally, slight changes were introduced. The first decided advance was the production of our "King George" dressing table. This was selected by the Art Committee and exhibited at the Palace of Arts, Wembley. The Queen Mary low dressing-table soon followed, and was exhibited at Olympia, 1925, when it created a marked impression on the public. These low dressing-tables were the very first ever made in England. Their subsequent influence on English furniture design is witnessed by the fact that at Olympia, 1928, practically every stand, featuring bedroom furniture, included a low type of wing-mirrored dressing-table. Many of these designs quite obviously were based on the Maurice Adams models.

The next step was the production of the Alexandra dressing-table (page 127), followed by the Alexandra bed. The latter design has had greater influence upon our subsequent designs than any other. The concave curve forming part of this particular design was now introduced into the top of the Alexandra chest, and instead of a moulded edge to top being returned at the sides of top in the usual way this moulding was returned down the front corners, thus constituting a decided advance in design.

The Alexandra chest led up to the Connaught series (pages 113, 134-136, 145). These have a raised edge at the top of the sides. The same raised edge used in connection with elliptically fronted tables developed the Grosvenor series (pages 28, 42, 43, 46-48, 54, 67-73, 75-77, 86, 87, 94, 95, 117, 118, 121-123, 131, 132, 143, 147, 148, 155).

The sequence of our designs has been in close association with the use of burr walnut. For effective display richly figured wood veneer must be used over wide unbroken surfaces. To emphasize and extend this principle, mouldings of every kind became gradually eliminated, and free curved surfaces were used wherever possible. Sharp corners gave place to rounded forms so that the main faces blend one into the other without the abruptness of a sharp angle. Our later productions have a marked feeling of rhythm. Beauty of line and form exactly proportioned find expression by thus employing the richest and most gloriously figured walnut procurable. The result arises from careful selection. Hence the splendid quality insured.

The curved unbroken surfaces in our later designs were made possible only by the use of laminated mahogany. The evolution of these designs has been brought about by utilising contemporary methods of construction and material in its modern form. For example, ten or fifteen years ago there was only one known way to construct a door, viz., by means of a solid wood frame enclosing a panel of thin wood. The joint between the frame and panel was either moulded solid on the frame or covered with an applied moulding. The construction of a Maurice Adams' door is entirely different. There is neither frame nor panel, but the door is formed out of a single board of laminated mahogany which is not ply-wood, but is formed with quarter-inch strips of mahogany glued face to face across the thickness of the board, under enormous hydraulic pressure. The grain of the wood is thus at right angles with the face of the board, insuring the maximum resistance to warping and buckling. Doors thus constructed need no frame, moreover, the entire surface may be covered with figured veneer without any risk whatever of either cracking or splitting. This method of construction is distinctly so revolutionary that it has changed the character of all furniture designing.

We have indicated how Maurice Adams' furniture has evolved from eighteenth century models guided by the principles and standards of art outlined above. This furniture is distinctly the product of its own time, the needs of which it is purposed to fulfill and express. No sudden break with the past was made. On the contrary full advantage was taken of the experience and guidance of the best designers of former days. Our work is in full sympathy with eighteenth century furniture out of which it has been evolved. It is our sincerest wish that this furniture, in the creation of which we had keen enjoyment, will bring pleasure also not only to its immediate purchasers but to those into whose hands it must inevitably pass in the years to come, when our work is finished, leaving to others to carry on the enterprise we have commenced; to go forward in their own day as we have endeavoured to do during the present.

# FIRST CONSIDERATIONS

This book deals primarily with figured walnut, and embodies a form of decoration in keeping with that material. This is because our own personal preference for figured walnut has led to its adoption by our clients. We do not wish it to be inferred that we only work in one material. No two woods have quite the same characteristics, and designs made specially for burr walnut are not suitable for other woods unless somewhat similar in figure. We have several types of design for use with mahogany and other woods. In the case of a yacht furnished by us (page 221 *et seq.*), the staterooms have distinctive woods—walnut, coromandel, bubinga maidou, flame mahogany and Bombay rosewood. Recently we have carried out various rooms in lacquer and painted furniture also. Considerable possibilities in this direction present themselves for clients having a flair for the unusual. Interesting furniture may be designed with the use of rare and uncommon woods. Furniture may also be gilded with unobtrusive and artistic results. Shagreen, skin and other like materials afford possibilities, but demand exceptional judgment in their use.

It is, however, with the use of familiar materials we propose to deal in these pages.

# THE FURNITURE

TWO matters have usually to be considered prior to the ultimate selection of furniture. The first is cost, and the second, the nature and aspect of the rooms to be furnished. It is possible to produce artistic and pleasing results in furnishing where outlay is at a minimum. In these pages, however, we propose to deal primarily with furnishing where the desired results are not unduly hampered by considerations of first cost. Ostentatious display is opposed to the spirit of art, therefore, lavish expenditure is not here advocated. Our intention, however, is to indicate possibilities by giving actual examples. Naturally some of our clients are very wealthy, but in these servantless days people of ample but moderate means wisely prefer to furnish and decorate a few rooms thoroughly well and possess a few good pieces of furniture, rather than to spread their outlay on furnishing indifferently more apartments than they actually propose to use.

The best home is where the house itself, its decorations and its furniture are designed together relatively as a whole. Only thus is perfect unity possible. Unfortunately circumstances rarely make this likely. When a new house is built there should be no reason why the furniture and decorations cannot be considered at the outset, and subsequent alterations avoided. In any event where possible the interior decorations ought to be arranged with the furniture. To decorate a room without any regard to the furniture is foolish. Fine furniture requires the right setting if it is to be seen to the best advantage. The creation of such a setting calls for artistic skill and experience. The best results are definitely not obtained by choosing haphazard papers, fabrics and colourings on the assurance of "I know what I like and want." One's taste may be excellent, but, lacking personal knowledge, it is apt to spoil good rooms and at best make success a thing of chance. Timely expert guidance and suggestions may change the effects desired from a matter of chance into a certainty.

In these days of wireless and motor-car, the countryside does not exist in the old exclusive sense. There is more inter-communication and less difference between a town house and a home in the country than hitherto. The character and nature of each house should nevertheless influence the choice of its furnishings. Suitability must ever be paramount everywhere.

In furnishing a single room the same procedure should be followed as with an entire dwelling.

The first consideration is the plan of the room to be furnished. Always remember that the furniture we propose to buy must fit into the particular apartment to be furnished. There is only one way by which we may make certain of this, and that is by means of a plan of the room drawn to scale on which is drawn the proposed furniture. This enables one to realize exactly how our scheme works out.

We shall do well to take briefly the various principal rooms in order, and note any matters which require special consideration in the allocation of the furniture.

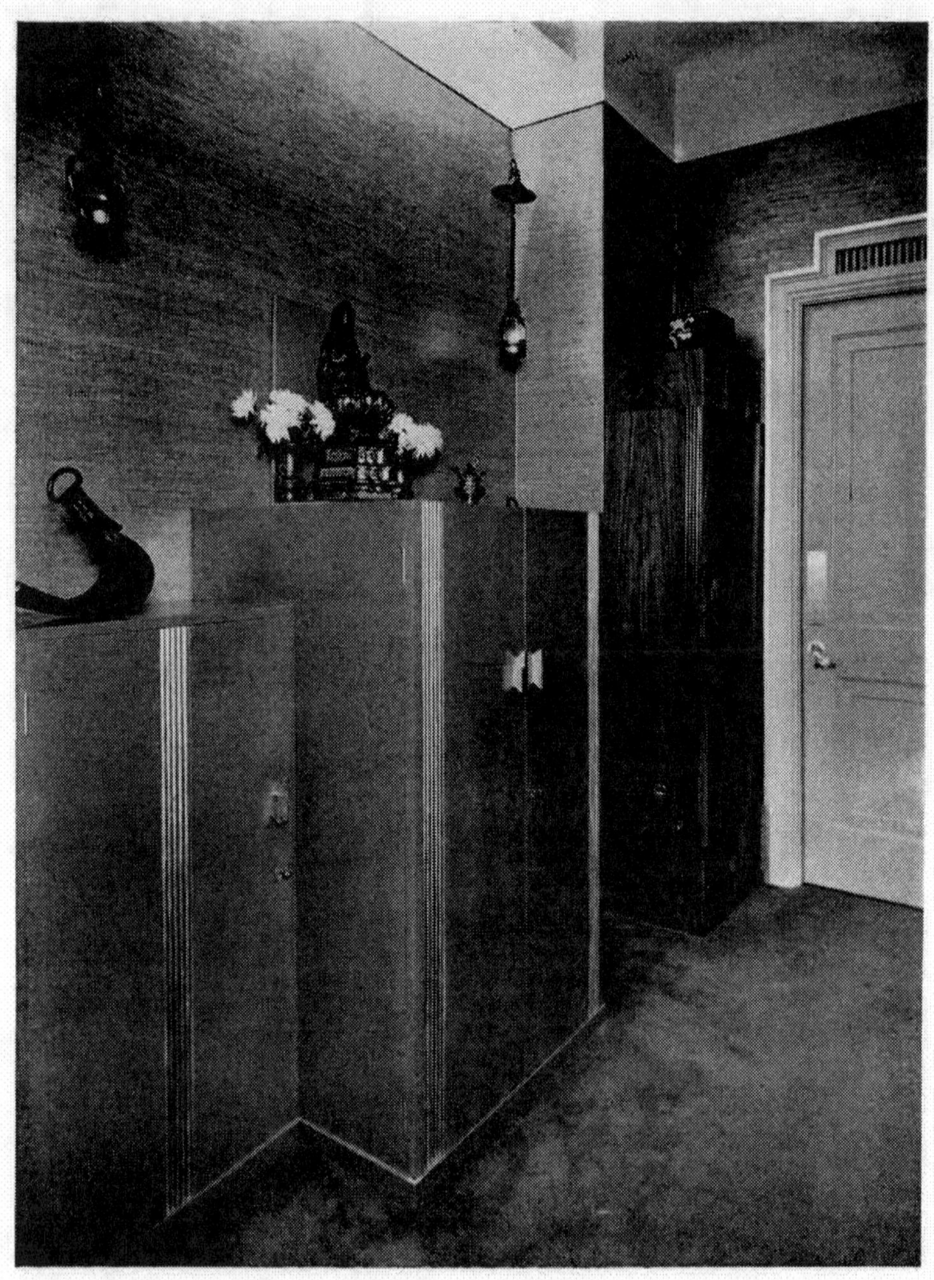

A LONDON FLAT—ENTRANCE HALL

# A LONDON FLAT

THE decorations and furnishing equipment of this 1929 flat were conceived on the artistic principles advocated in this book, although differing so greatly in appearance from the other work herein illustrated.

These interiors are worthy of careful study as illustrating the present-day spirit of freedom from furnishing conventions. We observe a fine sense of fitness; an appreciation of colour harmony; real craftsmanship and a knowledge of how to bring out the inherent beauty of material. We become conscious of artistic atmosphere different yet entirely sensible. We find nothing extreme or unusual merely for its own sake.

A brief description of the materials used in this flat is as follows :—

*Hall*

Walls are covered Japanese grasscloth. Carpet deep pile close fitted mauve Saxony. Doors and ceiling painted putty colour. Skirting fillet finished golf leaf. The Hall photograph shows cabinet in coral lacquer with old gold bandings. This cabinet encloses Frigidaire. The tall cabinet beyond is of walnut. The hall is lighted by a screened ceiling strip-light above the lacquer cabinet. Waxed walnut is used for the rest of the Hall furniture.

*Living Room*

Walls covered mauve Japanese grasscloth. Ceiling and house joinery painted to match. Carpet close fitted deep pile black Saxony. The illustrations of this room show the walnut and Macassar ebony sideboard. Note the gilt framed wall mirror above sideboard flanked by black glass panels obscuring tubular electric lights. Richly figured walnut is used for the dining table, while the dining chairs are of walnut upholstered old gold canvas cloth. The two tall cabinets in this room are finished black lacquer. The settee has covering of green cord material, and feet and plinth finished gold leaf. The low walnut and ebony occasional table is topped with silvered glass. The walnut nested tables at side of settee have old gold tile tops.

Indirect lighting is used throughout the flat. Tubular lights are fitted behind the wood pelmets to windows. Screened tubular lights are also fixed on either side of the pier between the two easy chairs.

*Bedroom*

The walls are covered with tightly stretched pale green linen. The ceiling is painted white. The carpet is black. The furniture in this room is natural oak veneered on mahogany and banded with ebony.

A special feature is the dressing table with its long mirror and diagonally set pedestals. The dressing stool has upholstered seat covered with python skin. The snake skin harmonises beautifully with the oak and ebony framework of stool.

Two attached wardrobes are provided in this room, one of which is seen in the illustration. Between the wardrobes a special chest of drawers is illuminated by an indirect ceiling light.

Radiators throughout the flat are painted silver or gold and are cased top, ends and plinth with putty-coloured marble. Radiator fronts have metal bands finished black and silver alternating. Our illustration shows one of the radiators next to dressing table.

Between the bedroom windows a large unframed mirror provides background for the perfume stand of wrot silvered brass. This stand supports a " sky-scraper " set of shelves constructed entirely of glass.

The twin beds have oak frames or boxes supporting mattresses and Vi-springs. The panne velvet bedspreads are dyed a special mauve shade.

*Studio*

This is a small room furnished for personal use. Walls are covered yellow Japanese grasscloth, the ceiling and house joinery being painted to

A LONDON FLAT—ENTRANCE HALL.

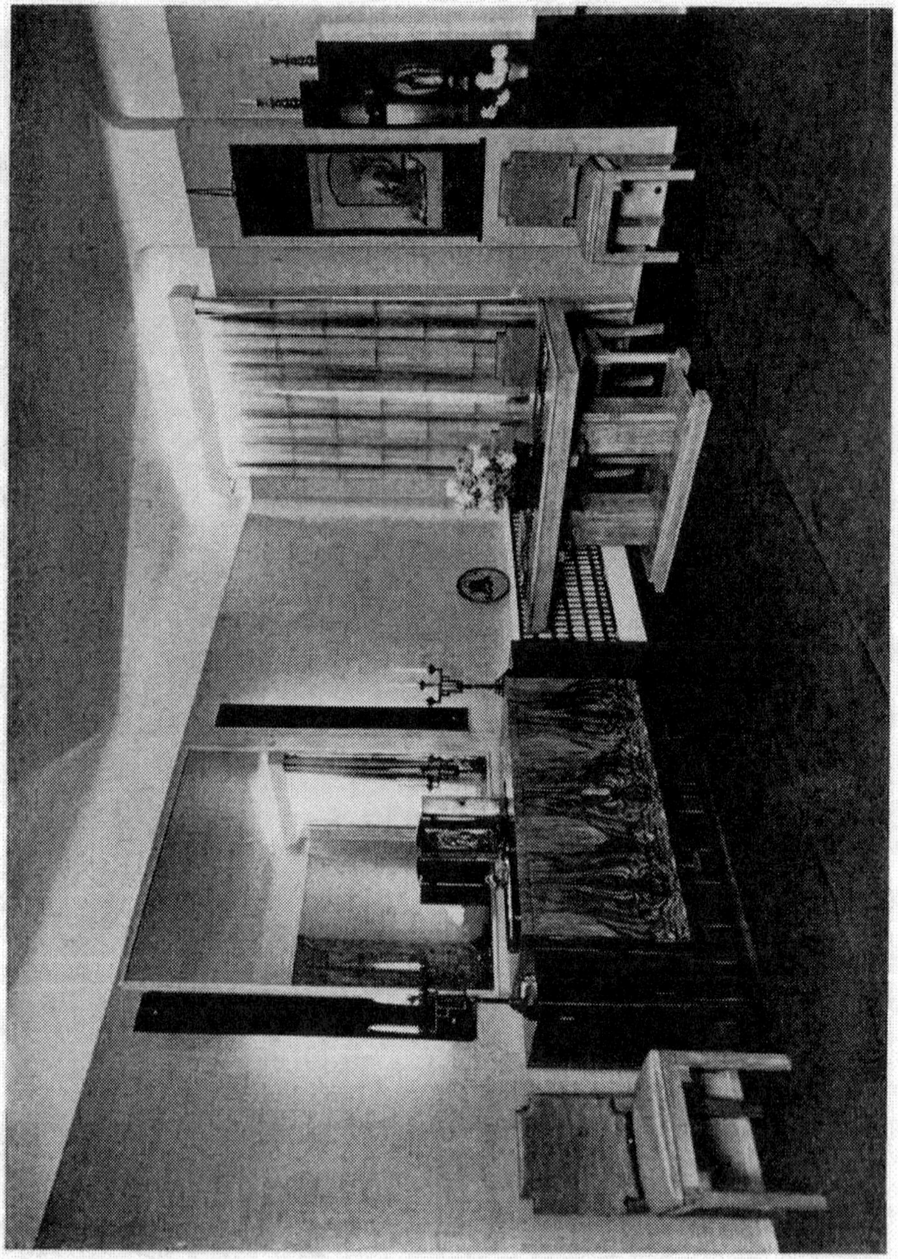

A LONDON FLAT—LIVING ROOM

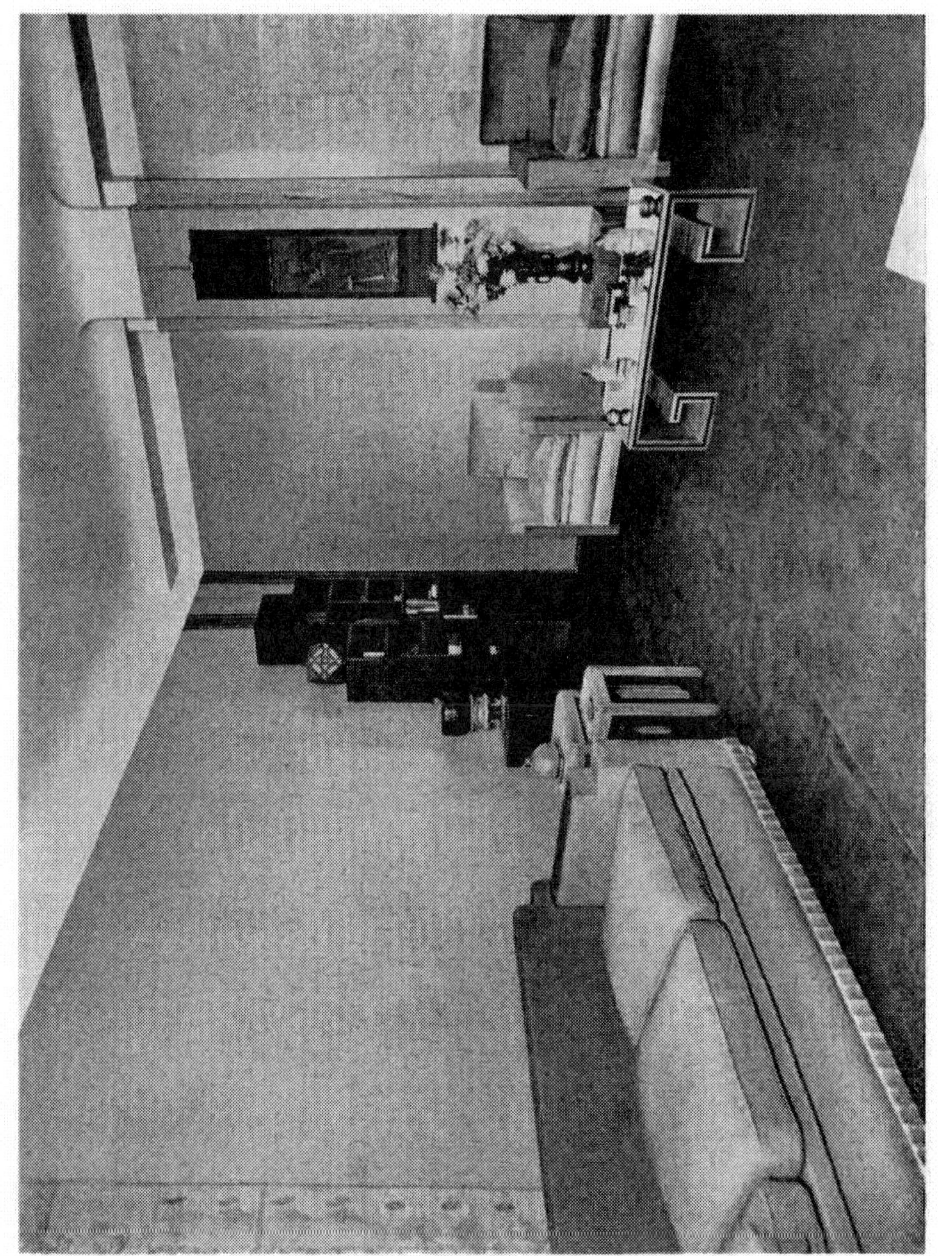

A LONDON FLAT—LIVING ROOM

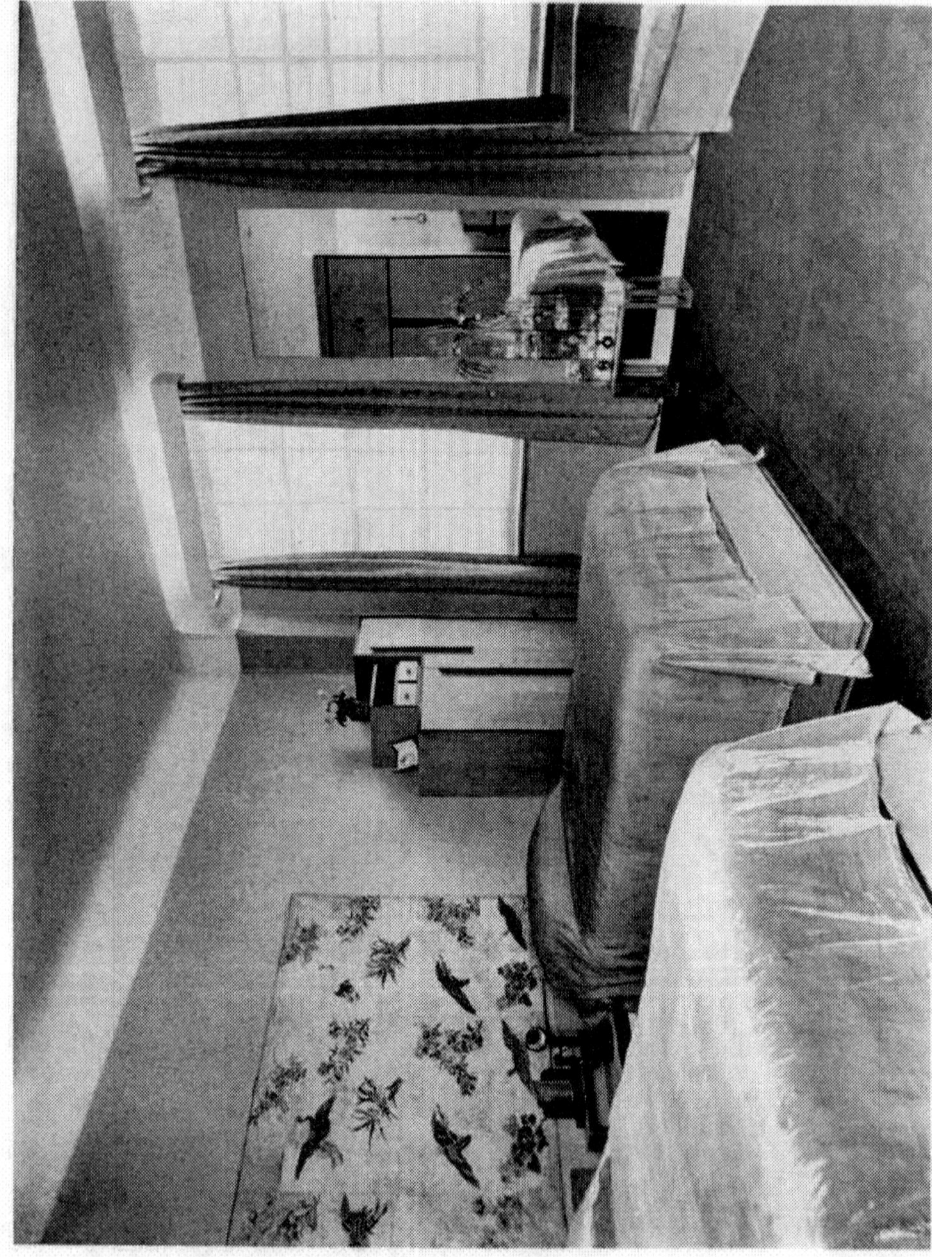

A LONDON FLAT—BEDROOM

match. The deep pile carpet is coral shade. The furniture consisting of wardrobe, sky-scraper bookcase and writing table, chair and divan are of walnut with ebony introduced to form contrasts.

These furnishings provide an ideal background and setting for the beautiful Japanese and oriental works of art belonging to the owner of the flat. Although European and modern it will be observed how much this type of decorative art has in common with oriental art.

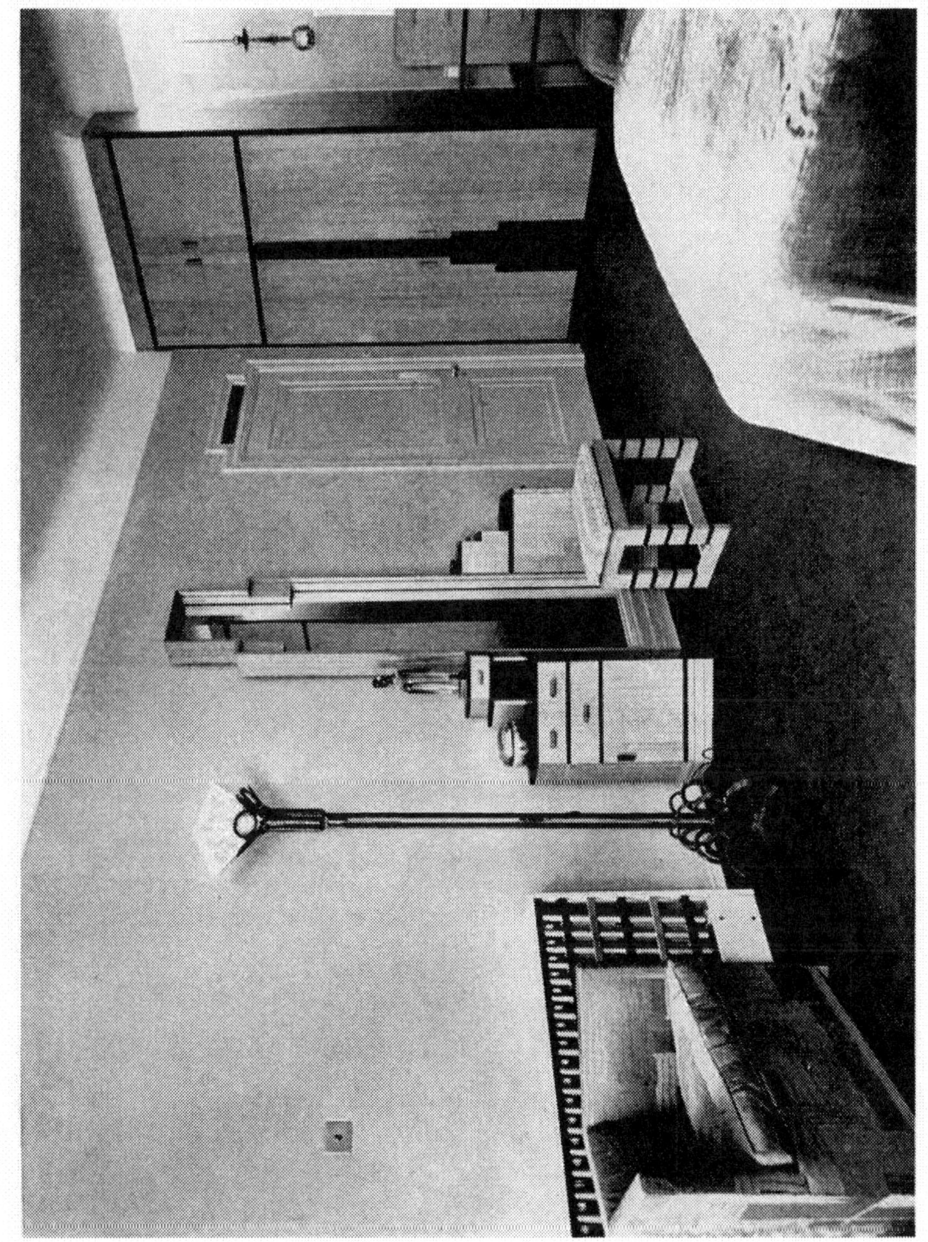

A LONDON FLAT—BEDROOM

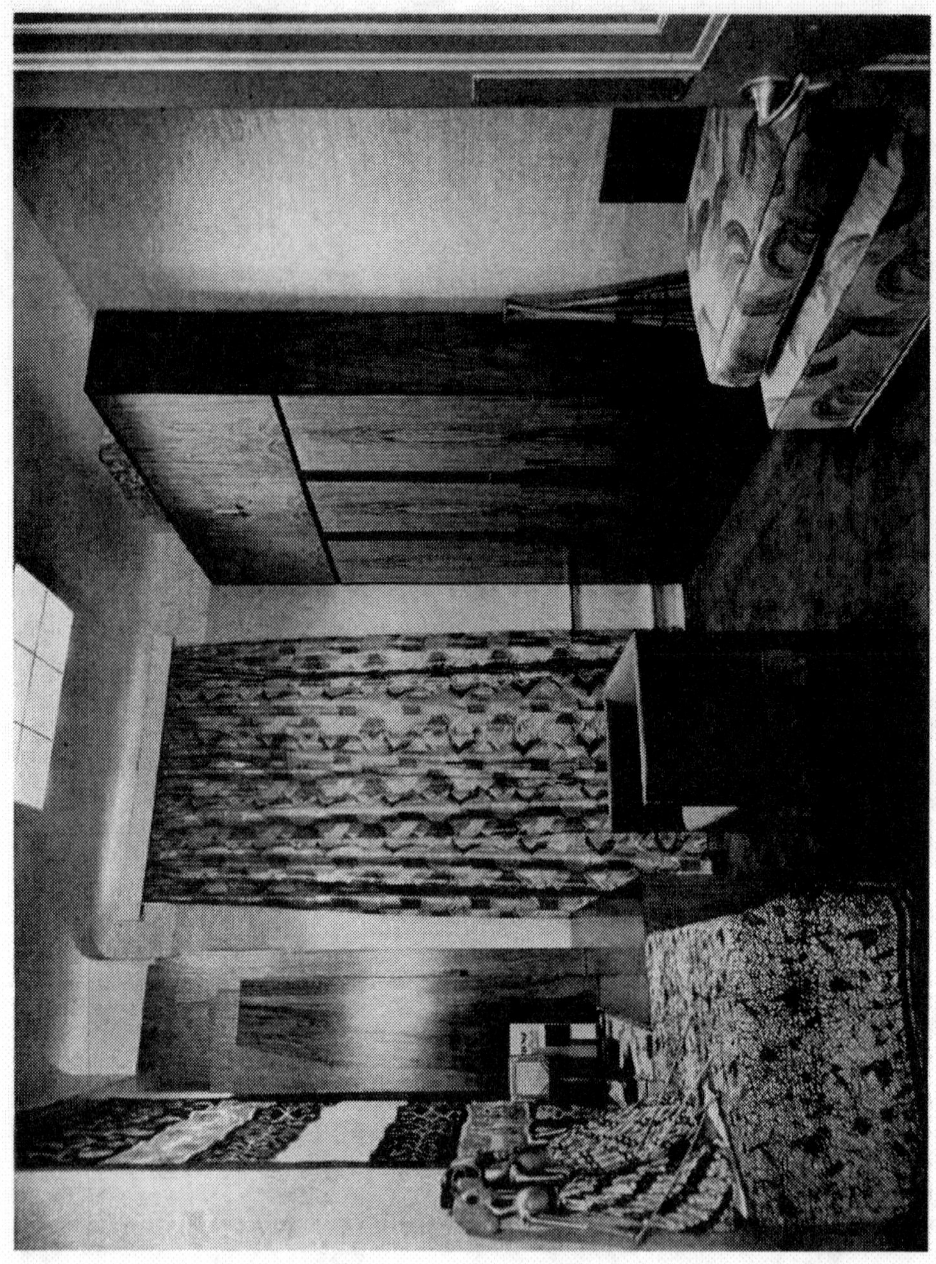

A LONDON FLAT—STUDIO

# THE HALL

IT is seldom that the hall gets sufficient attention, yet no part of the house is more important as regards artistic appearance. Too often the sitting rooms are elaborated at the expense of the hall, which is left to look after itself.

As regards hall furniture, the less, the better, will be the rule. Practically considered, the only furniture required will be a suitable chair for visitors not received in the drawing room, a small table for letters and cards, and a wall mirror. Hat racks, coat and umbrella stands should find no place in an entrance hall. If there be no cloak room or lavatory, then hats and coats should be kept in a small hall cupboard having a definite position in the scheme.

Decorate your hall properly, and no furniture beyond these essentials will be required to suggest a homely appearance. Your floor should be of polished wood, covered with an oriental rug of good quality. The hall windows should be provided with well cut and properly hung curtains, while the hall walls may be either panelled and painted, or covered with decorative wood as described for the dining room. Plain walnut, pine or natural colour oak are suitable as wall coverings for the hall. Panelled plaster walls may be made very effective. The ceiling and frieze may be enriched with raised ornament and painted. Omit all superfluous and unnecessary detail in your hall. Treat your walls consistently in the decorative sense. Have just one or two furniture items distinctive for their quality, practical suitability and artistic interest, and the result should more than justify the expenditure. The artificial lighting should be silk shaded. A warm or orange-toned light suggests comfort. Never have patterned wall paper in the hall unless conditions be exceptional. The stair carpet should usually be plain colour. Grey or blue pile carpet looks as well as anything. Stair carpet requires a more durable quality to wear well. The best grade should be selected.

The decorative treatment in the hall may, with advantage, be carried up to the first floor for landing and passages. If a panel treatment, the panels require skilful handling where these meet the staircase. Ordinarily it will be advisable to let the ground floor panels retain their normal height next the stairs, and not attempt to rise with the steps. Take care to keep the first floor panels level with the first floor. The panels immediately on the staircase will then adapt themselves between the lines of the ground floor and first floor panels. It will, otherwise, be difficult to avoid irregular and awkward shapes in the staircase panels.

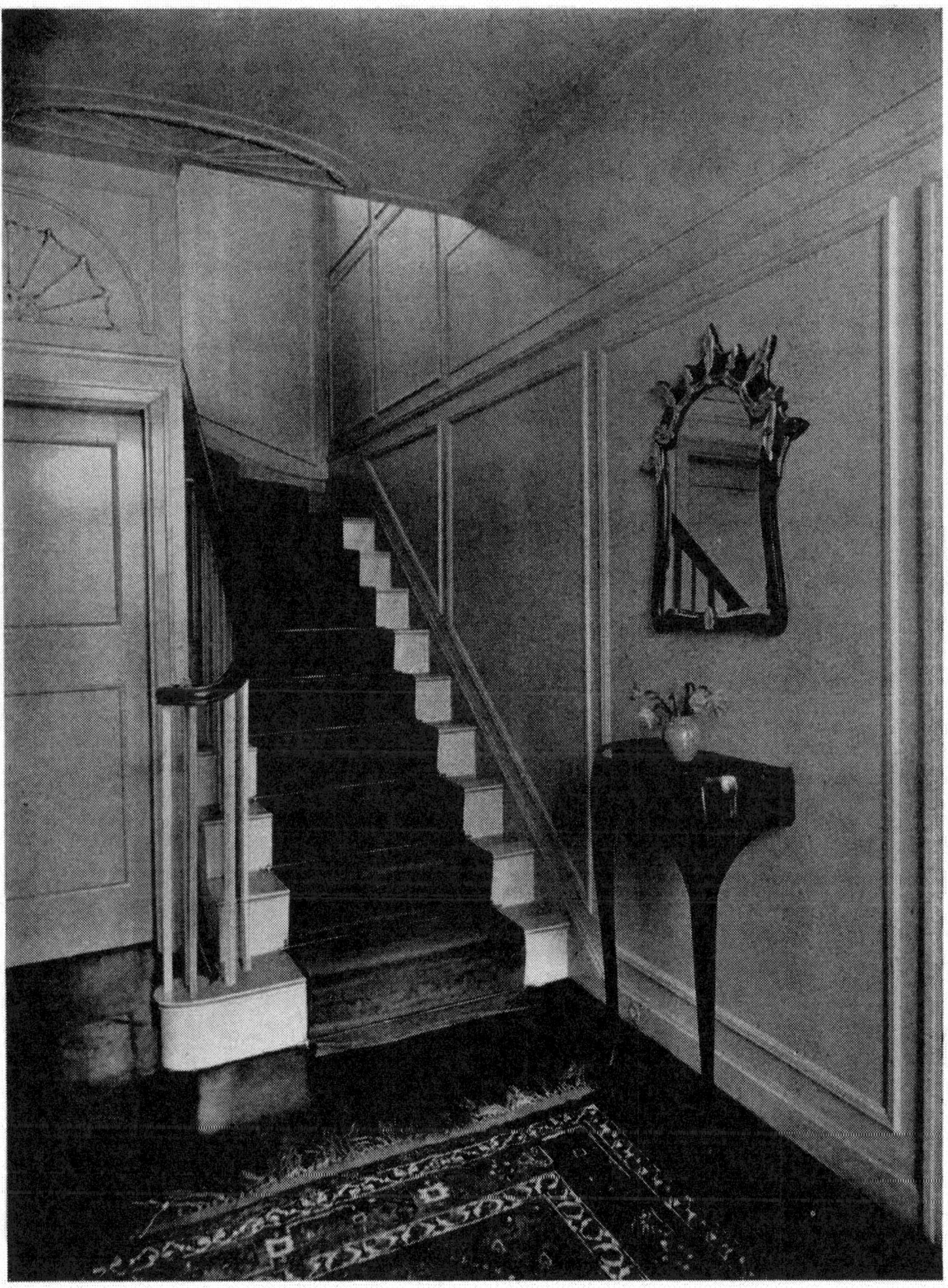

ENTRANCE HALL DESIGNED BY MAURICE ADAMS

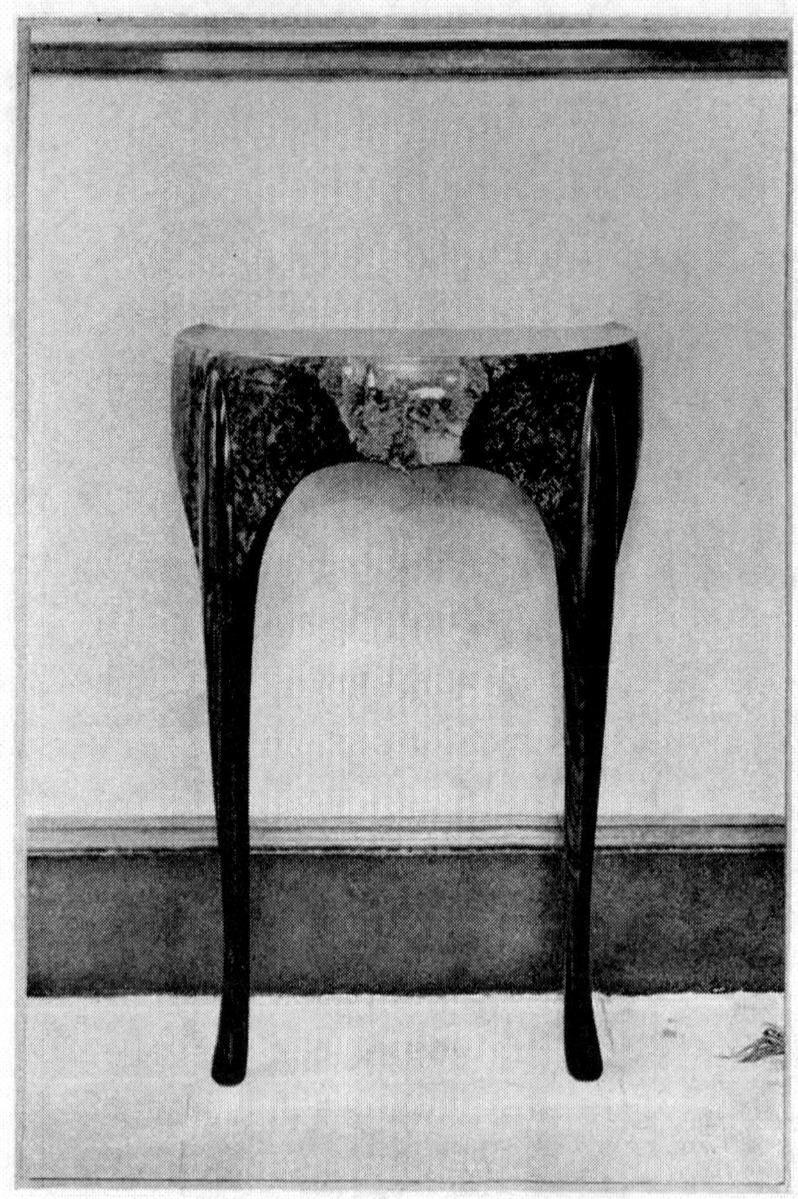

GROSVENOR CONSOLE TABLE, NO. 669-C BURR WALNUT

MAURICE ADAMS

# THE DINING ROOM

ATTENTION will first be given to the average number of persons taking meals together under normal conditions. Most householders entertain to a certain extent, and at ordinary times, there may be visitors taking meals in the house. At Christmas and other special occasions the numbers will naturally be considerably augmented.

In our view, it is a mistake to furnish the dining room treating special occasions as if they were normal. If four people ordinarily dine together, then we would plan the room for four individuals with, say, space for two visitors. Unless the dining room be very large it is a mistake to put up with the inconvenience of too large a table all the year round, when a smaller one would suffice for everyday requirements and make service more convenient. Another point is that two or three people dining at a large table can hardly avoid a feeling of isolation. Extending tables have their advantages and in some measure overcome this difficulty.

Dining tables are ordinarily placed in the centre of the room. There should, if possible, be not less than three feet clear space all round the table to allow of convenient service. Of course, some form of side table or sideboard will be necessary. Other factors will be the fireplace, the door or entrance and the various windows.

If possible five feet should be allowed between the dining table and fireplace, and space around the door should allow convenient access for table service during meals. In small rooms particularly the position of the door will require careful attention. A servant carrying a tray requires the door to open wide. If the door opens immediately opposite the dining table the open door will itself reduce the passage between the table by approximately 2 ft. 6 ins.

A bay window near by, by widening the space around the table, will materially increase the effective size of the room. It is very convenient in smaller dining rooms for the sideboard to occupy a recess. This arrangement must necessarily be planned when the house is built. With ordinary construction, a recess in one room entails corresponding projection in the adjacent room. In the case of a kitchen adjoining a dining room, intervening recesses in the kitchen may conveniently be utilized by fitted cabinets or cupboards. A serving hatch or cupboard should always be provided as a convenience of service, particularly in these days when servants are difficult to obtain.

The plan of the room will, therefore, generally determine the best form for the dining table. A circular table is excellent in square rooms but not otherwise. In narrow rooms it may be an advantage to place the sideboard or dresser at the end of the room, out of the way and not interfering with table service. Nothing is more disturbing than to have one's chair continually knocked by the servant in attendance and this cannot be avoided unless sufficient gangway is allowed for around the table.

The rounding or curving of the table top at the ends will add to the size of the room without reducing the convenience of the table. Oval tables, if made to extend, lose their oval shape. It is better in this case to make the table ends round or segmental. Where a large table is necessary in a small room, the usual sideboard may be dispensed with, and its place taken by two cabinets placed in the corners of the room. This treatment is effective and adds interest to the scheme. Where there is a projecting chimney breast, the side recesses may be filled by two small sideboards fitted into these spaces. This will make the room larger by keeping the main walls free of fitments.

The use of finely figured woods for dining tables has led to the cloth being dispensed with and lace mats used instead. In some houses plate-glass tops have been used, but a better plan is to have the table top polished with cellulose. This produces an excellent table surface which will not easily mark, and will stand moderate heat without discolouring.

Artificial lighting in the dining room is of special importance, though it seldom receives the attention it deserves, since the comfortable use of the room largely depends upon the nature of the lighting. In arranging this the aim should be to throw a good but softly-shaded light directly upon the table. Anything in the nature of a glare is best avoided. Concealed lamps giving light by reflection on the ceiling produce excellent results. In some cases a sinking, corresponding with the top of the dining table, may be formed in the ceiling for this purpose. Indirect lighting in this manner requires, of course, to be much stronger than direct lighting, and the number of lamps must accordingly be increased.

Many people prefer to dispense with electric light during dinner; light being provided by wax candles placed on the table. This can only be conveniently arranged when the table is large enough to allow room for the candle-sticks without unduly crowding the table.

The most usual arrangement is to have a large bowl or similar lamp directly over the dining table. We will not go so far as to say that this cannot be done effectively, but, under ordinary circumstances, this method is the least artistically attractive method to adopt.

Popular commercial-made hanging bowls and lamps are, generally, very ugly and spoil any room where used. Apart from this the difficulty is to make the lamp large enough to be effective without dominating the room. The lighting is very important, but the fittings themselves do not constitute the chief furnishing items. If too large they will dominate the scheme and detract from the furniture and spoil the decorations. A better way is to have wall lights suitably placed and shaded. In a panelled dining room, appropriate fittings arranged in the panels around the room are very effective. Examples of this method of lighting are shown in the accompanying illustrations. Silk shades for direct lighting should always be used. Their colour may be cream, pale yellow, orange or rose, to suit the colour scheme of the room.

Ordinarily the dining room furniture will consist of dining table, small chairs, armchairs and sideboard. In large establishments the carving is usually done in the kitchen. Where the carving takes place in the dining room it is an advantage to have either a carving table or a buffet table for this purpose.

Suitable woods for dining room furniture are burr walnut, plain figured walnut, figured mahogany and oak. From this choice, selection usually is made. Where there is much entertaining, burr walnut, by reason of its rich tones and figurings, is particularly suitable. Plain figured waxed walnut suggests refinement without over elaboration. It is most suitable for everyday use in any dining room. Figured mahogany continues to be favoured by many. The figure, however, is quieter than that of walnut. Some form of carving may be rightly introduced unless plain furniture is preferred. Oak furniture should be left in its natural colour. Furniture of natural coloured oak in modern design may be made effective for the dining room, particularly when dark walnut or ebony beading is neatly introduced around the drawers and cupboards. Light oak for dining rooms should have the grain filled and be either French polished or polished with cellulose. Otherwise the furniture will soon take on a dirty appearance.

Those favouring something unusual in style have a choice of numerous beautiful woods. Pre-eminent among these is Bombay rosewood on account of its beautiful colour. This is similar to mahogany but less aggressive in tone. Natural ash combined with plain walnut; coromandel and walnut, also Bubinga Maidou deserve mention as providing great possibilities in dining room furniture.

The leaves of extending dining tables should be provided with "aprons" or pieces at the sides. This avoids the unsightly appearance which results when the table construction is exposed to view.

As regards the dining room decorations, the form of treatment will be determined largely by the nature of the room itself. An irregular plan, or where the wall surfaces are broken by large bays, oriels and other windows, suggests a much simpler treatment than a room presenting large unbroken wall surfaces. Rooms having many features will require a plain and rather severe treatment of the wall spacings.

For wall finish the facilities of choice consist of wood covering, panelling, cloth covering, painting, papering.

Before the introduction of ply and laminated wood, the use of wood for wall coverings necessitated a wainscot treatment. A wood framing was prepared covering the wall surface; the spaces in the framing being filled with panels. From the design point of view, this construction had several disadvantages, the chief being the narrow widths of the panels and the large proportion of structural framing.

Solid wood framing and panelling was also very much subject to atmospheric changes, and was, therefore, liable to appreciable movement between the framing and panels. This resulted in open joints in the framing and cracks in the panels themselves. The cost of solid wood panelling was also considerable.

Walls may now be covered with wood by using either plywood or laminated material. Plywood is formed with three or more veneers, *i.e.*, sheets of thin wood glued face to face forming a single board. Plywood varies in thickness from about one-eighth to half-an-inch. As with laminated wood quality depends both on the veneers from which it is made and the cement or glue. Cheap or poor quality plywood is quite useless for panelling. Its use leads to defective work due to warping and twisting, blistering and the like, which cannot be cured or made good subsequently. Plywood for panelling must be of the very best quality and made with waterproof cement. It must be of sufficient thickness, or buckling will result in undulating and faulty surfaces.

Laminated wood is entirely distinct and different in construction from plywood. This is not made with veneers but from thin strips of wood glued face to face, so that the grain is at right angles with the face of board. The advantages are considerable. For such purposes as wall coverings, this board may be made of pine or soft wood faced both sides with a veneer of mahogany or other hard wood. The degree of warping, twisting, shrinking and other usual defects is negligible. It may be used in large boards several feet wide and of full height without visible joints. The cost of framing and panelling is avoided. Laminated wood may be faced with any kind of decorative wood and may be polished or painted. The walls and ceilings in modern yacht construction are now formed with laminated wood, providing a smooth unbroken surface entirely free from after movement or shrinkage.

Walls may, therefore, safely be treated with laminated wood to suit the decorative effect desired. Walls may be covered their full height if need be. This facilitates large unbroken surfaces of plain or decorative wood hitherto impossible. Designers to-day certainly possess a wealth of material providing unlimited scope.

A decorative wood treatment is eminently suitable for the dining room, and has advantages not to be found in any other material. Its use may be classified into two groups, plain and figured, and must, of course, accord with the furniture. It is difficult to lay down hard and fast rules as to how woods should be used for wall coverings, because the exact effect aimed at in each design will largely determine both the selection of the wood and its manner of use.

As a setting for richly figured furniture, either plain or figured woods may be appropriately used for the walls. If plain wood be selected, then a slight contrast obtained by some other wood lighter in tone than the furniture is preferable. With burr walnut furniture, for example, pine or ash as wall covering would be most suitable. These woods are much lighter in tone than burr walnut. Panel mouldings may or may not be desirable according to the nature of the room itself. The height for the wall covering will, in most cases, be from one to two feet below the ceiling, and may be capped by a small moulding or flat band of wood. It is not desirable that the old type of frame panelling should be imitated. Mouldings may be introduced, if at all, solely for the purpose of breaking up too large a surface, creating a line, or to give special emphasis to a piece of furniture or other feature of the room.

Should figured wood be preferred, this should correspond with the furniture, and should be used solely in conjunction with figured wood furniture. It is best to avoid all mouldings when figured wood is employed for the walls. The less broken the surfaces, the better will be the artistic appearance.

A less costly wall treatment for the dining room is to panel the plastered walls by means of applied panel mouldings. This method may be made very effective. The whole wall surface should be painted in oil paint and be stippled and shaded.

The dining room frieze and ceiling may be enriched with applied raised ornament as shown in the examples illustrated herein, or these surfaces may be painted white, clouded in blue or other colour, to match the room.

Cloth wall coverings are not to be recommended in the dining room. Plain leather and similar papers have possibilities. They are cheaper than paint but nothing like so effective. Low cost is their chief recommendation.

Large dining rooms may have their walls arranged as large panels painted to represent landscape or foliated effects. This treatment must be very well executed to be artistically satisfactory, and necessarily is very costly. It will only be in exceptional cases where anything of the kind will be attempted or made satisfactory.

The dining room floor should preferably be covered with parquetry wax polished. Any rugs or carpets will be of oriental manufacture. Persian runners on either side of the dining table are effective and economical. In place of parquetry, the floor may have close fitted pile plain colour carpet, but with this proviso, that quality must be the best as wear in dining rooms is usually heavy. One disadvantage of close fitted plain colour carpet for dining rooms is that it marks badly when liquids are spilled, which may easily happen. Close fitted hair grey carpet looks well in a meal room, particularly when there are one or two good Persian rugs. A further alternative is dark brown linoleum, wax polished and partly covered with oriental rugs.

# DINING ROOM FURNITURE

WE illustrate two main types of dining room furniture. One type in plain figured walnut and one in burr walnut. In the former series the main faces are veneered with vertical strips of walnut. This method of veneering emphasizes the main lines of these designs and relieves the otherwise severity of style. The drawer and door margins are of ebony. This style is favoured by many for dining rooms on account of its " practical " appearance. These designs may suitably be made also in oak, mahogany or rosewood.

Attention is directed to the chairs with wood seats and loose squab cushions. The dished or " saddle " seats give distinction. With this type of chair wood seats are particularly suitable. The loose cushions are comfortable and their covers easily cleaned or changed. Wood seats cannot sag.

The Grosvenor burr walnut dining room furniture illustrated is unique for distinctive appearance. There are no sharp corners to knock against, no mouldings or ornament to harbour dust and dirt. It requires a minimum of labour to clean. The burr walnut veneers are the finest specimens procurable and mounted on mahogany throughout. The tables and sideboards are supplied in any size desired to suit particular rooms. The dining tables have loose leaves. The leaves have side " aprons " which hide the table framework whether open or shut. The table top veneers are very carefully selected so that the pattern of the markings in the burr walnut are properly balanced whether the table is closed or extended. These tables and sideboards may be supplied with cellulose polish to tops. With this finish table-cloths are unnecessary as this polish will not mark easily with either moisture or heat.

The design of the Grosvenor dining room chairs is interesting. They are unlike historic examples, yet their definitely modern appearance is entirely natural and in perfect good taste. The drop-in seats may be suitably covered to match colour scheme of the room.

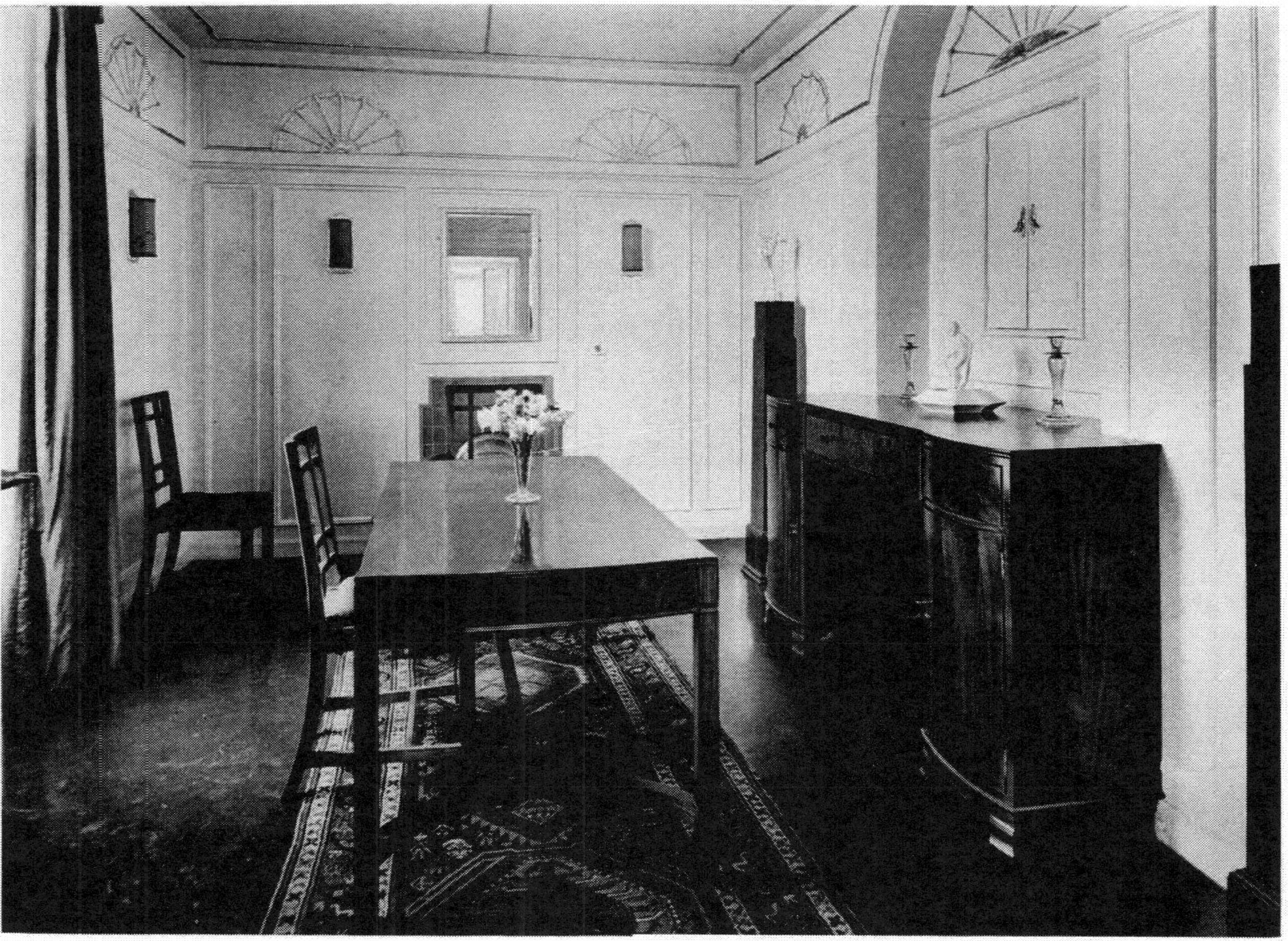

DINING ROOM DESIGNED BY MAURICE ADAMS

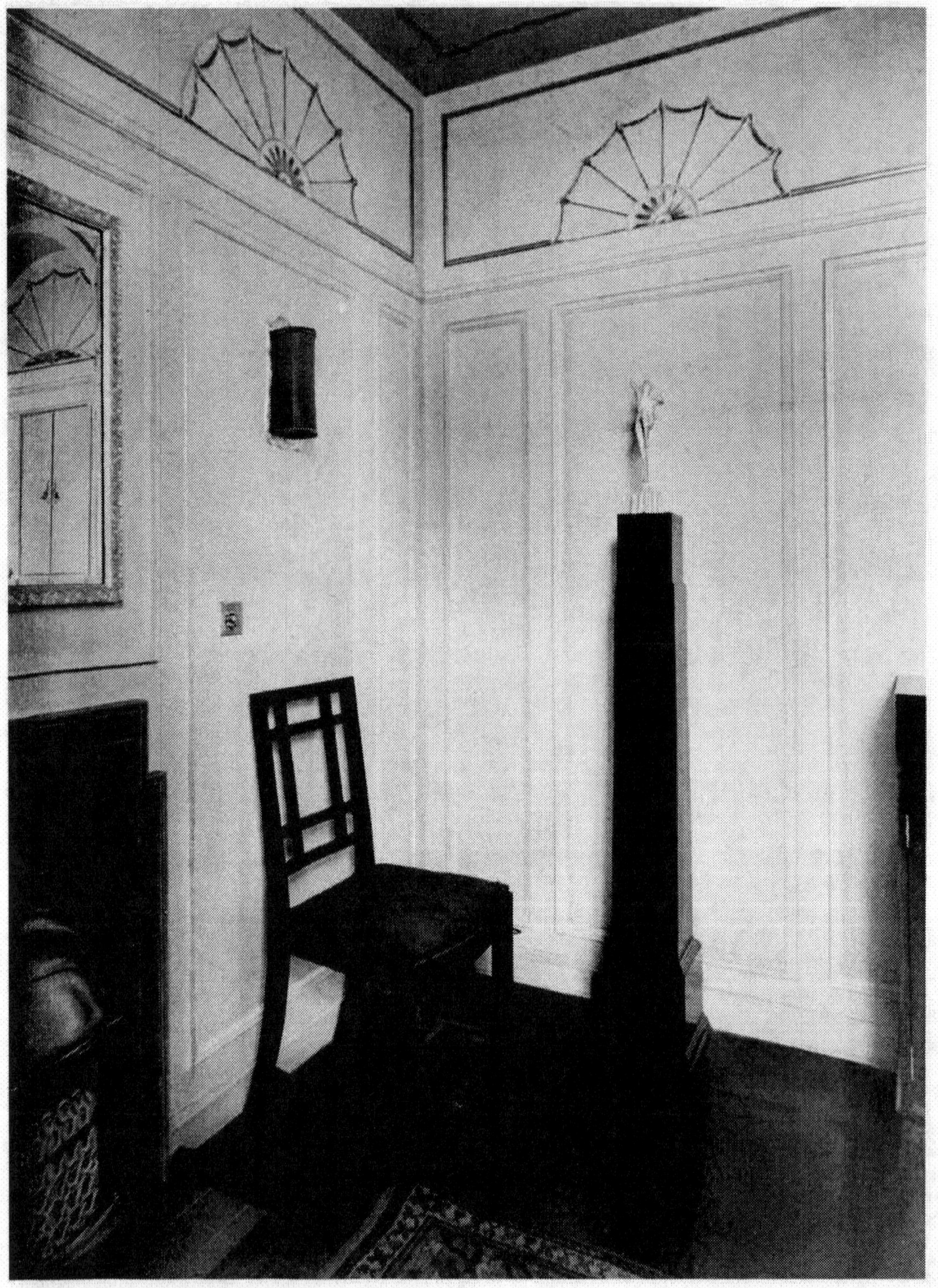

CORNER OF DINING ROOM DESIGNED BY MAURICE ADAMS

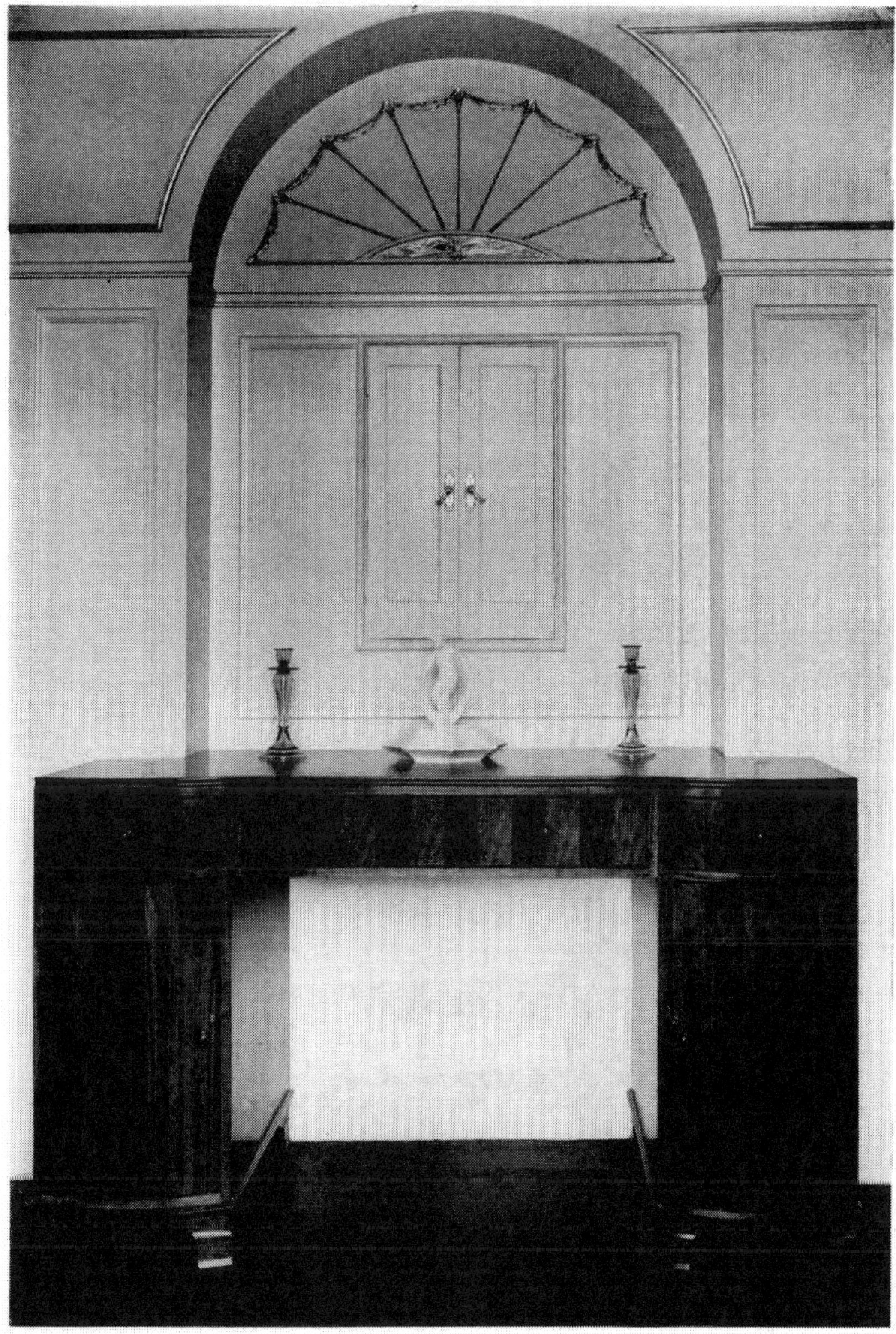

SIDEBOARD AND SERVING HATCH — DESIGNED BY MAURICE ADAMS

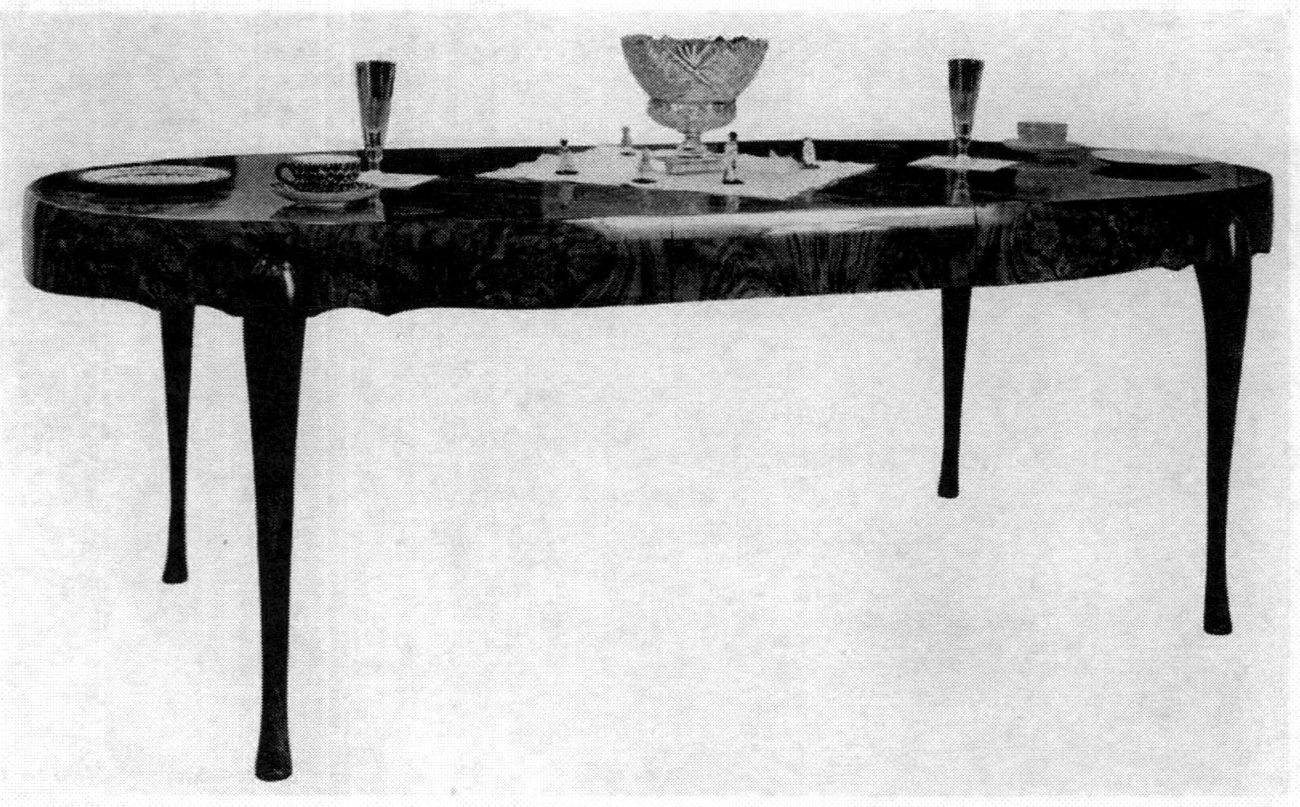

GROSVENOR DINING TABLE, NO. 535-C
BURR WALNUT

MAURICE ADAMS

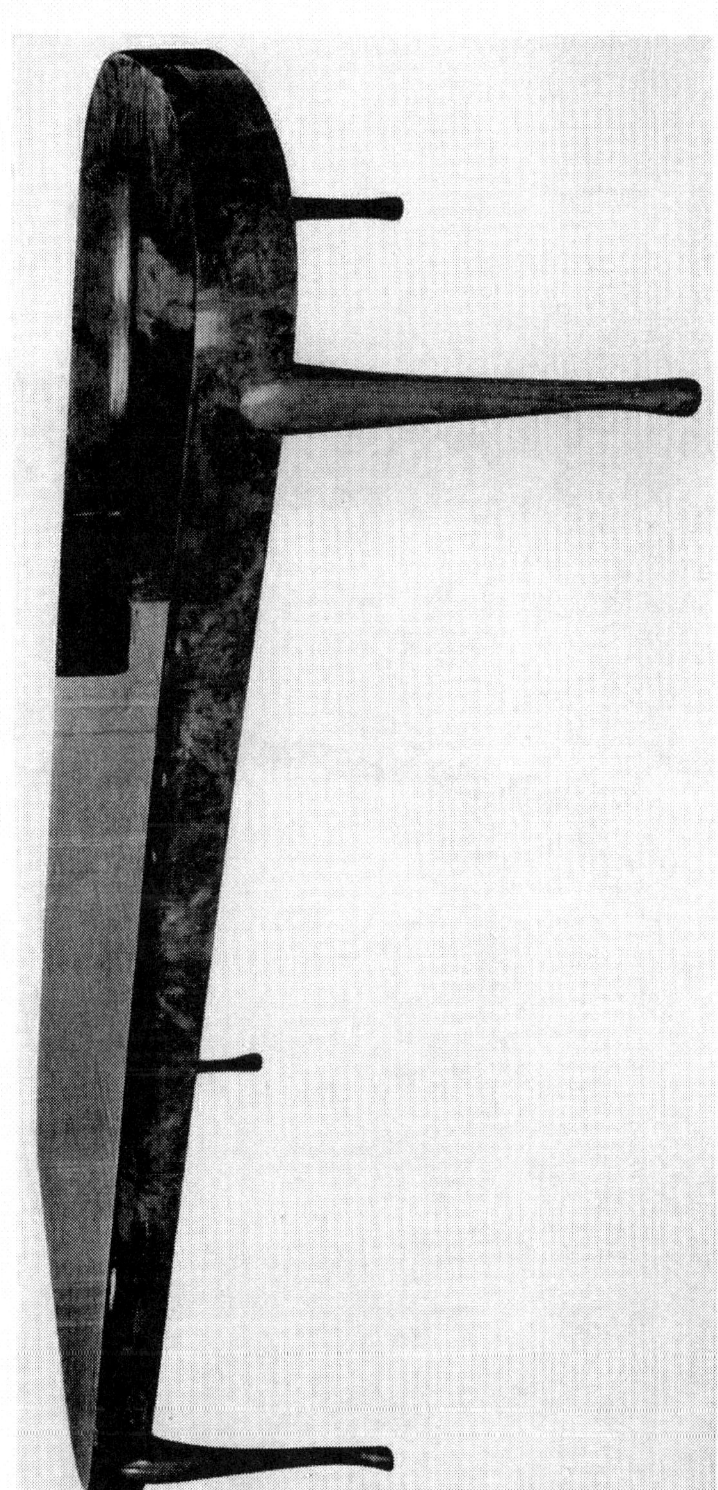

GROSVENOR DINING TABLE, NO. 463-C
BURR WALNUT

MAURICE ADAMS

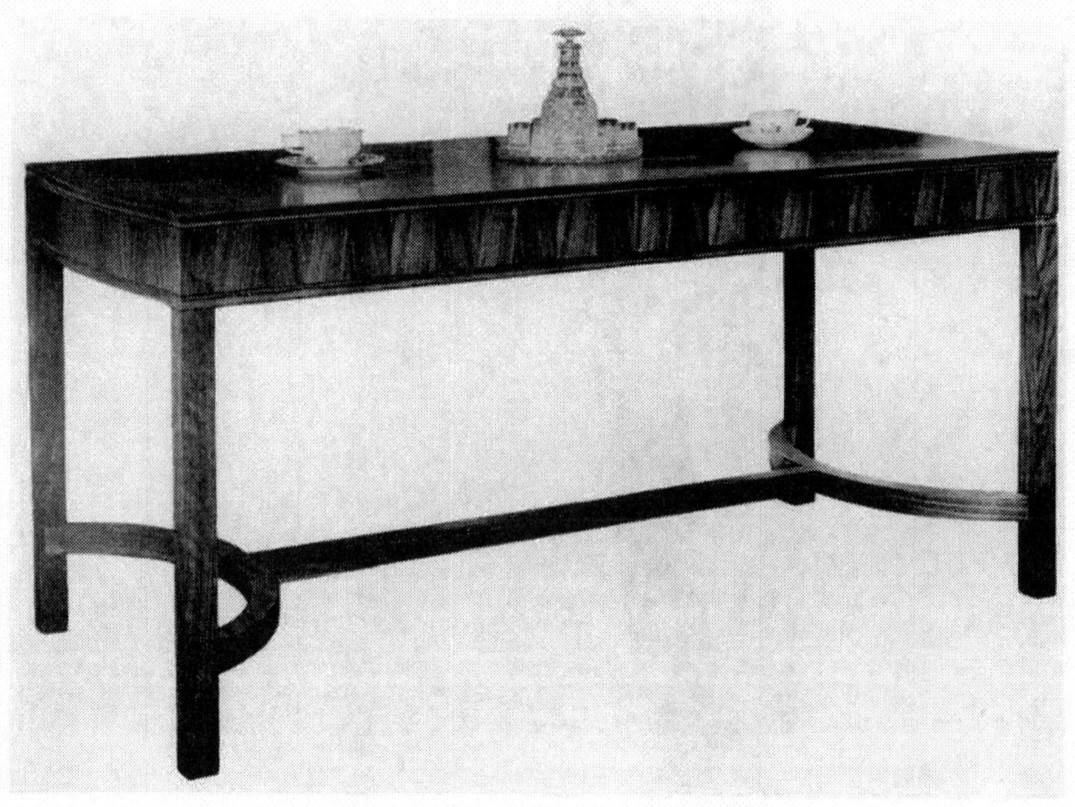

WAXED WALNUT DINING TABLE, NO. 457-C MAURICE ADAMS

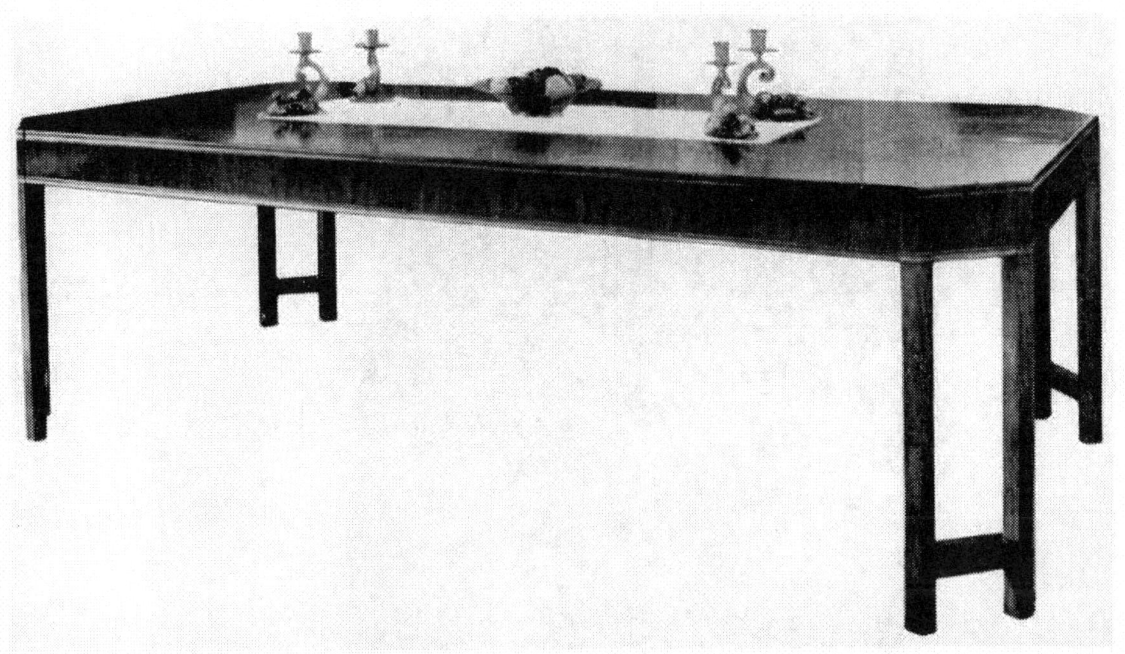

WAXED WALNUT DINING TABLE, NO. 543-C MAURICE ADAMS

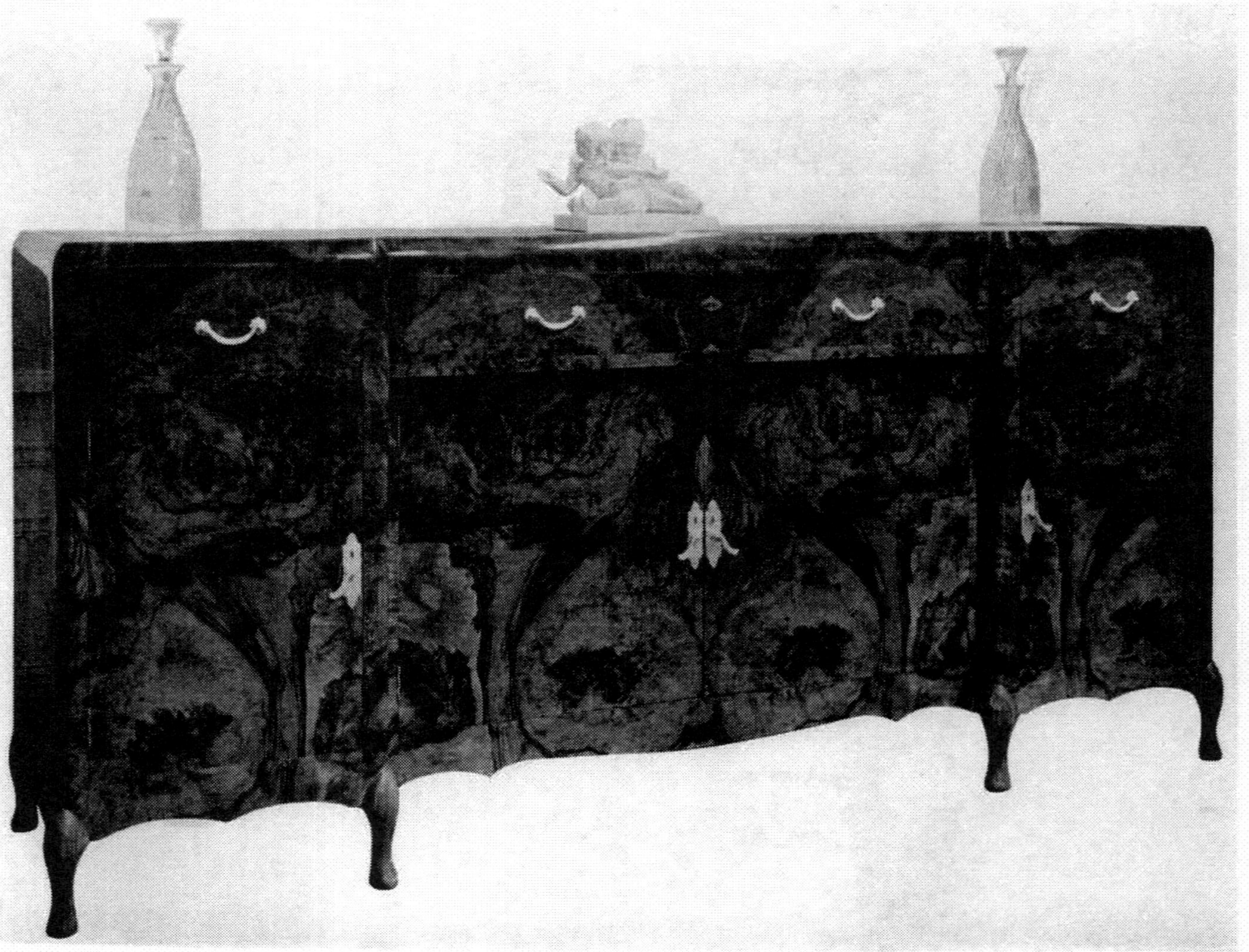

GROSVENOR SIDEBOARD, NO. 460-C
BURR WALNUT

MAURICE ADAMS

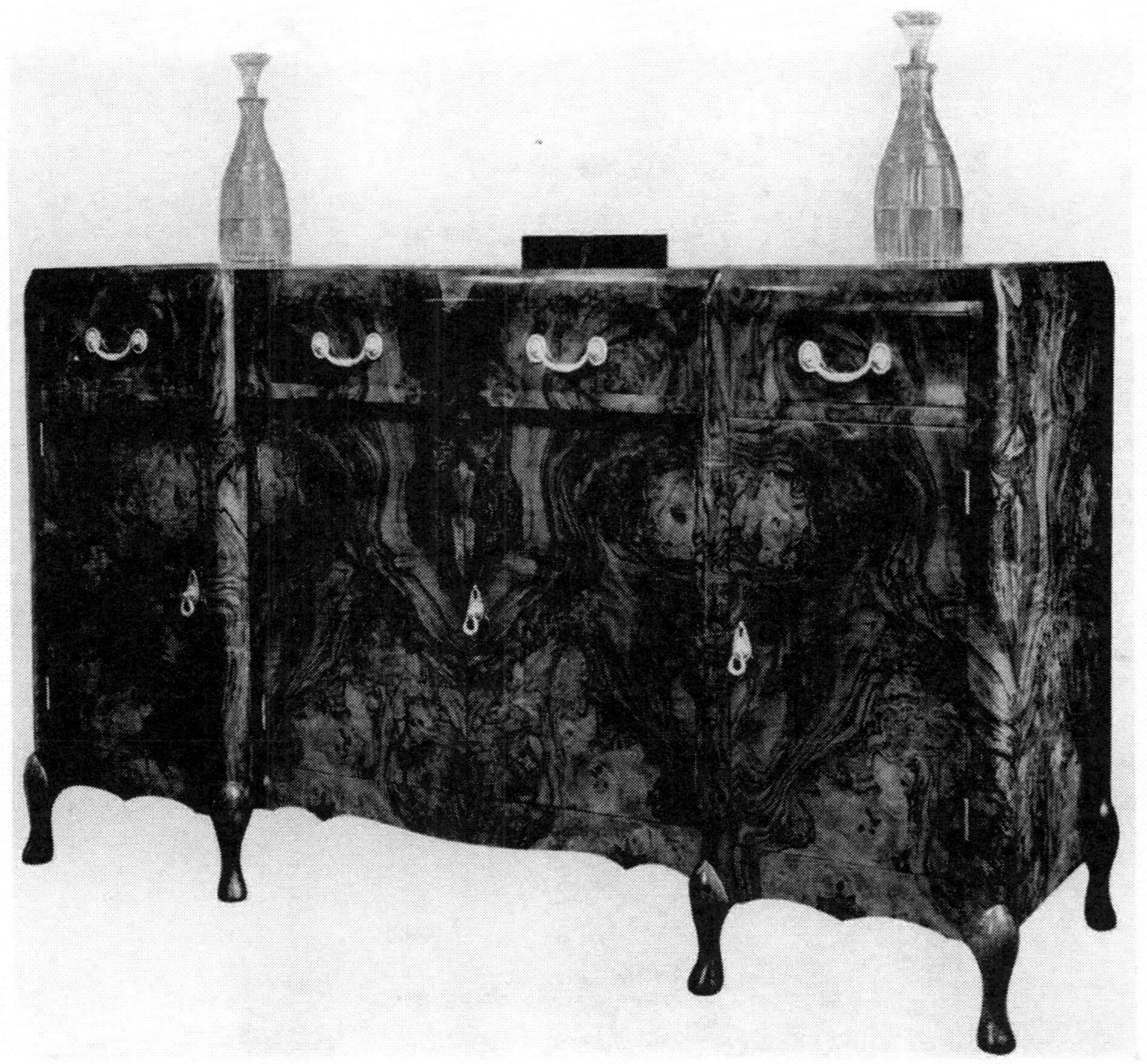

GROSVENOR SIDEBOARD, NO. 462-C
BURR WALNUT

MAURICE ADAMS

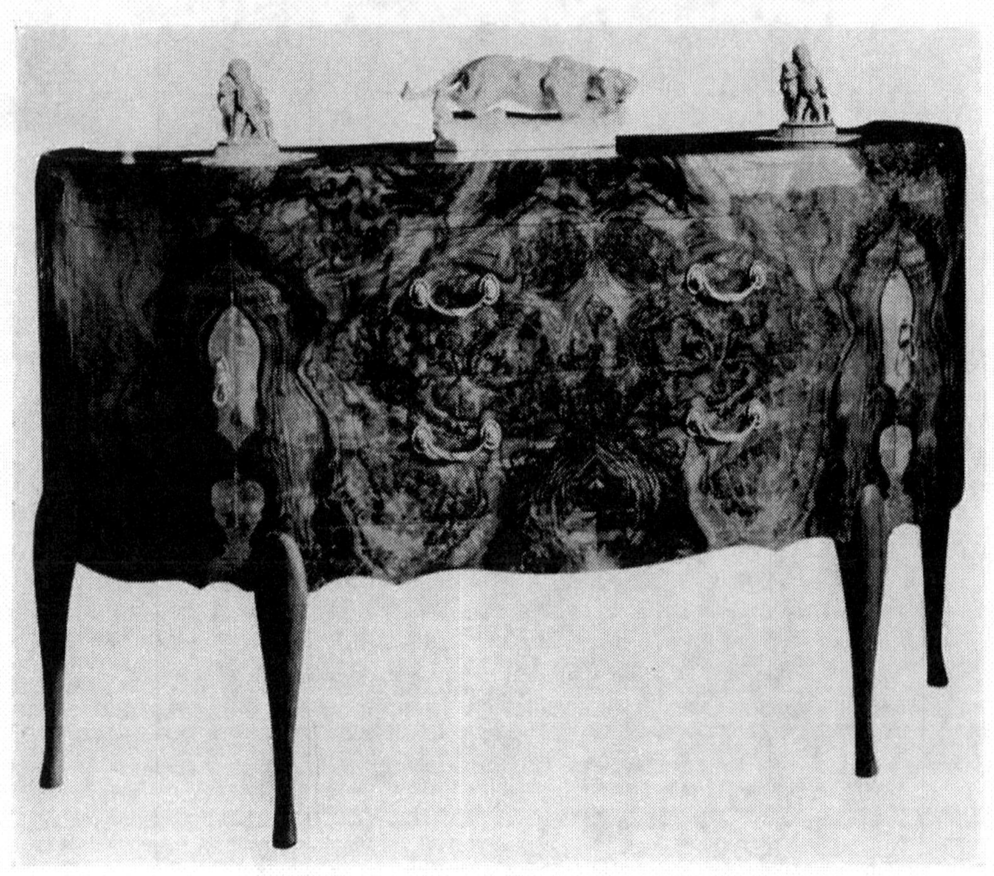

GROSVENOR SIDEBOARD, NO. 533-C.
BURR WALNUT

MAURICE ADAMS

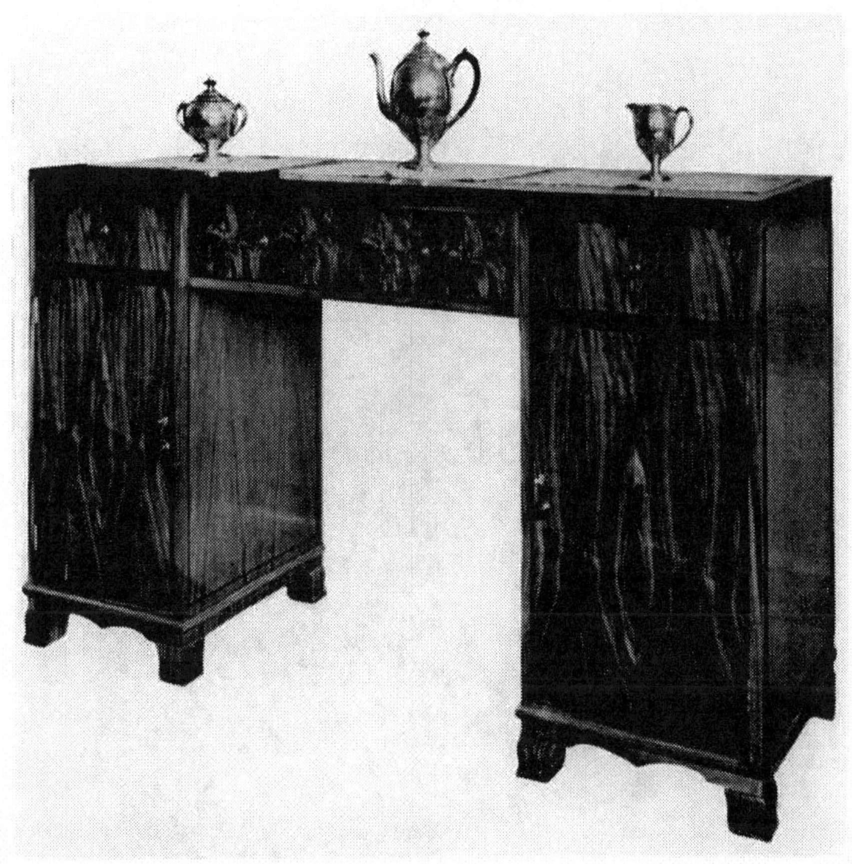

WAXED WALNUT SIDEBOARD NO. 544-C MAURICE ADAMS

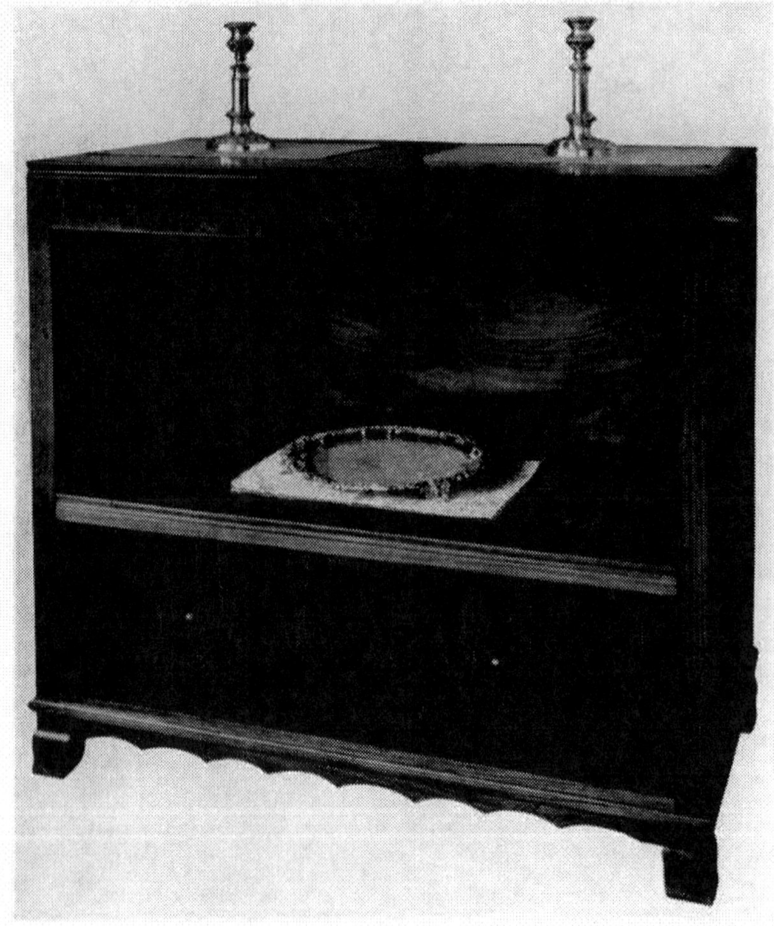

WAXED WALNUT BUFFET, NO. 546-C MAURICE ADAMS

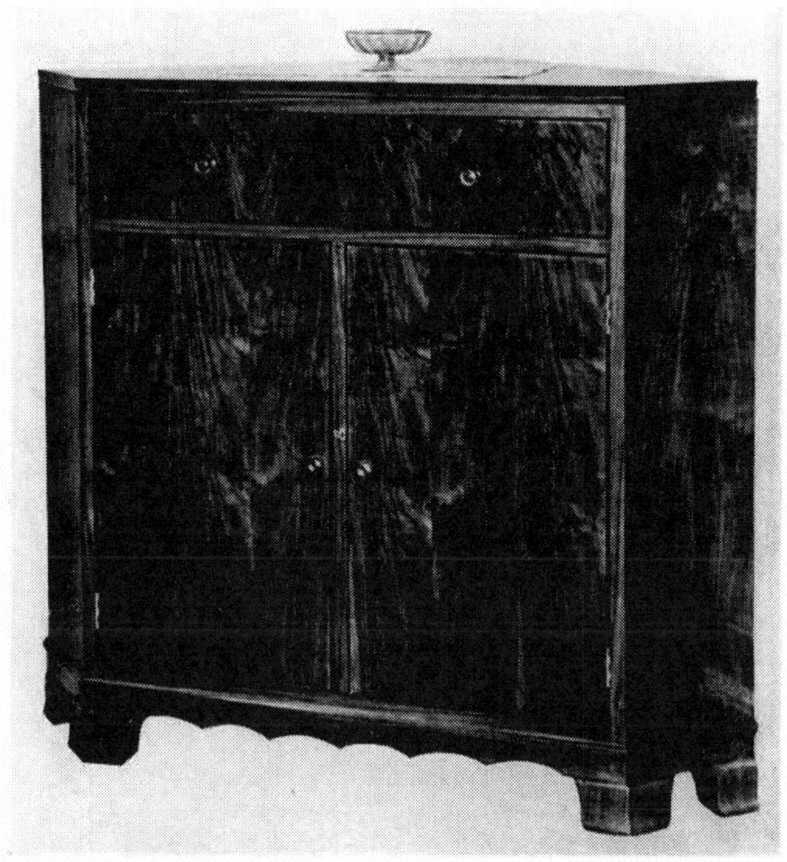

WAXED WALNUT CORNER CABINET, NO. 545-C MAURICE ADAMS

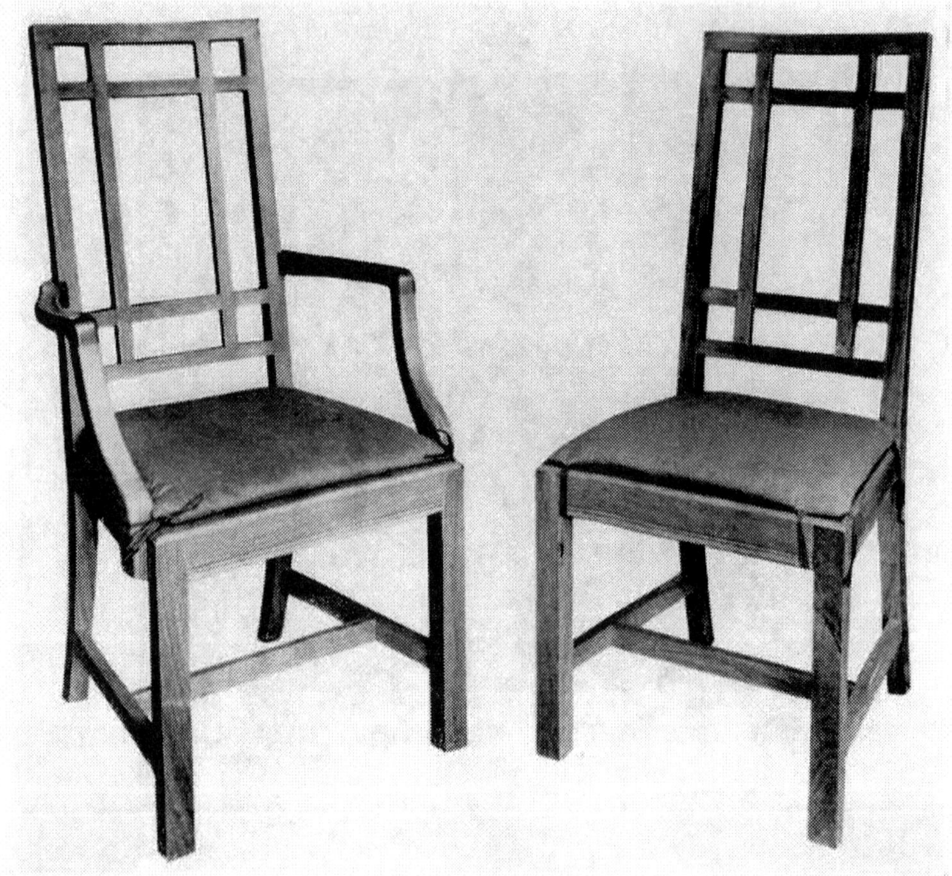

WAXED WALNUT CHAIRS, NO. 551-C, WOOD SEATS, LOOSE CUSHIONS MAURICE ADAMS

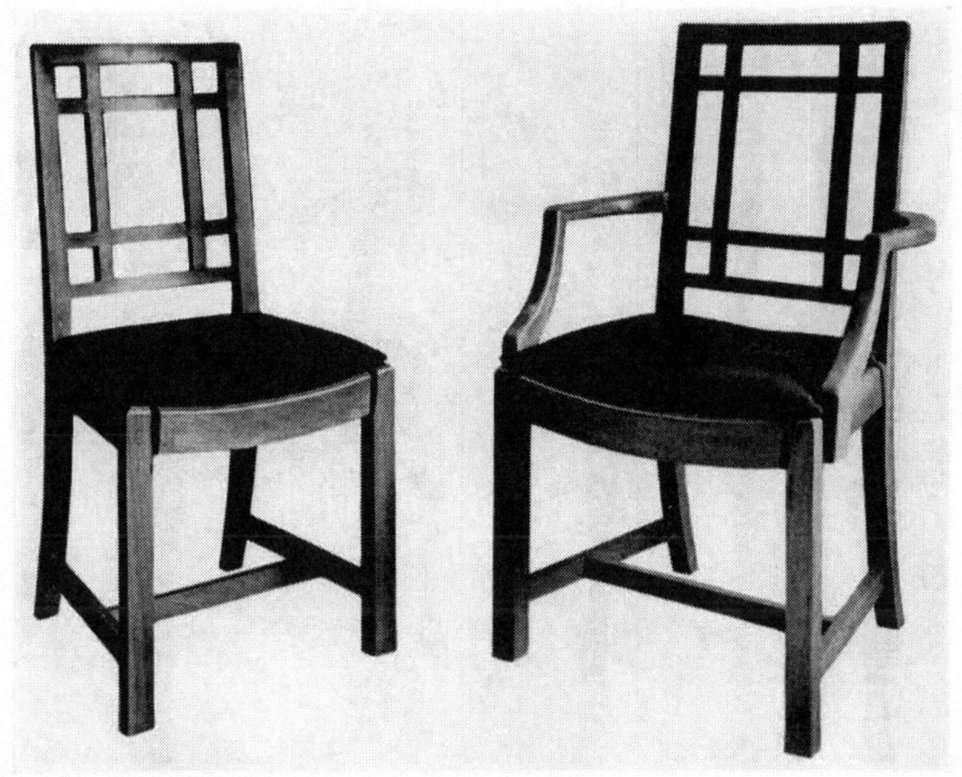

WAXED WALNUT CHAIRS, NO. 405-D, SADDLE WOOD SEATS, LOOSE CUSHIONS MAURICE ADAMS

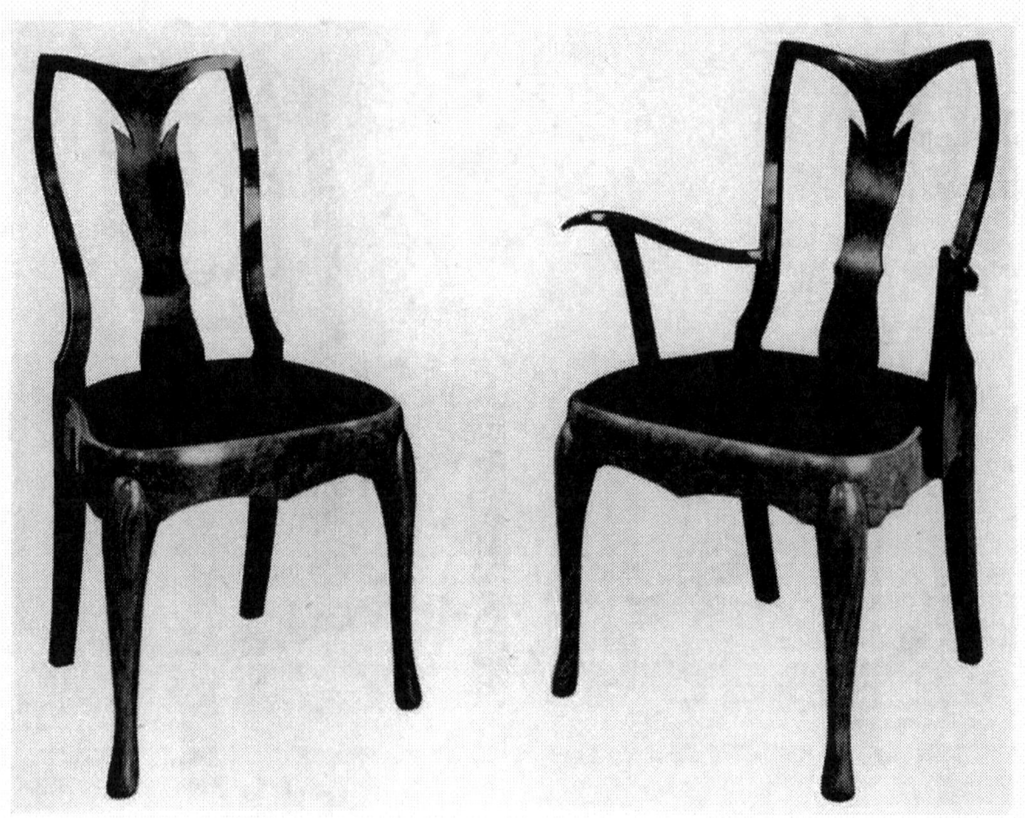

GROSVENOR CHAIRS, NO. 484-C MAURICE ADAMS

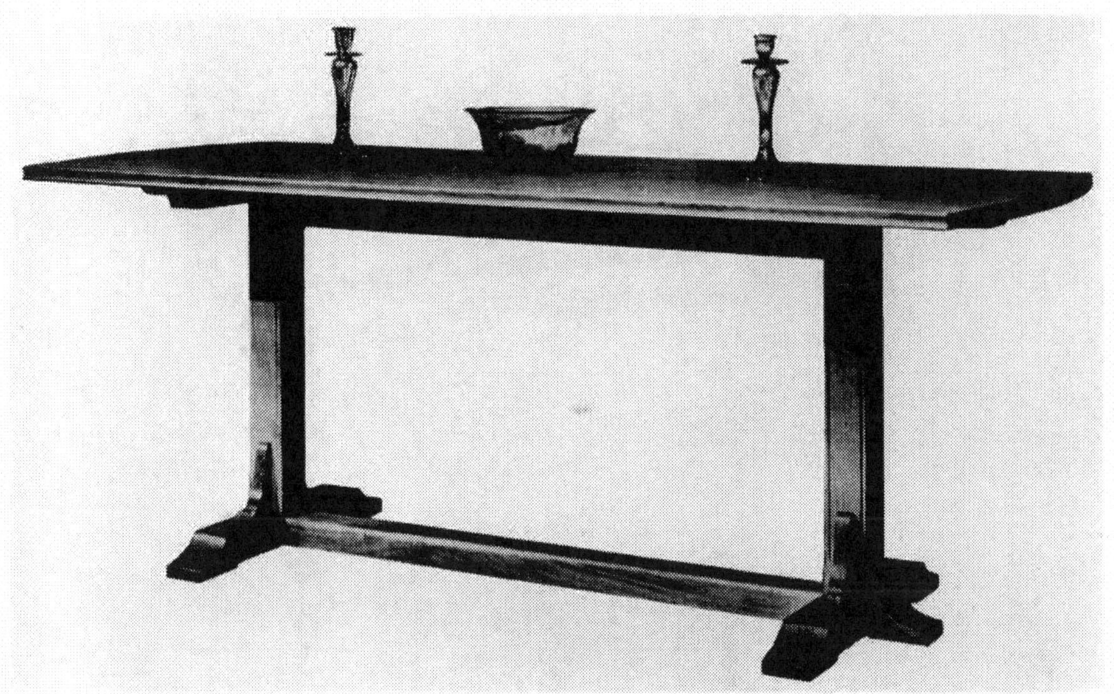

NATURAL OAK TABLE, NO. 407-C MAURICE ADAMS

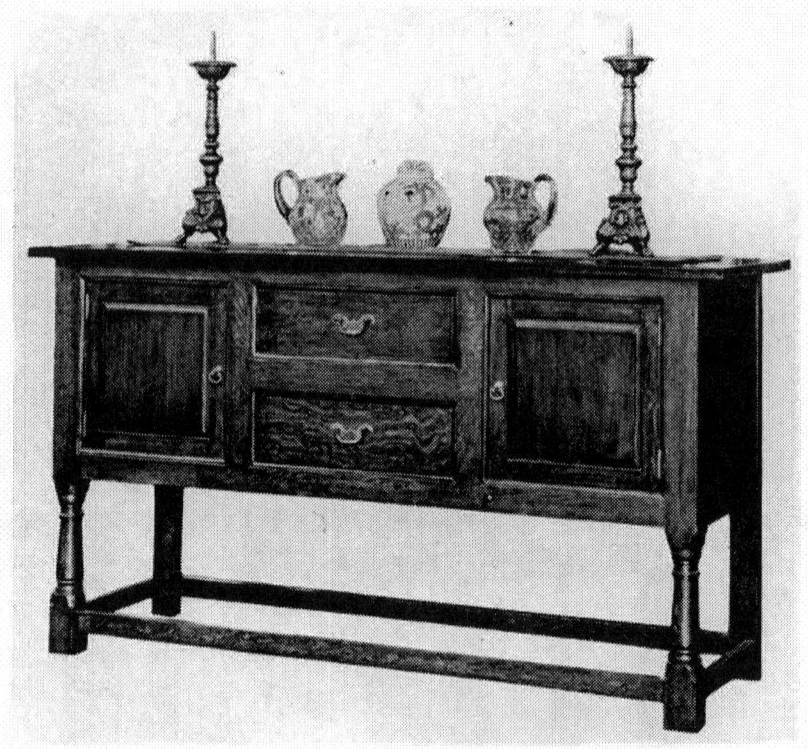

OAK SIDEBOARD, NO. 118-C MAURICE ADAMS

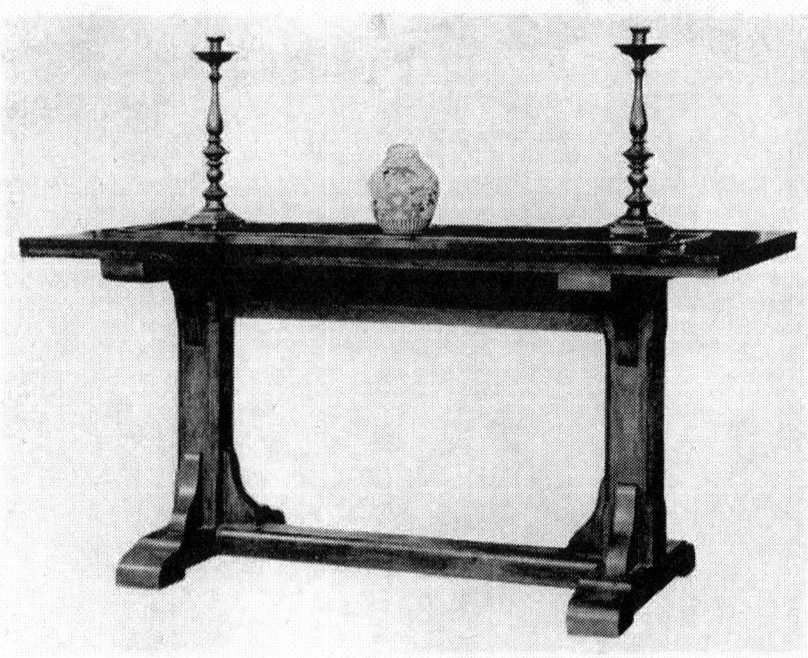

OAK DINING TABLE, NO. 243-C MAURICE ADAMS

# THE LIVING ROOM

# THE LIVING ROOM

FOR the drawing room, or as this room is now sometimes called the living room and by others the Lounge, the first furniture essentials are one or two really comfortable easy chairs and a settee. For large rooms the settee may be 6 ft. long. In medium and small rooms, 4 ft. 6 ins., 5 ft. or 5 ft. 6 ins. will be better sizes. Settees and easy chairs should be stuffed all hair, have double sprung seats and real down loose cushions to seat and back. The Grosvenor settee (page 72) and chair (page 73) illustrated herein are particularly comfortable. They require less floor space than the "saddle-bag" type and are more attractive by reason of their special design.

One or two occasional chairs will be necessary. These may suitably have arms with upholstered backs as well as seats. Our Grosvenor occasional chair is suitable and may be covered to match the upholstery. To complete the furnishing of drawing rooms we may add a dwarf circular tea table and tray about 2 ft. diameter, a round magazine table 2 ft. 6 ins. to 3 ft. 6 ins. diameter, a side cabinet with cupboard and one or more tall cabinets.

To illustrate our ideas and suggestions as to the manner in which a modern drawing room should be furnished, we refer the reader to the views of drawing room at Moor Park, illustrated herewith. This room serves as the principal living room. As such it is used for reading, music, including wireless, and the reception of visitors. Our aim was to make the room interesting and artistically satisfying—above all, comfortable and easy to keep clean.

The room presents a well furnished and even luxurious appearance, yet it will be noted that there is not a single article which has not its definite use, place and purpose. Everything in the room is of a quality in keeping with the scheme. A single purpose artistically expressed engenders a restful feeling.

Comfort is provided by a 5 ft. 6 ins. settee, double sprung and having loose back and seat down cushions, and one easy chair to match. These are covered with black poplin, all cushions being faced with black and gold dragon silk. There are two upholstered occasional arm-chairs covered to match. The other furniture comprises circular Grosvenor dwarf tea table and tray, (page 73) 2 ft. 6 ins. circular Grosvenor occasional or magazine table (page 76).

4 ft. 6 ins. Grosvenor side cabinet with cupboard (used for music) page 71, two tall Grosvenor side cabinets with open compartment, containing novels, magazines and reading material generally, radio cabinet taking radio and wireless gramophone. Grosvenor boudoir grand piano and music stool. Artificial light is provided by two silver fittings above the mantel-piece and one floor standard. There are no pictures, their place being taken by four carved walnut mirrors. The room is panelled and painted pale apple green; the panelling being arranged to suit placing of the furniture. The ceiling is richly ornamented with raised ornament finished with silver leaf. The four French circular-headed windows have red silk taffeta curtains, lined and interlined and finished with pelmets of the same material embroidered and fringed with silver. The floor has a small Chinese carpet in which crocus yellow predominates. All the furniture is of very choice burr walnut. The door handles and electric switch plates were specially designed. They are finished silver. Apart from the furniture and decorations, the only ornaments in the room are three china figures on the mantel-piece; one piece of china in each tall cabinet, and three pieces of china on the side cabinet.

The Grosvenor piano in this room is of special interest, demonstrating that there are no technical difficulties or reasons why a piano should not be made a work of art. Artistically furnished rooms are often spoiled by the introduction of an ordinary commercial piano. This example shows that we are able to both design and make the piano case to suit the style of furnishing.

We do not advise polished or figured wood as panelling or otherwise for drawing rooms. Neither do we favour cloth panels arranged with contrasting borders or framing. Many have a strong objection to cloth wall coverings of any kind, but artistically speaking, wall draperies provide an excellent ground for the effective display of furniture. Silk or other damask of soft colour and subdued pattern may be stretched tightly over the drawing room walls without breaks of any kind.

Drawing room floors are adapted to parquet. Alternatively they may be covered all over with deep pile plain colour carpet. In either case one or more first quality oriental rugs will be desirable.

Large drawing room windows by reason of their size, should receive more than ordinary care in their treatment. Heavy damasks and brocades may be used for long curtains, but thin silks and taffetas may also be used if interlined as well as lined. Care and judgment must be exercised in selecting materials for drawing room curtains. A rich feeling of luxury should be aimed at. It is advisable to test the material in the actual room before the material is cut because its effect will depend largely upon the number and arrangement of the windows. Rooms lighted from one side only are difficult in this respect because the curtains are seen in shadow against the light. On the other hand rooms lighted from two or more sides and rooms with bay windows do not present the same difficulty. The richest effects are only to be obtained by the use of real silk, and a real feeling of luxury will not be possible without rich silk window curtains, and in most cases braided and fringed pelmets, plain or embroidered, will also be necessary. For those, however, who cannot afford silk there is now an excellent range of really beautiful materials in artificial silk costing about 15/- a yard. In other cases, art silk taffeta costing about 6/- a yard may be used. Curtains will never look well unless they be properly cut and made. This calls for expert work and rarely can this satisfactorily be done at home. The slight additional cost of professionally made curtains and pelmets will be amply repaid both in appearance and durability.

For short windows, pelmets present a top heavy appearance, but for long curtains and tall windows pelmets are necessary to hide the curtain rods, and they add a well dressed appearance to the windows. The improvement created by well proportioned pelmets is considerable.

The shape and depth of pelmets cannot be decided by rule. The windows should be measured and drawn out on paper to small scale. The drawing will also indicate the position of floor and ceiling. Over this drawing the proposed pelmets will be roughly sketched until the most suitable shaping and size for the pelmet is arrived at. From this full size outline drawings will be made of the pelmet. The shaping and size of the pelmet must be carefully proportioned to suit the window. The above method leaves nothing to chance, so that both curtains and pelmet will appear exactly as intended. The reason why pelmets so frequently are badly proportioned is that sufficient trouble is not taken in their preparation.

The pelmet's contour must harmonize with the proportion and type of window. Square-headed windows present little difficulty, but circular-headed windows require special treatment. Pelmets to circular-headed windows should follow the curve of the window opening, otherwise the pelmet edge will cut off the top of the window and give an unsightly appearance. An example of pelmets to semi-circular-headed windows is shown in the photographs of the drawing room at Moor Park herein.

Over elaborate braiding is not advised either to curtains or pelmets. Pelmets should always have fringed bottom edges and braided top edges. The top may have ½ in. cord edge in addition. Plain pelmets embroidered with applique purpose-designed embroidery, as at Moor Park, greatly enrich the decorative appearance of any room.

Pelmets need only a slight projection, otherwise they will appear top heavy. 4½ ins. will usually suffice. The curtains may be carried on ½ in. brass rail attached to underside of pelmet board. Patent curtain runners may be used, if desired, in place of the rods.

The best form of light fitting for the drawing room is the silk shade carried on a wood or metal plate. Examples, both of metal and wood light fittings, are illustrated in these pages. The hand-made metal fittings, finished old silver, are by far the best, artistically speaking. Such fittings are ornaments in themselves and materially beautify the room. Silvered wood and compo. plates are, however, cheaper and can be made both artistic and effective. In no case should ordinary commercial fittings be used as they will spoil any artistic furnishing scheme. The light points may be arranged in the wall panels. Their design may form an essential part of the decorative scheme. If there is no panelling the light fittings may be placed in positions corresponding with the principal pieces of furniture.

Centrally-placed hanging bowl lights are best avoided. Silk shades fixed direct to the ceiling may effectively be arranged about three feet from the four corners of the room.

An ornamental ceiling such as may be seen in rooms herein illustrated obviously is a great asset by adding an appearance of luxury.

# LIVING ROOM FURNITURE

MENTION was made earlier in this book of the Grosvenor boudoir grand piano. The instrument is a standard "Collard and Collard" fitted in case designed and made by us to harmonize with our Grosvenor drawing room furniture. All exposed surfaces of the case, including inside of lid, are veneered with exceptionally fine burr walnut. All metal parts of case are silver-plated. Any make of piano may be supplied in this style of case. We can also design special cases to harmonize with any style of furnishing.

There is now little demand for the old-fashioned type of china display cabinet. This no doubt is largely due to the more general use of this room as principal living room or lounge. The Grosvenor tall cabinet No. 492 C (page 69) affords an interesting example of a present-day cabinet taking the place of the earlier type. Rich burr walnut and interesting design combine to make the cabinet ornamental. The drawer for magazines, and the cupboard for books and novels make the cabinet useful. The open compartment for the display of one or two pieces of fine china or glass, stamps this definitely as a drawing or living room article of furniture. Cabinets of this type may be arranged to suit any particular position by varying the dimensions and accommodation.

Some form of side table or cabinet is necessary in every drawing room. For this purpose our Grosvenor cabinets of which Nos. 480 C (page 67), 425 C (page 68), 709 C (page 70), 493 C (page 71), and 424 C (page 72) are examples may be supplied in any desired size. These are fitted with cupboard in which may be stored books or music.

The circular Grosvenor magazine (page 75) and occasional tables (page 76) are supplied in a variety of sizes and also as small coffee stools. They are decorative as well as useful.

The dwarf circular tea table and tray No. 413 C (page 73) is now an essential item of the well-furnished lounge.

The Grosvenor settee (page 72) and easy chairs (page 73) are double sprung and stuffed all hair. The loose down cushions to back and seat are added for greater comfort. The arm facing-pieces are of burr walnut. They are supplied also in mahogany.

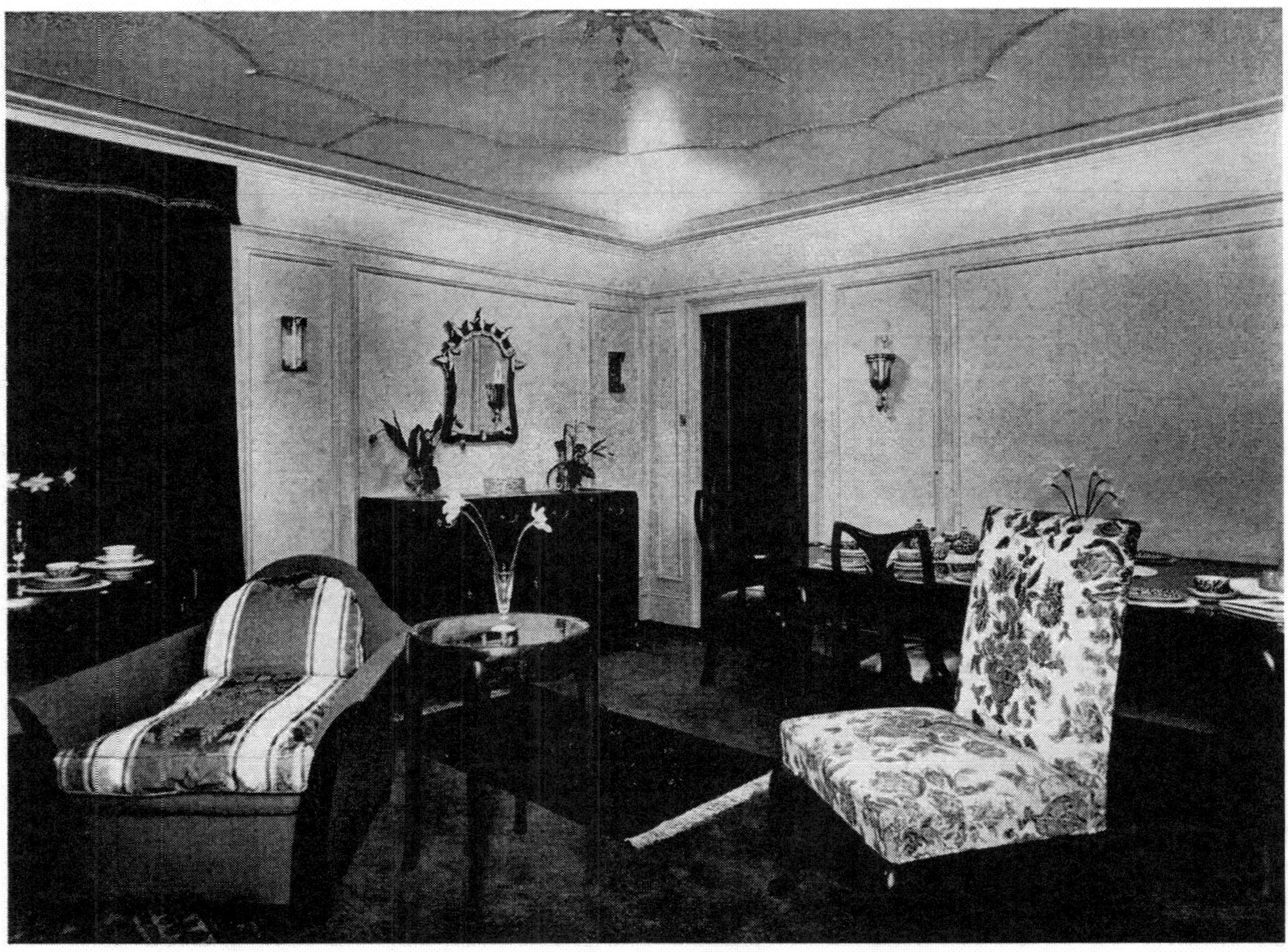

LIVING ROOM

DESIGNED BY MAURICE ADAMS

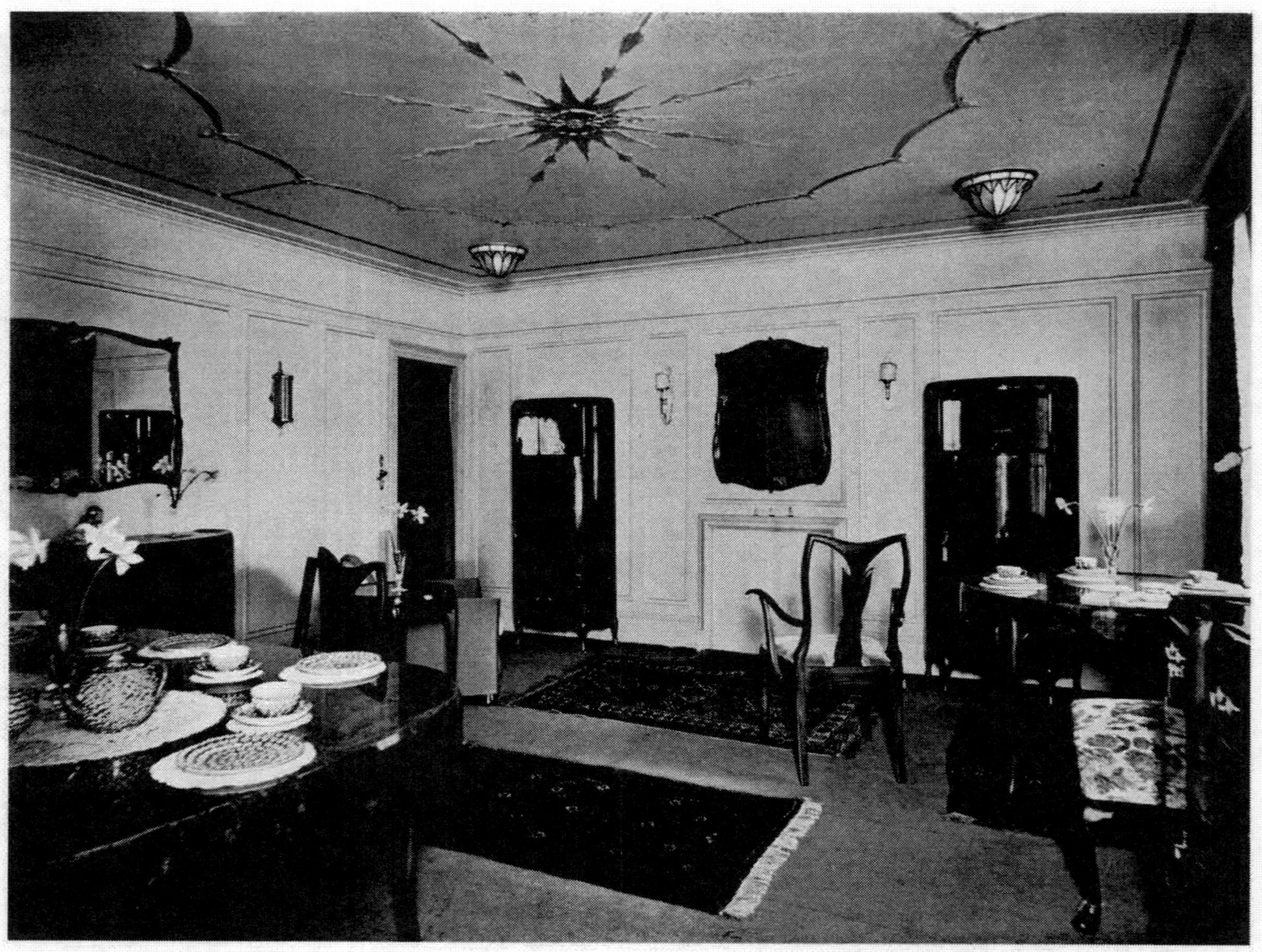

LIVING ROOM

DESIGNED BY MAURICE ADAMS

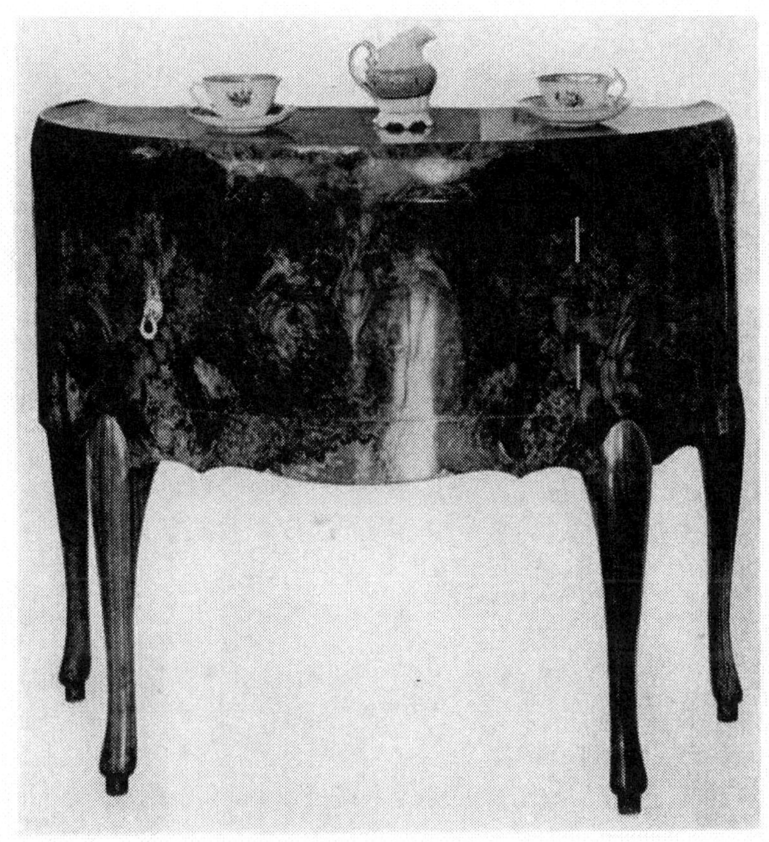

GROSVENOR COMMODE, NO. 480-C
BURR WALNUT

MAURICE ADAMS

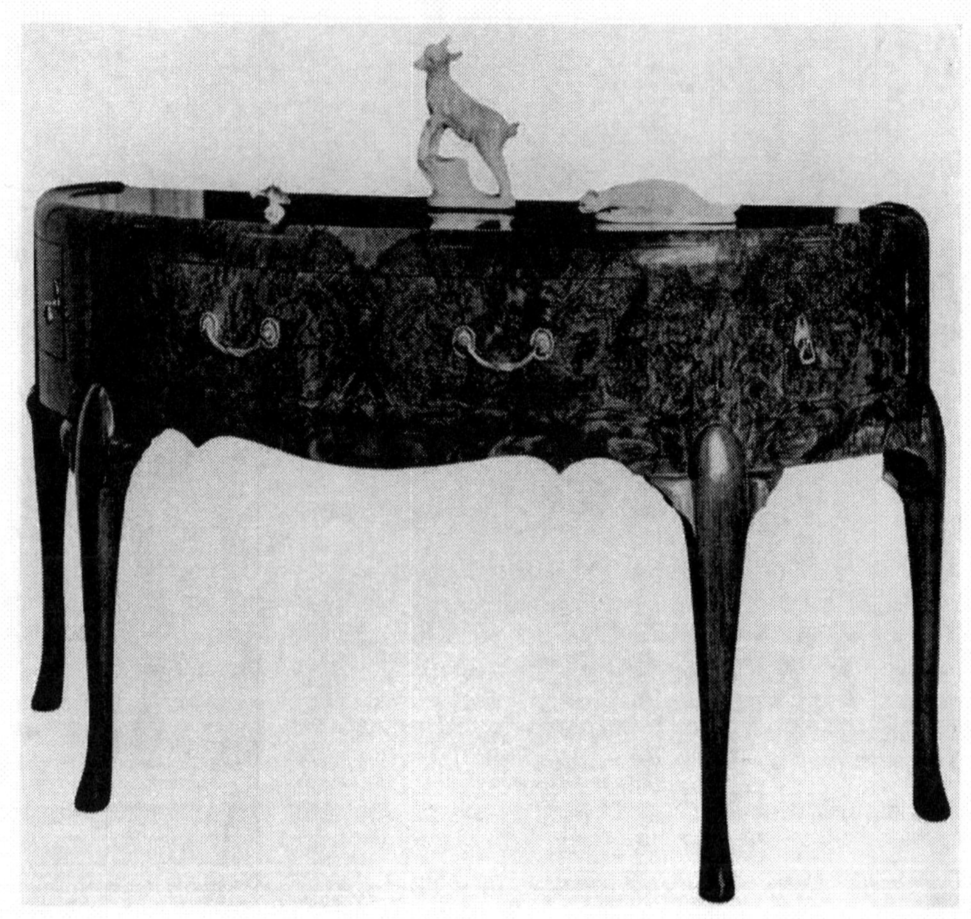

GROSVENOR SIDE TABLE, NO. 425-C
BURR WALNUT

MAURICE ADAMS

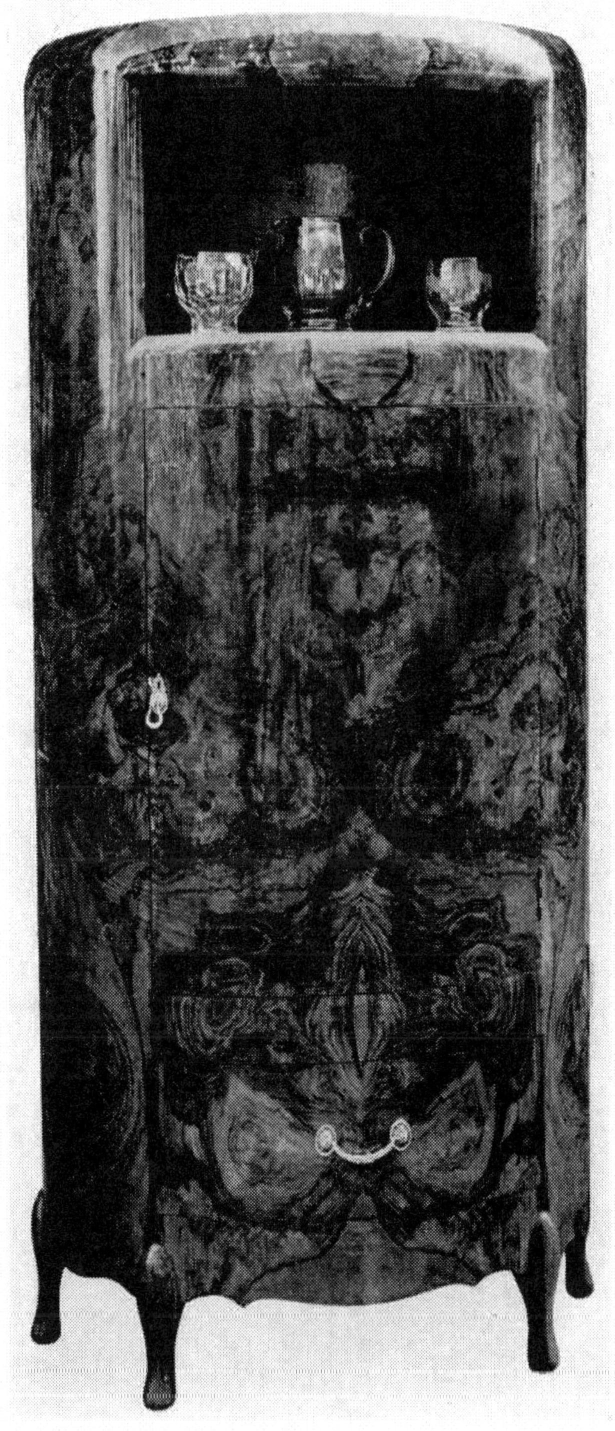

GROSVENOR TALL CABINET, NO. 492-C MAURICE ADAMS

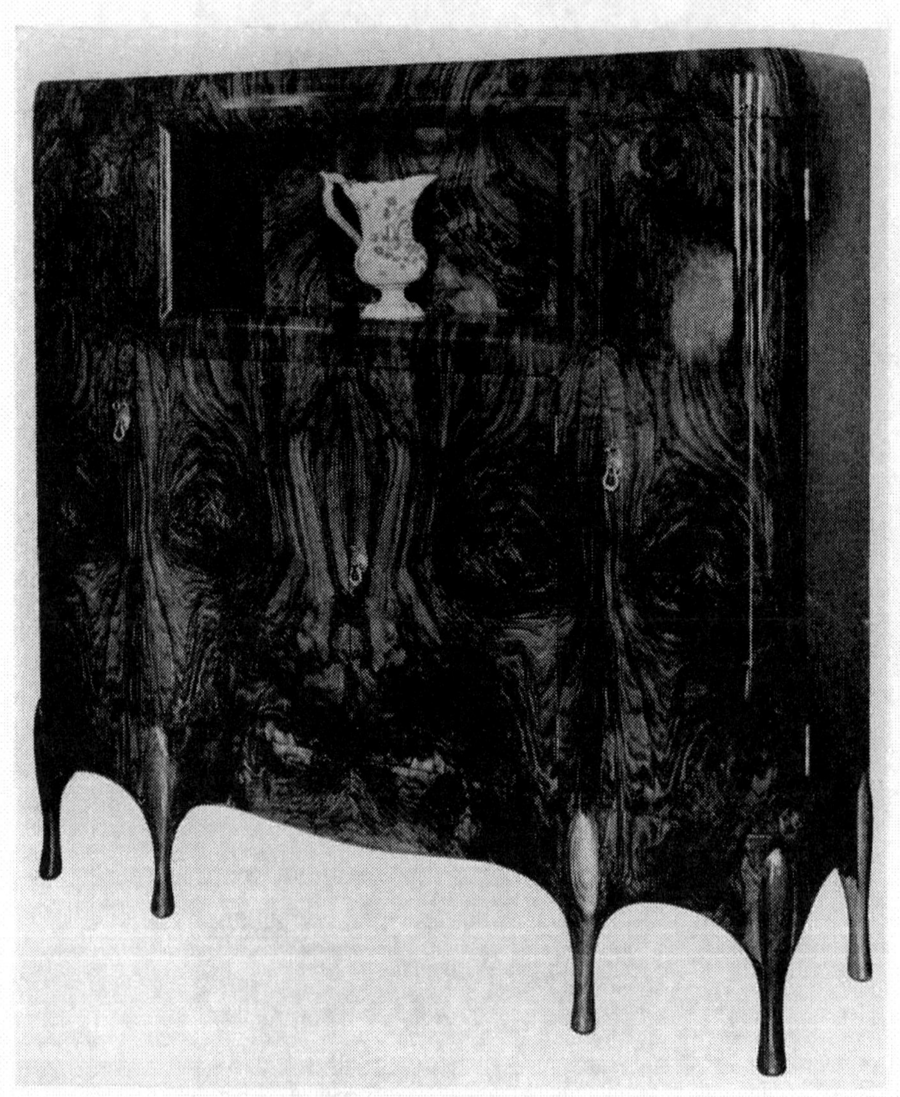

GROSVENOR MUSIC AND BOOK CABINET, NO. 709-C MAURICE ADAMS
BURR WALNUT

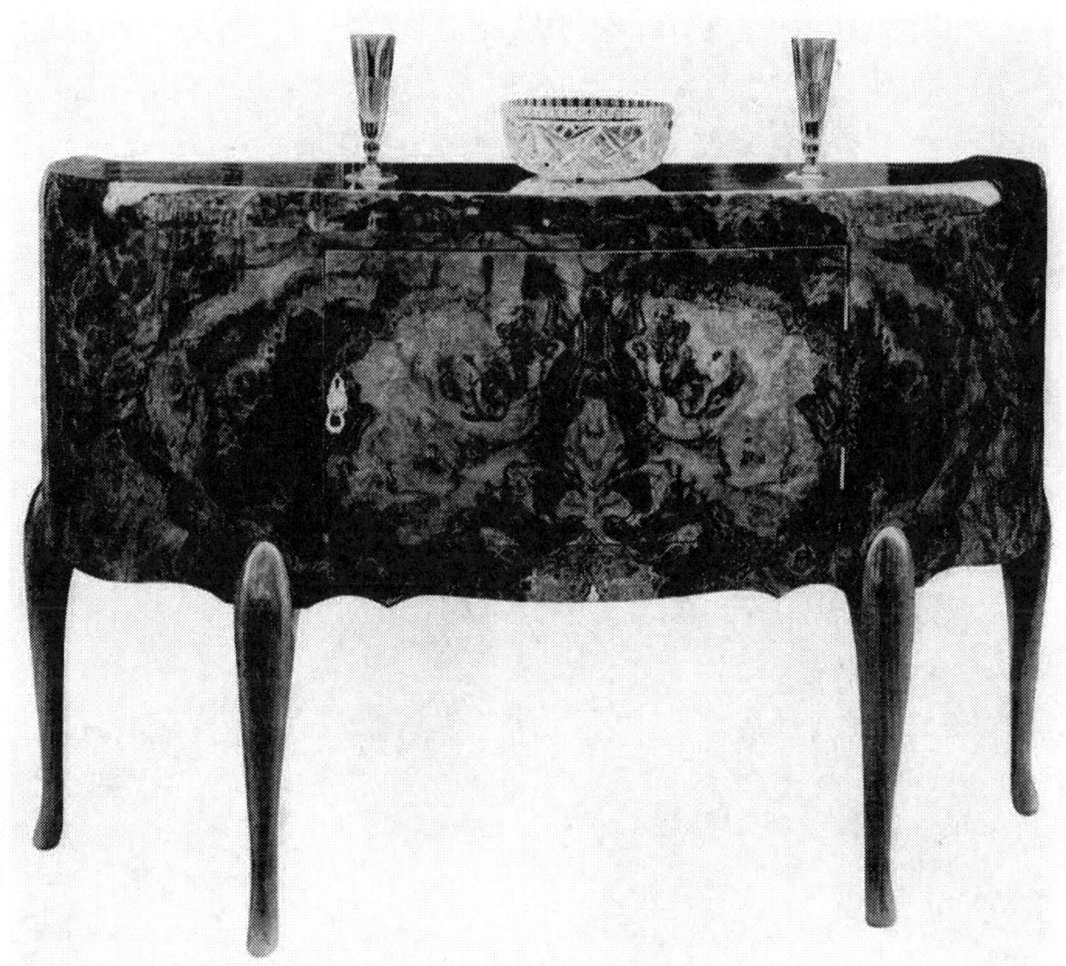

GROSVENOR SIDE CABINET, NO. 493-C
BURR WALNUT

MAURICE ADAMS

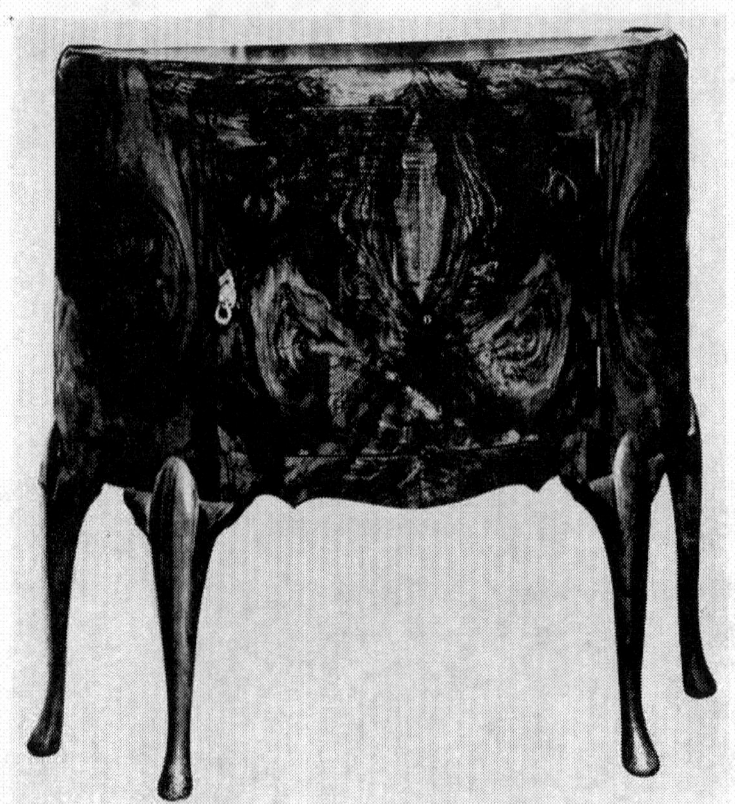

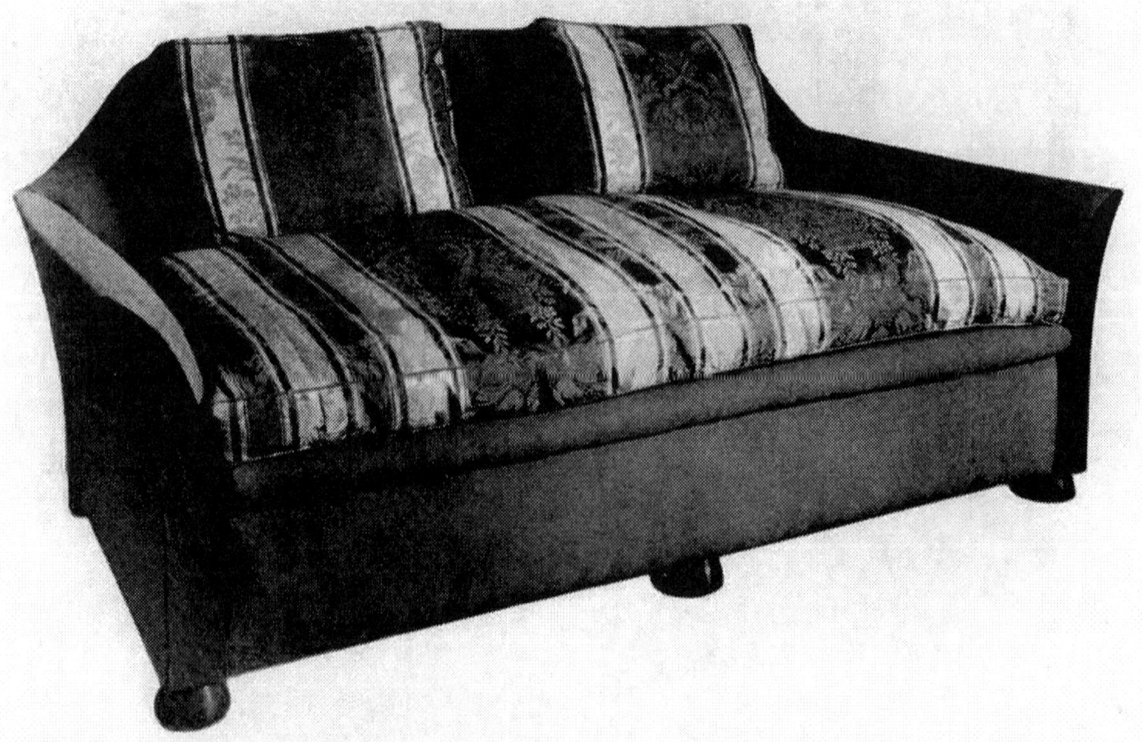

ABOVE—GROSVENOR SIDE CABINET, NO. 424-C
BELOW—GROSVENOR SETTEE, NO. 413-C

MAURICE ADAMS

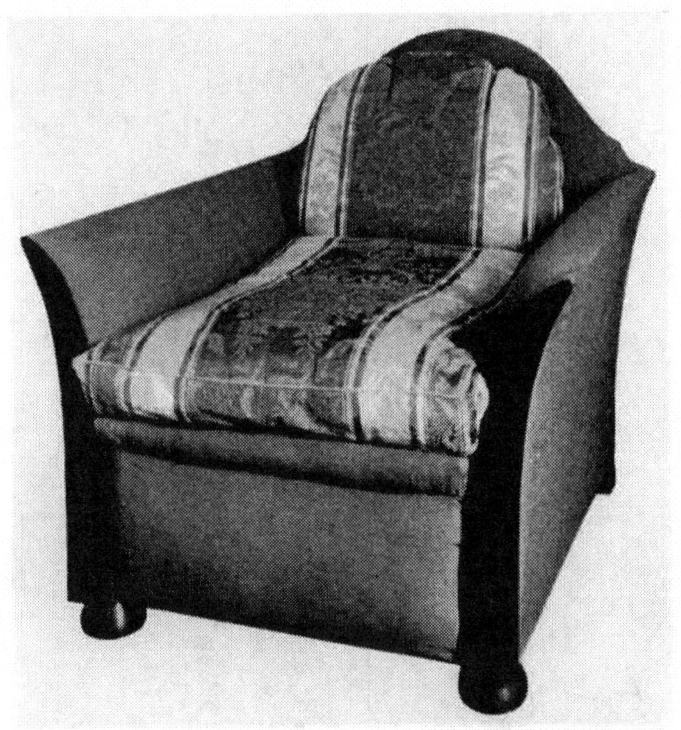

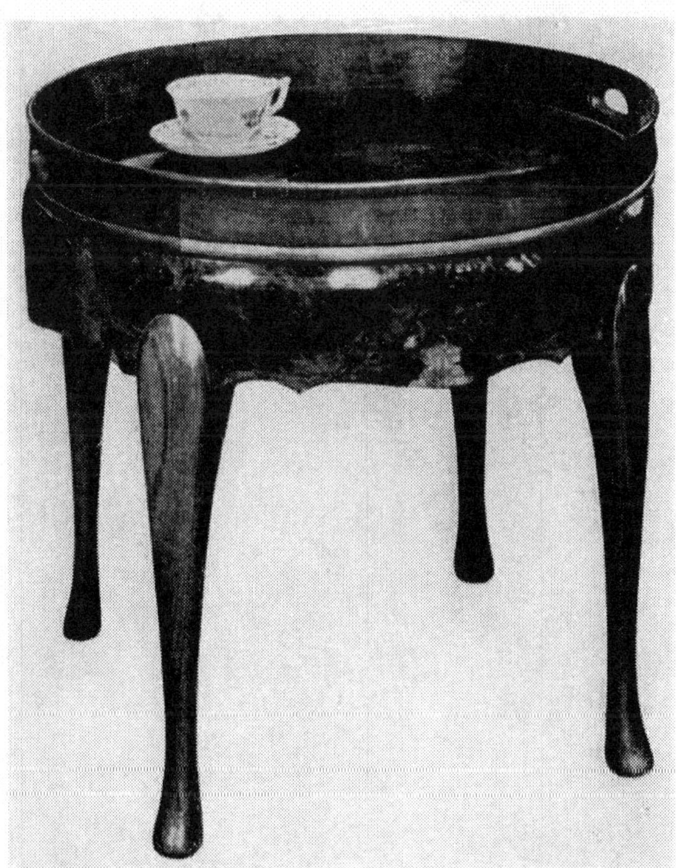

ABOVE—GROSVENOR EASY CHAIR, NO. 413-C MAURICE ADAMS
BELOW—GROSVENOR TEA TABLE AND TRAY, NO. 450-C

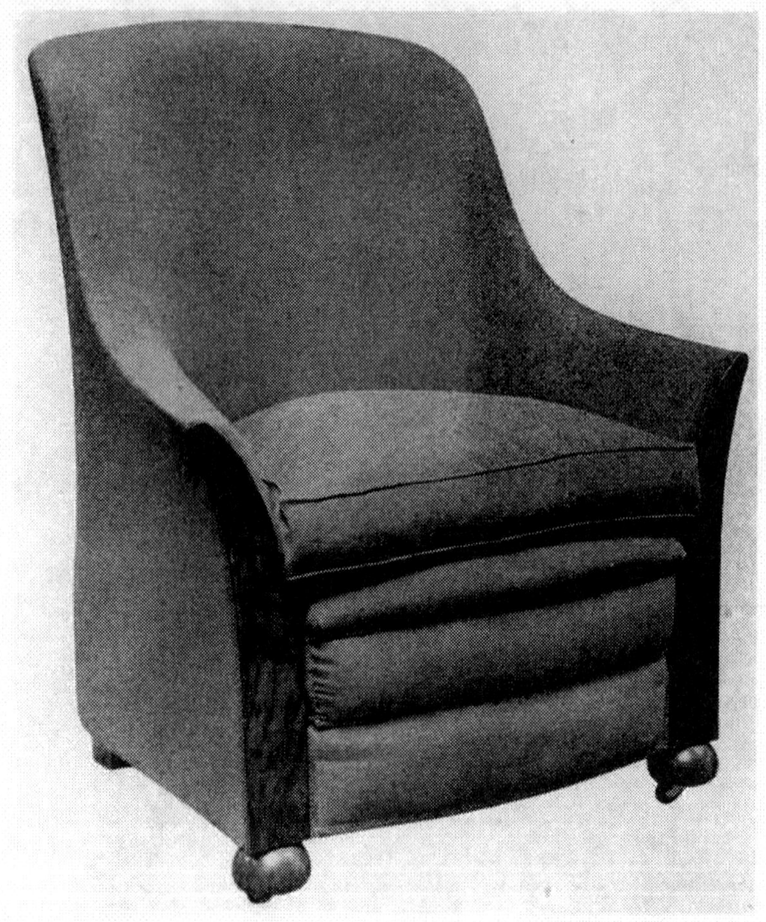

SPOON BACK CHAIR, NO. 402-C MAURICE ADAMS

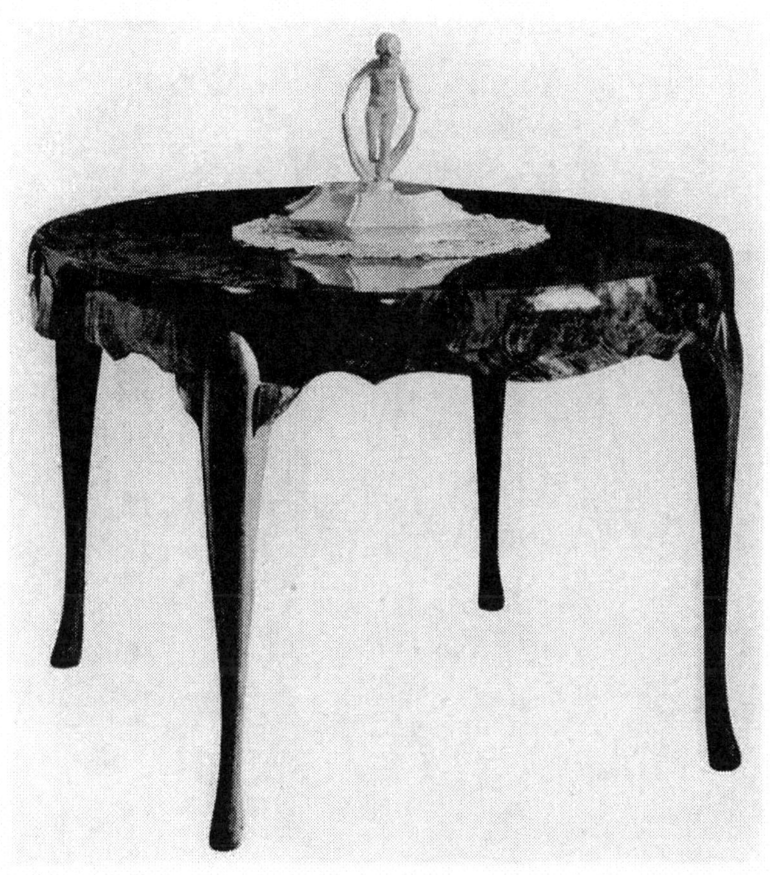

GROSVENOR MAGAZINE TABLE, NO. 451-C MAURICE ADAMS
BURR WALNUT

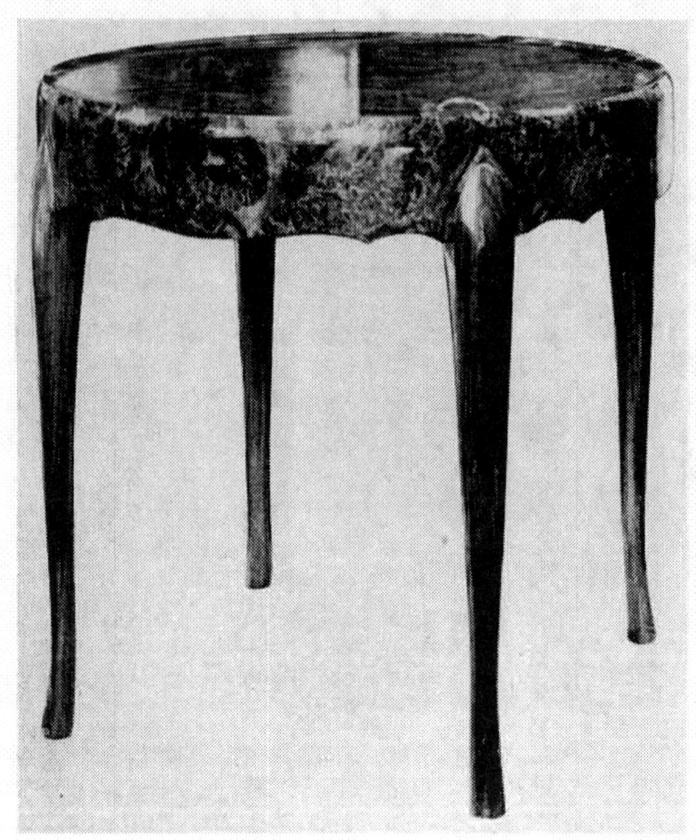

GROSVENOR OCCASIONAL TABLE, NO. 494-C. MAURICE ADAMS
BURR WALNUT

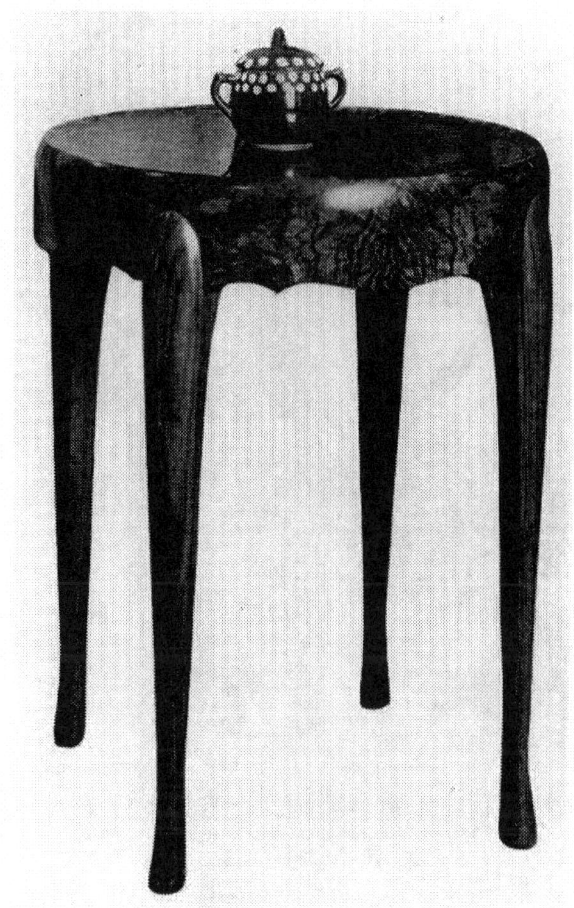

GROSVENOR OCCASIONAL TABLE, NO. 529-C.
BURR WALNUT

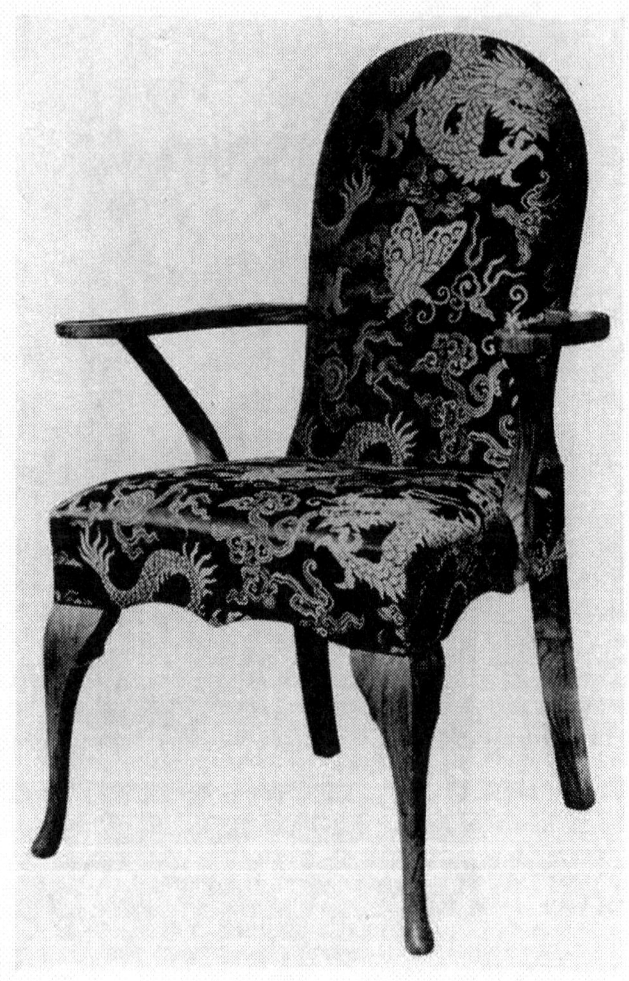

ARMCHAIR, NO. 452-C MAURICE ADAMS

# THE DRAWING ROOM

WE have exhibited each year since the war at the Ideal Home Exhibitions, held at Olympia. We include two interior views of specimen room at Olympia 1929, which measured 25 ft. by 12 ft. 6 ins. The walls were panelled and the ceiling enriched by means of applied raised ornament. The colour scheme was pale blue painted walls, stippled and shaded upwards; ceiling in paler shade of same colour, all ornament above the wall panelling being finished with silver leaf. The carpet and curtains are purple. This room illustrates the Maurice Adams form of interior decoration, and was furnished with selected examples of Maurice Adams' burr walnut furniture in our Grosvenor manner.

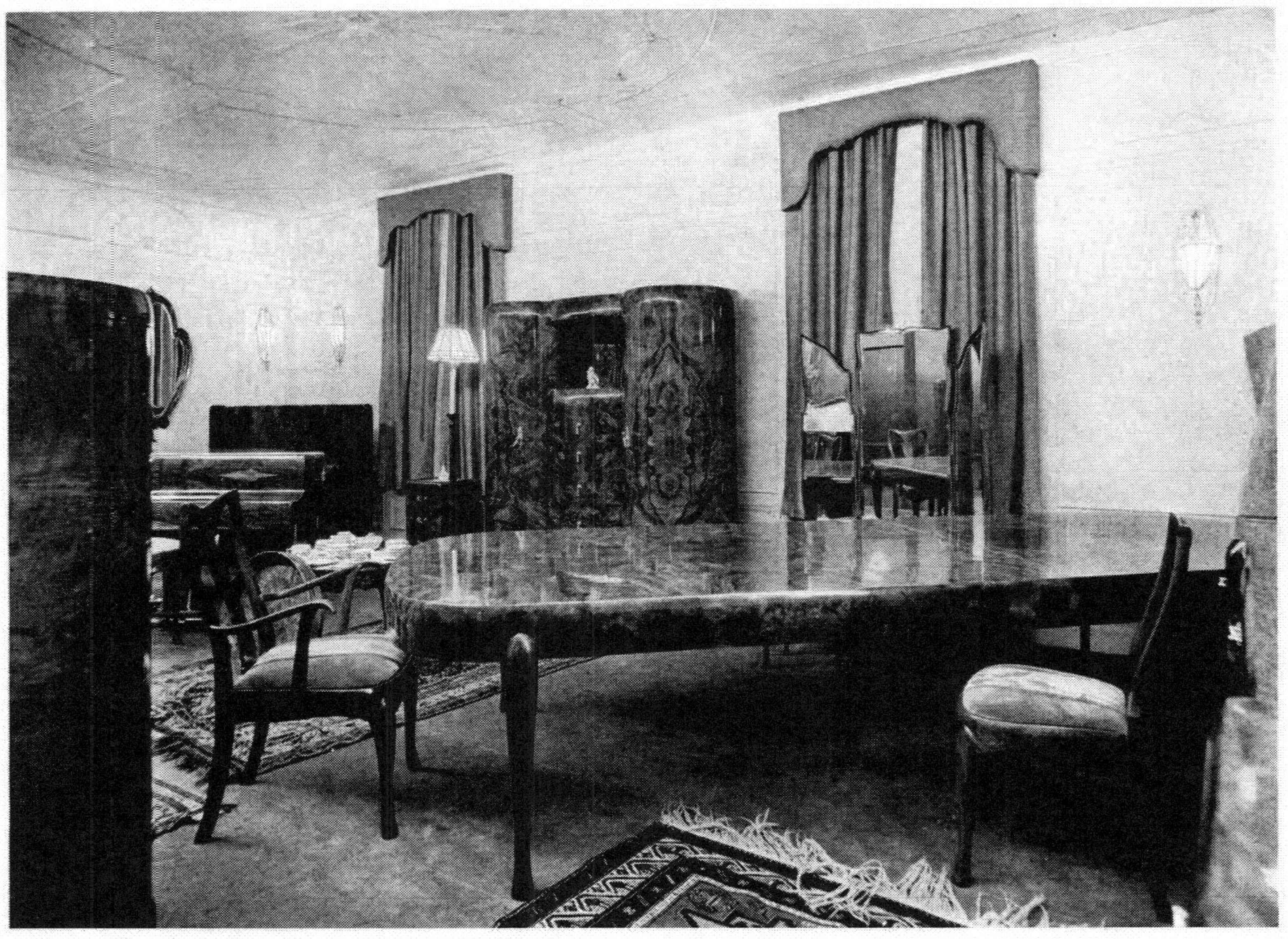

SPECIMEN ROOM, OLYMPIA, 1929
WALLS AND ORNAMENT, BLUE AND SILVER

DESIGNED BY MAURICE ADAMS

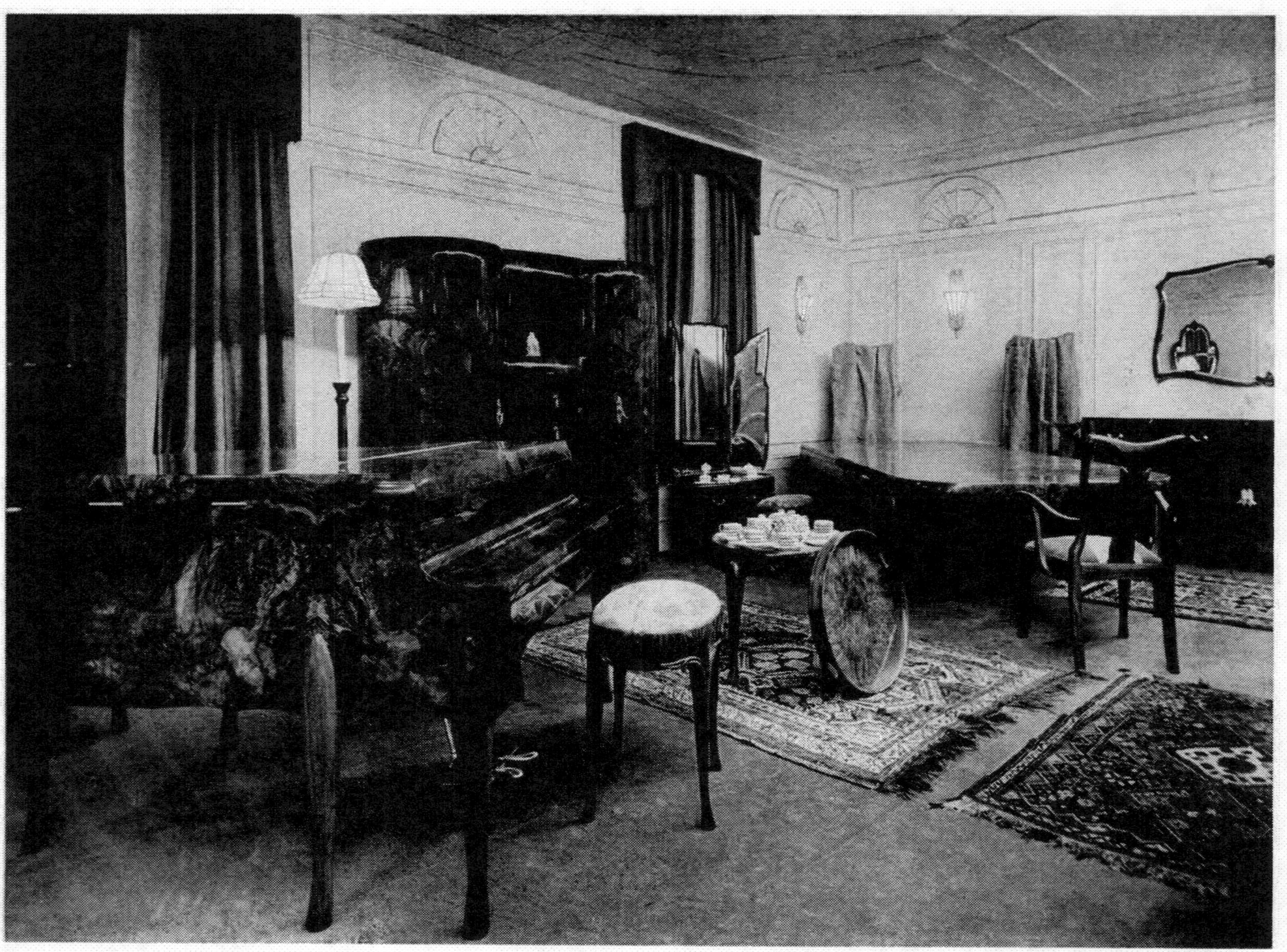

SPECIMEN ROOM, OLYMPIA, 1929
BURR WALNUT FURNITURE

DESIGNED BY MAURICE ADAMS

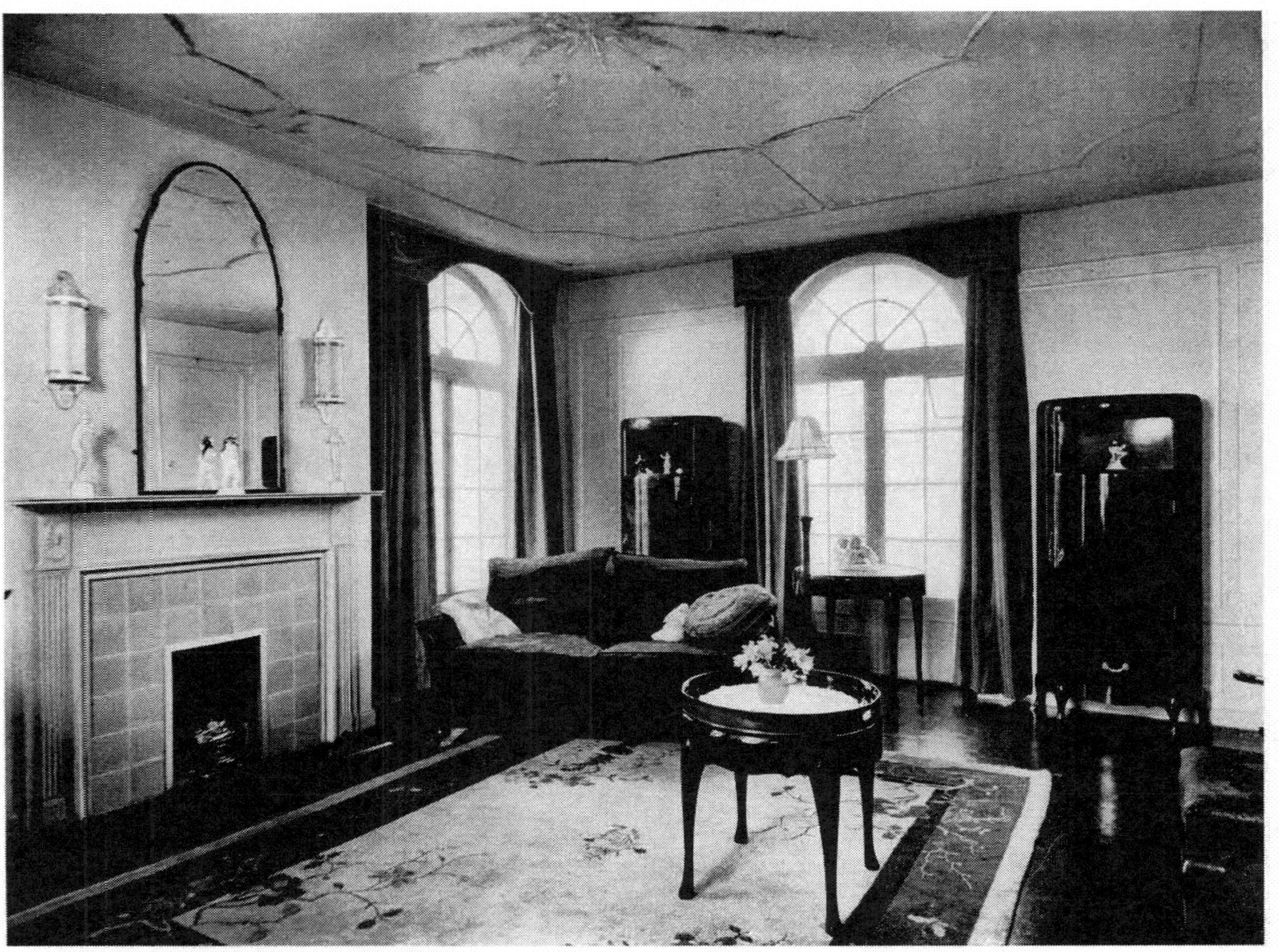

DRAWING ROOM

DESIGNED BY MAURICE ADAMS

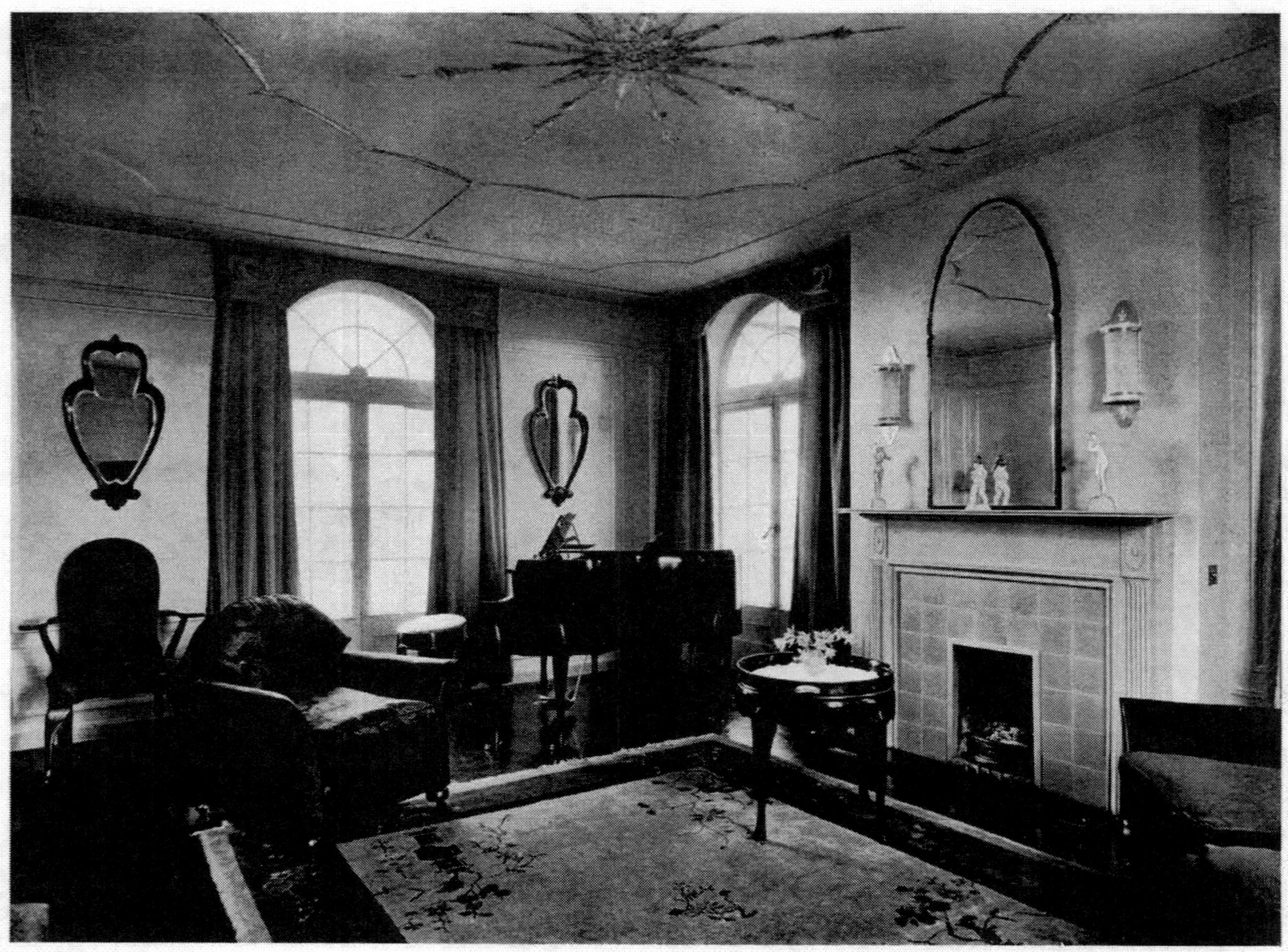

DRAWING ROOM — DESIGNED BY MAURICE ADAMS

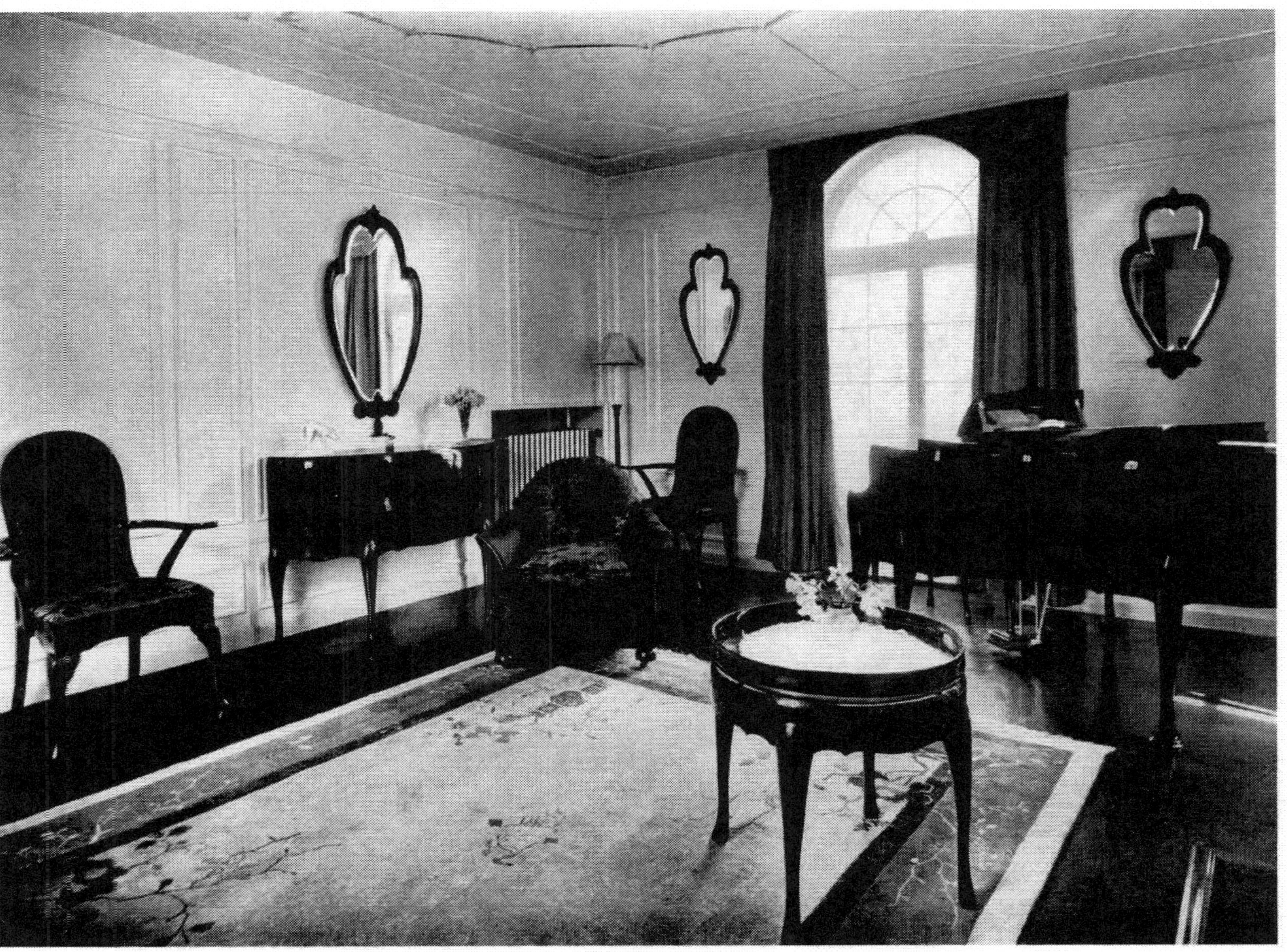

DRAWING ROOM

DESIGNED BY MAURICE ADAMS

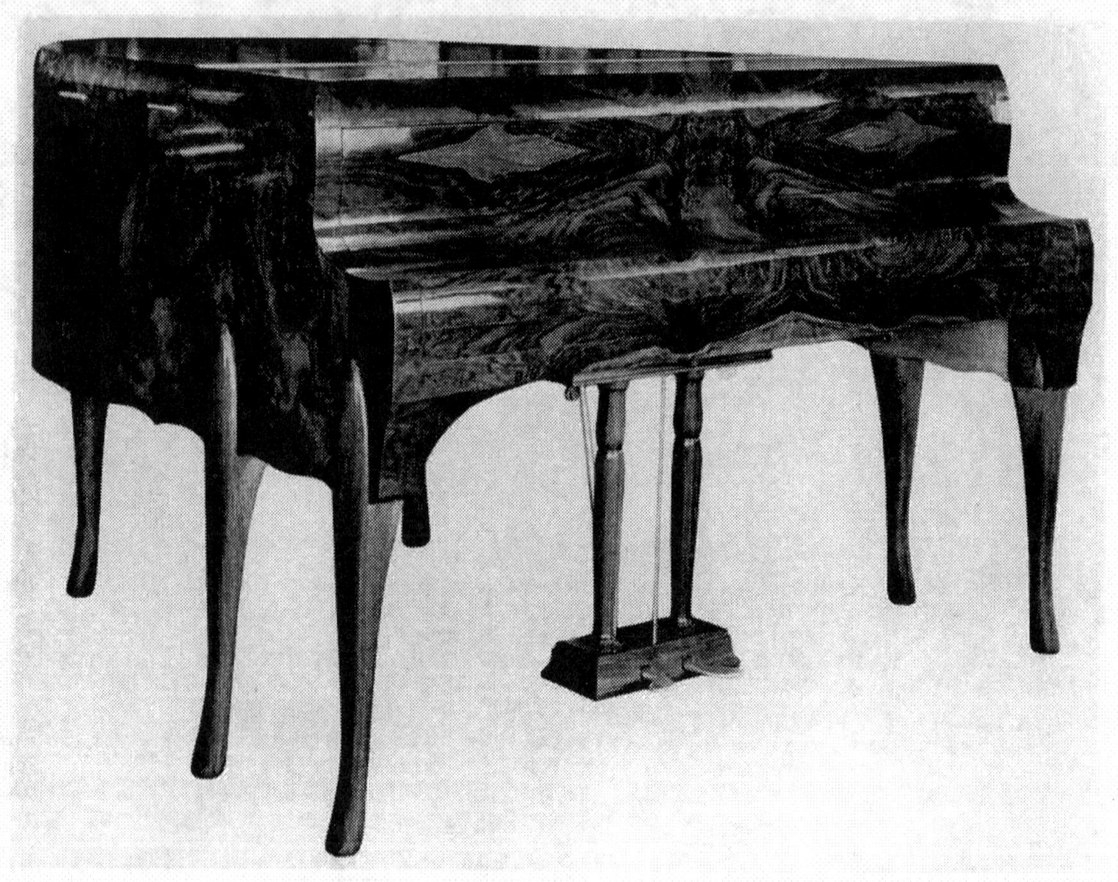

GROSVENOR BOUDOIR GRAND PIANO, NO. 658-C
BURR WALNUT

MAURICE ADAMS

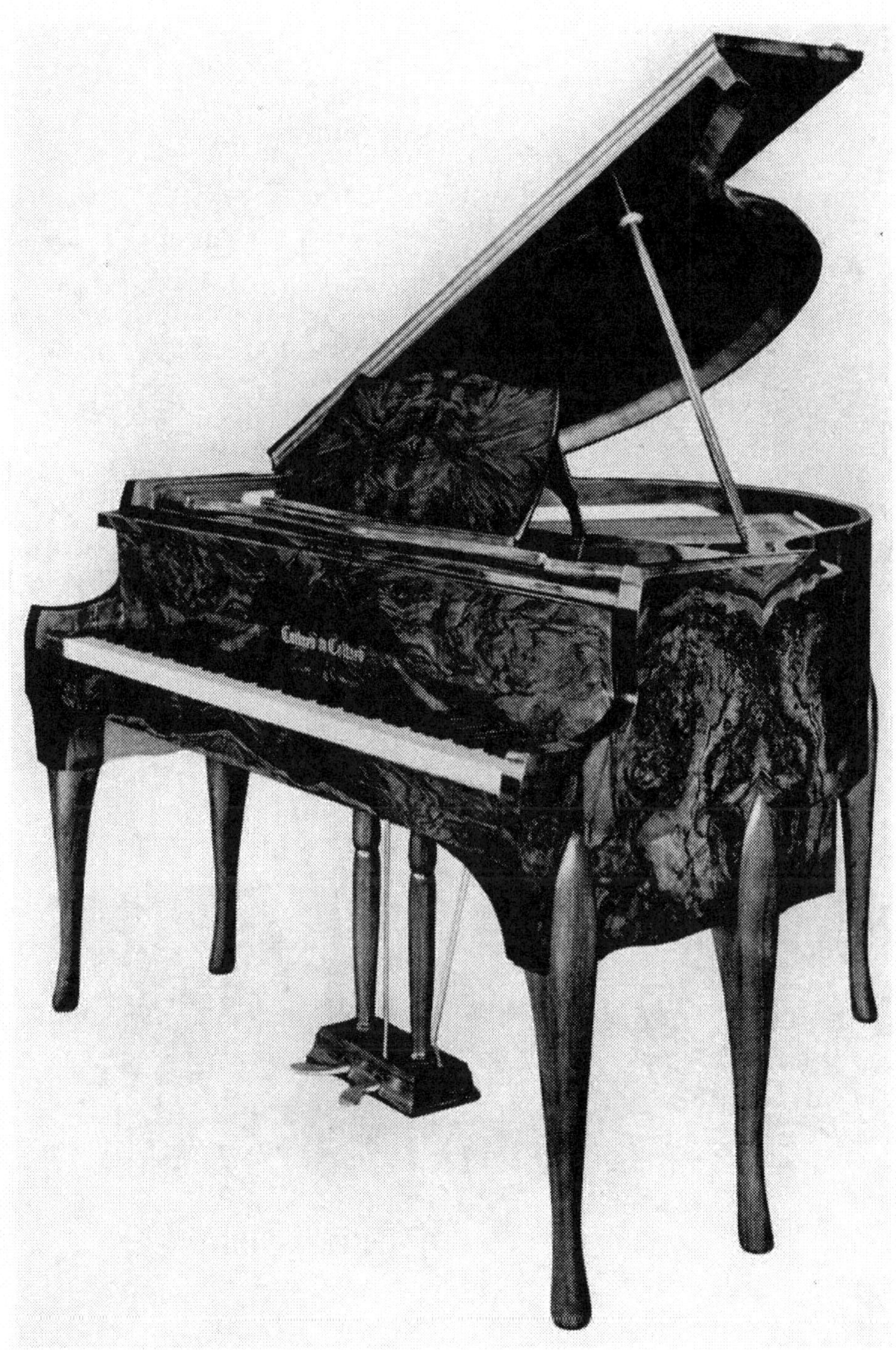

GROSVENOR BOUDOIR GRAND PIANO, NO, 658-C
BURR WALNUT

MAURICE ADAMS

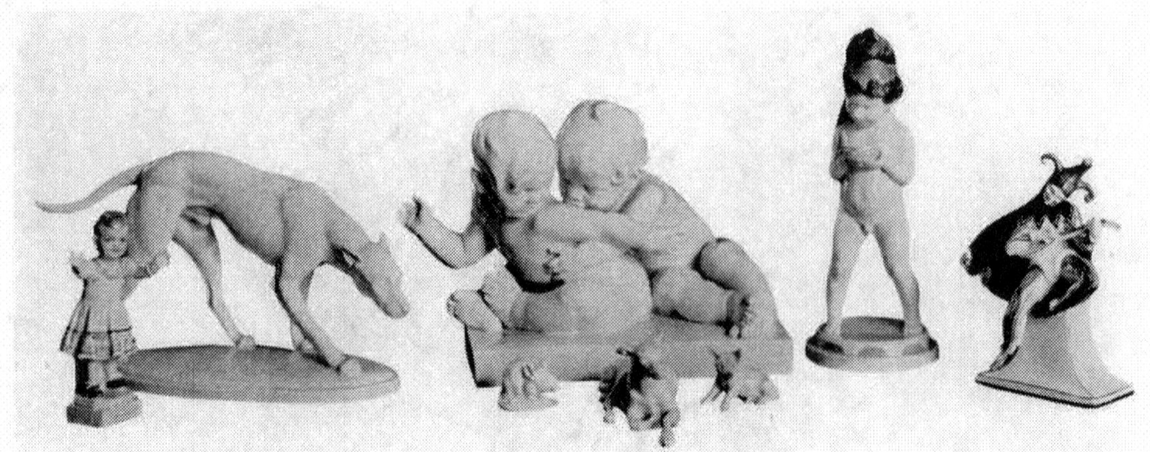

WELL-MODELLED CHINA ORNAMENTS

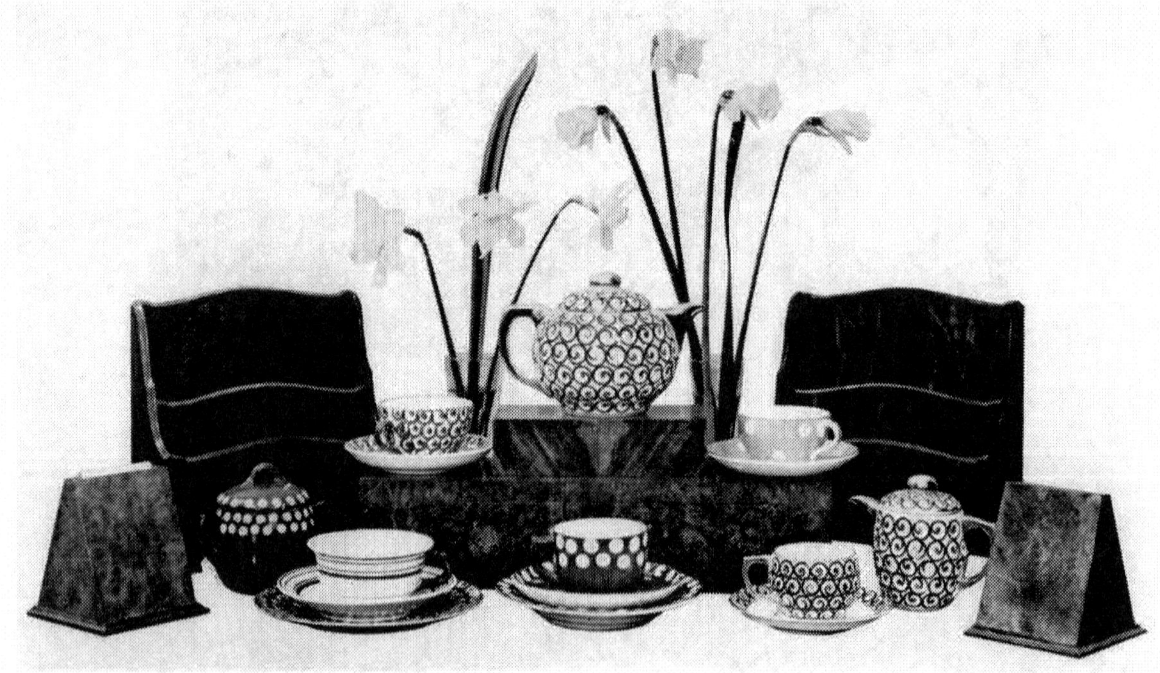

MODERN POTTERY AND CHINA

WALNUT STATIONERY STANDS, CIGARETTE AND GLOVE BOXES, TEA SERVICES

# THE LIBRARY

THE library on the "Coronet" illustrated by scale model and photograph (page 226) may be studied as indicating the right artistic "atmosphere." The walls are panelled with plain figured waxed walnut. A large book-case occupies practically the whole of one side of the room. This panelling, by virtue of its beautiful surface and dark tones, is particularly restful and is eminently suitable in a study or where much reading is done, because it does not attract attention. Richness is introduced by carved architraves to door heads and book cabinet, and also carved walnut " drops " in the wall panels. The silver light fittings aid this decorative idea. In contrast with the plain wall panelling the ceiling is elaborately enriched with radiating fan-shaped features. The furniture of plain waxed walnut is veneered with strips of figured wood. The design suggests refinement and repose in keeping with the studious character of the apartment. The carpet is a beautiful shade of jade green, and the silk window curtains correspond in colour.

For libraries generally we advocate a wall covering of dark-toned wood such as walnut. A panel treatment is suitable because this may be made to correspond with the design of the book-cases. Where possible these should be built into the walls. It is necessary to remember that books are very heavy. The cases must be placed close to the walls. By this arrangement overloading of the floors is avoided. From all points of view book cabinets are best made as attached or built-in fitments. There is no reason, however, why they should be ugly. Their design and manufacture should receive the same skill and care as elsewhere.

For the library wall lights are best. One or more floor standards should also be provided.

# WRITING TABLES

THE four writing tables illustrated are typical of leading types. Grosvenor writing table No. 534 C (page 94) has nine drawers and one cupboard (inside the kneehole). The character of the design makes this table suitable for use in a drawing room or sitting room. It is an ornamental as well as useful piece of furniture.

Grosvenor writing table No. 468 C (page 95) is a beautiful piece of cabinet work. All surfaces including sides and inside faces of kneehole are veneered with richly figured walnut. It is suitable for use in a drawing room or lounge.

Writing tables Nos. 406 C (page 96) and 464 C (page 97) are suitable for use in professional offices, libraries or writing rooms. The almost severe type of design brings out the fine quality of the workmanship. No. 406 C has nine drawers fitted with automatic locking device controlled by centre drawer. It has also two pull-out rests. This table is constructed of mahogany veneered with figured oak fixed in vertical strips for decorative effect. Such fine quality craftsmanship would be impossible in solid oak.

Table No. 464 C is constructed of mahogany veneered with strips of plain figured walnut. The drawer margins are of ebony. Observe the stationery racks and ink stand on this table, producing a beautiful and complete appearance.

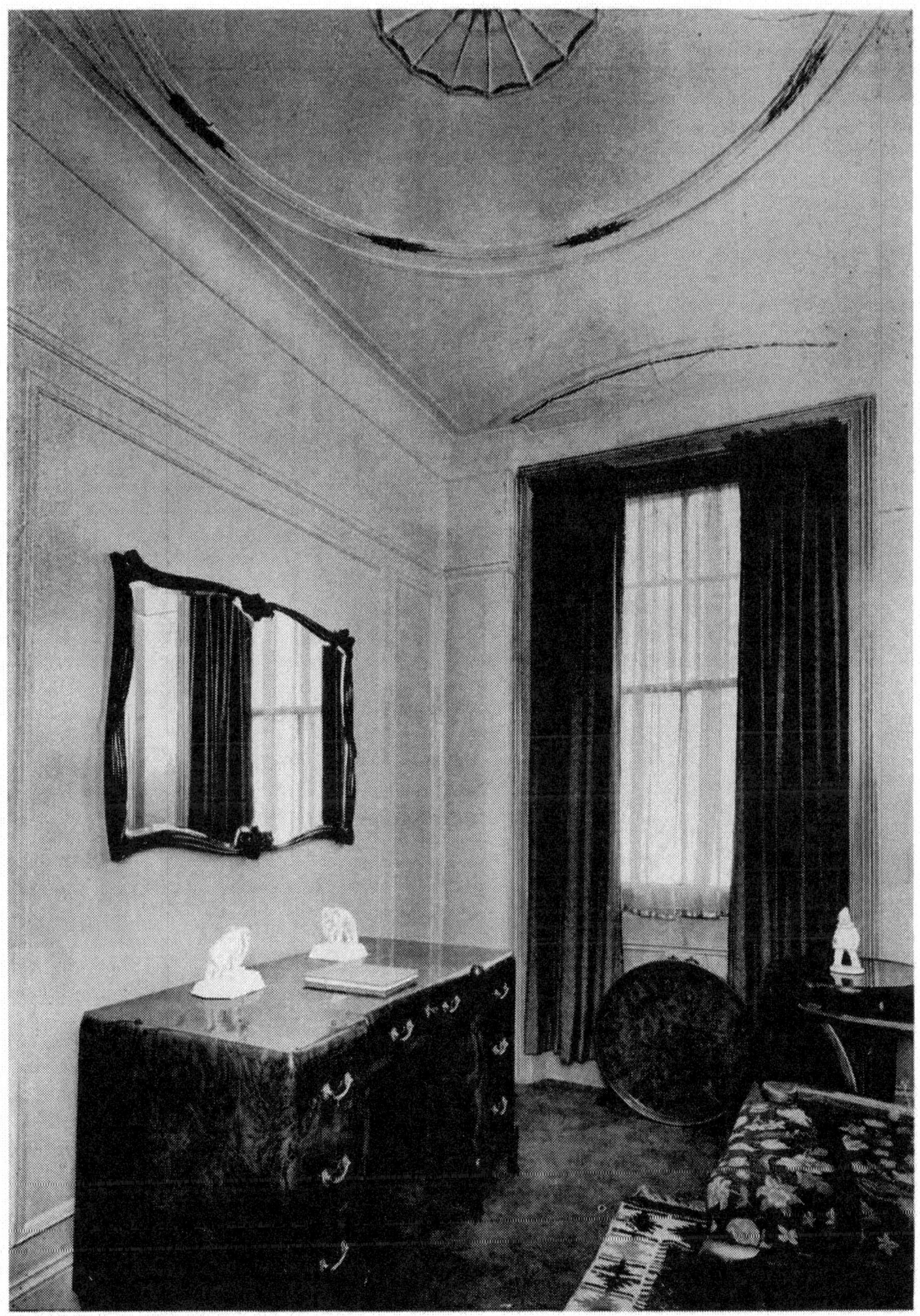

A SMALL WRITING ROOM DESIGNED BY MAURICE ADAMS

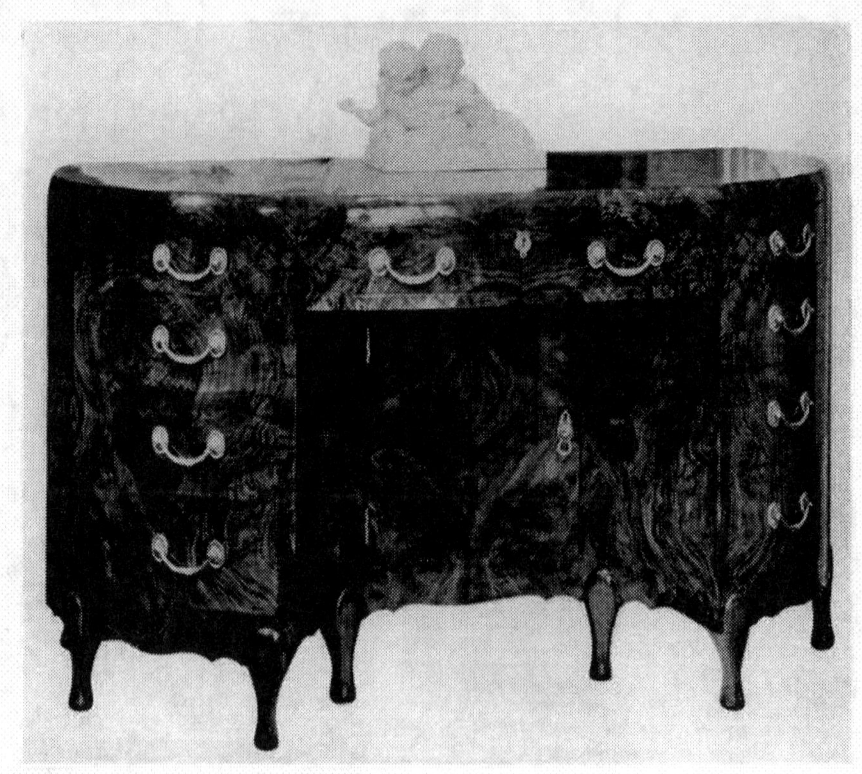

GROSVENOR WRITING TABLE, NO. 534-C MAURICE ADAMS

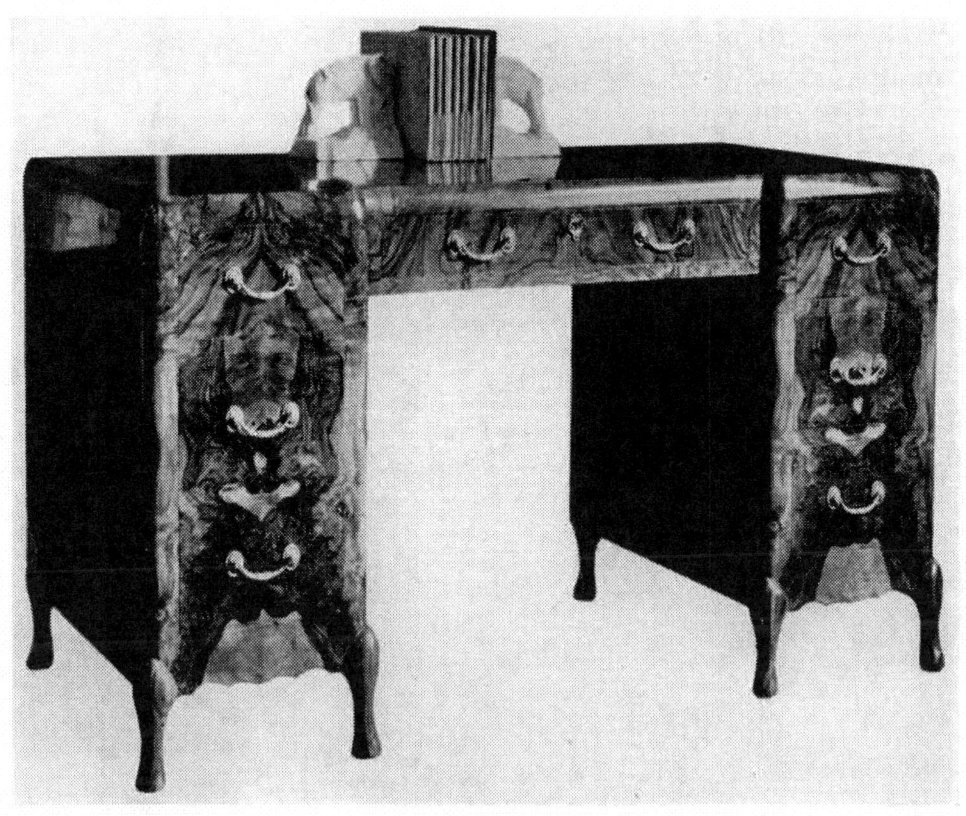

GROSVENOR WRITING TABLE, NO. 468-C MAURICE ADAMS

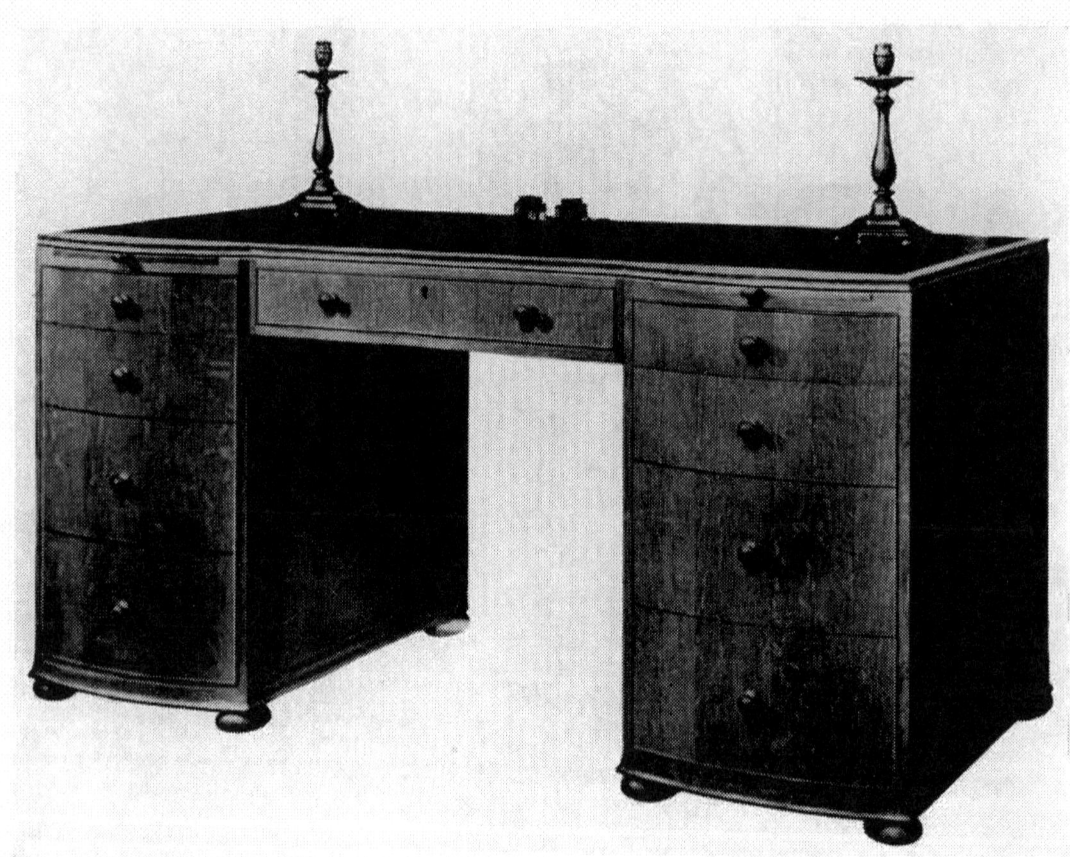

NATURAL OAK WRITING TABLE, NO. 406-C MAURICE ADAMS

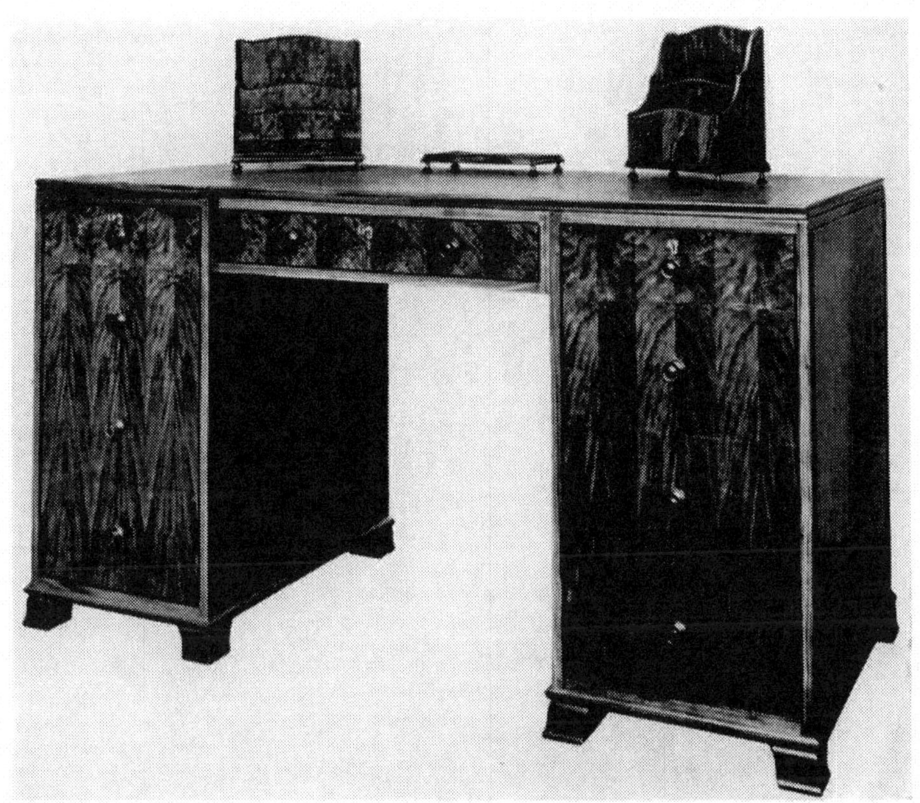

WAXED WALNUT WRITING TABLE, NO. 464-C. MAURICE ADAMS

# BEDROOMS & DRESSING ROOMS

MORE attention is now usually given to the principal bedrooms than formerly. A degree of luxury in these rooms is now expected, the like of which was never dreamed of by our forefathers. The well-equipped bedroom of to-day is central heated and has, in addition, either a gas or electric fire. The bed equipment includes super-soft box-spring mattress supporting white wool and pocket-spring mattress. The bedside table is arranged to take tray, telephone and book cupboard. Bedlight, with separate switch, now forms part of standard requirements.

Each principal bedroom probably has its own bathroom with hot and cold water supplies and shower. The bathroom will also be fitted with a radiator and towel airer. Adjoining dressing room is also provided.

Appropriate luxury in bathrooms is now the vogue. The bath itself will have marble or other enclosure of similar character. The walls will be lined with marble, mosaic or glass. We do not advocate either a panel treatment or dado in these places. The wall covering should be carried right up to the ceiling. Even in large bathrooms the size of room is too small to permit of effective panelling. Whether the scheme be marble or other material, employ as few breaks or joints as possible. Where practicable the ceiling may be "stepped" or domed, the lighting being concealed in the ceiling. One of the most effective ceilings for the bathroom is a parabolic section dome. When painted or decorated to represent a clouded blue sky, and illuminated by tubular lights hidden at the base of the dome, the effect is startling in its realism. The parabolic section or curve reflects the light over the dome surface in an even manner not achieved in any other way.

Bathroom fittings, including lavatory basin, should be enclosed and decorated to match the walls. The usual difficulty of unsightly taps may be overcome by dispensing with ordinary fittings and arranging taps on the pipes below the basin.

In setting out the bedroom furniture the same procedure should be followed as already described in the dining room. A small scale plan of the room showing position of windows, doors and fireplace, should be prepared on which may be set out the furniture proposed. This method at once insures the most suitable arrangement and some idea as to the size of furniture the room will allow. If twin beds are proposed these will require a width of 6 ft. for the actual beds and not less than 2 ft. between them, making a minimum of 8 ft. in width overall.

The position of windows should also be considered in relation to the beds.

The standard width for a double bed is 4 ft. 6 ins. In very large bedrooms the bed may be 5 ft. wide, but it is a mistake to have a larger bed than the room will conveniently accommodate. Detachable French castors have large wheels. These support the bed independently of head and foot panels, and allow the bed to be easily moved for dusting. Beds are now usually made much lower than formerly. A low bed increases the apparent size of small bedrooms. The exact height should, however, be governed by the bed design. Box springs are not less than 9 ins. deep. With the overlay the depth is 15 ins., in addition to which must be added the bed clothes. For low beds, the side rails must be fixed quite low down, or else well-sides provided to the box spring. The lowest possible type of bed can be arranged by having a Staples mattress on iron frame. Box springs should be made to fold, otherwise there may be difficulty in getting the mattress upstairs or round narrow passages.

In some cases a small pedestal chest of drawers takes the place of bedside cupboard. Alternatively, this may have one drawer and cupboard or open compartment for shoes or books. The bed-light and switch is best attached to the wall. This leaves the bedside table-top free for books or telephone or tea tray. A small pull-out rest is also convenient to take the early morning cup of tea.

The wardrobe will necessarily be of the largest size the room will allow. 6 ft. is a good width for large rooms; 4 ft. 6 ins. is a suitable width for medium rooms; and either 3 ft., 3 ft. 6 ins., or 4 ft. for smaller rooms. Curved fronted wardrobes in the smaller sizes take up much less space without reducing accommodation. The wardrobe should be divided into one-third shelves and two-thirds hanging. The shelves may be fitted to personal requirements with drawers. Extending hangers are best in narrow wardrobes. Rails are best in wardrobes over say 3 ft. wide. For narrow, deep wardrobes, Everitt's long-bar hanger gives maximum accommodation and convenience in use.

Special attention is directed to the " Carlton " wardrobe illustrated on page 133. It will be observed that all main surfaces are curved and that there are no mouldings. The development of the curved surfaces around the open compartment above the central chest is particularly pleasing. The bottom of the open compartment contains a secret jewel box, only to be opened by first opening the top drawer of the chest. This contains a secret catch opening the jewel box. At the back of the recess is a further curved-fronted jewel or scent cabinet. This wardrobe is constructed in three sections for easy handling. It is unquestionably a remarkable piece of cabinet work, and displays to full advantage the very exceptionally fine burr walnut veneers with which it is decorated. The handles are silvered and specially designed.

Maurice Adams originated the low type of dressing table with large cheval mirrors. This idea has been copied by practically all English furniture manufacturers and so has attained considerable vogue. The most artistically successful of these dressing tables thus made at our works is our Grosvenor wing dressing table (page 121). Here design is simple yet avoids any feeling of unnecessary restraint. Compare the rhythm and beauty of its graceful flowing lines with the abrupt " meat-safe " forms at present favoured elsewhere. The flush-fronted curved surface to the drawers is not easy to produce, therefore, workmanship must be of the finest.

The " Coronet " dressing table (page 124) is of similar type but is designed to stand in a corner. It is, therefore, specially suitable for use in small bedrooms. The " butterfly " wings of the side mirrors are particularly charming in a small bedroom.

The " Grosvenor " beds and " Coronet " beds designed to go with these dressing tables are also herein illustrated (pages 117 and 112).

Wash-stands are seldom used now, having become almost a relic of former days. Chests of drawers remain in favour, but are now frequently fitted with a cupboard for hats or shoes above the drawers, thus forming a tall chest-cupboard. Examples are illustrated herein.

As an interesting example of modern design, our " flame " mahogany bedroom furniture deserves mention. These designs were specially made to suit the " curl " veneers which form part of the design. These veneers are placed in rows, face and reverse, on the furniture fronts ; a treatment purely decorative, original and distinctive. This furniture may suitably be used in the second or third bedroom.

Another distinctive type of design occurs in the carved natural colour oak dressing table and wardrobe to match. This furniture is constructed of laminated mahogany veneered with figured oak attached in strips. Relief is provided by a small ebony bead around the margins of drawers and doors. These designs depend for effect largely upon their very fine and accurate workmanship, only made possible by this method of construction.

For those who have a decided preference for more exceptional things, our painted bedroom furniture presents great possibilities on account of the wide selection of colour and decorative treatment. We illustrate examples in these pages which deserve study. This furniture is constructed exactly in the same manner as our burr walnut furniture. We use cellulose paint and lacquer for the main surfaces. The ornament is raised and finished in darker tone of colour employed. In other cases the ornament is finished gold or silver. The handles to doors and drawers are of wood or ivory. The painted beds illustrated are very pleasing and may suitably be used in conjunction with burr walnut for the other furniture.

Attention is directed to the bedroom chairs illustrated. These are more substantial and of greater interest than earlier types. The dressing stool with carved " plant-growth " leg, should be noted, as this represents our latest development in design at time of publication, and may have considerable influence on our future designs. In our earlier designs we used the cabriole leg in its original Queen Anne form. This leg is of animal origin and has relationship with a claw-footed animal leg. The hoof-foot first used on our horn-foot beds, following the shape of a horse's leg, is curved differently, which quite alters the character and contour of the leg. From this leg our King George V. leg was arrived at. This is of the spread-foot type. We now made a decided departure from earlier design by developing the leg from the face of the furniture instead of, as in the cabriole leg, making the leg an attached and supporting member. Thus the leg became part of the structure, and not merely a support. These legs now went through various stages of evolution and commenced by omitting the " ears," or side pieces, usual in the cabriole leg type. Later, the first stages of plant-like growth were reached, by springing the furniture from the sides of the leg until we see in the above-mentioned stool the ultimate development, where the entire character of the leg has changed from the animal form to one of plant-like growth.

For larger bedrooms an easy chair makes a desirable addition. This should be smaller than for living rooms yet luxuriously comfortable. The spoon-back type of easy chair is suitable for this purpose, of which our Grosvenor easy bedroom chair is an example.

Bedrooms should be illuminated by hidden lamps or by wall brackets. In larger rooms one or a pair of floor standards may be used to illuminate the dressing table.

Bedroom floors should be close covered with deep pile plain colour carpet. This provides the right ground for the furniture. Avoid borders or margins to create disturbing lines around the furniture, and the soft pile creates a feeling of luxury. A Persian or Chinese rug may be used over the pile carpet in front of the dressing table or at the end of the bed. A patterned carpet is seldom suitable for bedrooms.

Bedroom curtains may be of silk or art silk damask in one colour. Soft pastel shades are best. Soft blue, soft green, ivory and rose are colours most in favour. Exposed curtain rods and sockets should be dull silver plated. The cost is trifling and appearance is greatly improved thereby. If pelmets are used these should be rather lighter than in the other rooms. Heavy pelmets are out of place in bedrooms. Plain window net will soften the appearance of the windows. Its use is recommended.

As regards decorative treatment much, of course, depends upon the nature of the room. Plain painted or papered walls lack interest unless broken up into panels or similar treatment. In some bedrooms there is a small amount of unbroken wall surface which makes a panel treatment less suitable. Patterned papers are seldom as effective as plain colour treatments. Much is possible by means of plain gold and silver papers, wiped, or shaded and stippled with oil colour. Aluminium paint may also be covered with stippled colour. The aim with these and similar methods should be to create a rich decorative background for the furniture.

Silks and damasks may be tightly stretched over the entire wall surfaces and should give a rich appearance. The patterns require to be subdued and the colourings soft. Ceilings may be stepped or enriched with raised ornament finished in silver or gold. Any silvering used for ceiling work should be done with silver leaf. Silver bronze powder, silver paper, or aluminium paint, look almost black when applied to ceilings. Special attention should be given to the lighting in all cases where the ceilings are coloured. Reflection must be allowed for. Even a pure white ceiling will appear tinted if there is much colour on the walls or in the carpet.

Where the house is large enough to allow of a boudoir, a freer treatment for both furniture and decorations may suitably be allowed in this room. There should be very little furniture in the boudoir. A low, deep divan and luxuriously comfortable easy chair covered with rich material and augmented by brightly coloured cushions, are first essentials in the boudoir. A large floor standard with silk shade, a dwarf tea table and tray, one or two pouffe cushions in bright colourings and possibly a writing table, painted or lacquered, may also be added to the equipment. There should be one or two lacquered or silvered wall mirrors, and special attention should be given to the floor covering. This may be a deep pile carpet in bold colourings. The treatment generally should be asymmetrical.

# BEDROOM FURNITURE

WE have made no more beautiful or more successful furniture than our Grosvenor series for bedrooms, of which a full range of photographs is here given. The Grosvenor wing dressing table (page 121) is probably the most generally admired of all our productions. As an example of superb cabinet work the Carlton wardrobe (page 133) is the finest individual piece of furniture we have so far made. This wardrobe has a secret jewel box inside the open compartment (beneath the china ornament in photograph). This box is secured by secret catch fitted inside the top drawer of central chest. There is also a jewel cupboard at back of the open compartment. Attention is directed to the way the various curved surfaces meet and blend together around the central open compartment. This wardrobe is constructed in three sections for easy handling. Everitt's long-bar coat hangers are fitted inside the two side hanging cupboards.

The Grosvenor wardrobe (page 132) is another beautiful clothing cabinet and may be used as an alternative to the Carlton. It is fitted two-thirds hanging and one-third shelves. The shelves may be fitted with one or more sliding trays or drawers to suit individual requirements.

The Grosvenor wardrobe No. 400 C (page 131) is suitable for smaller rooms or where space will not allow of a larger cabinet. In some rooms two of these may suitably be used in place of a single larger wardrobe. This is fitted with hat shelf and single hanging compartment. Small shelves may be fitted on either side of hanging space if desired.

It is usual now to have at least one chest cupboard in the more important bedrooms. The Grosvenor and Coronet designs herewith (pages 147 and 149) are alternative. Each has three drawers and hat cupboard above.

We originated the low type of wing dressing table in England. The long mirrors make an additional cheval glass unnecessary. This type of table is eminently practical, and artistically has great advantages over the usual type of dressing table. Examples of the higher type of dressing table are given for those who, for various reasons, prefer the more usual type.

Our Grosvenor beds now illustrated (pages 117 and 118) are among our most artistically successful pieces. The box mattresses and overlays are shaped to fit the curved sides. They may be fitted with French castors to order.

The Coronet bed (page 112) shows an interesting development in design, having a form of palm leaf carved inside the sides of head and foot panels.

The carved dressing stool No. 720 C (page 156) shows the "plant-growth" leg about which we wrote in the general text of this book. This leg is entirely original and of special interest in view of its possible further developments.

We give illustrations of our Carlton and Grosvenor bedroom chairs (page 153) and also Grosvenor easy chair (page 73). It has taken us several years to evolve these designs, which we think are very satisfactory.

We are including several further examples of our Connaught series of bedroom furniture not previously illustrated, as well as one or two examples of our standard Connaught and King George V. models. The full range in both series is given in " My Book of Furniture " and " My Connaught and Marlborough Furniture."

Coromandel is a form of ebony with light and dark markings. It is a beautiful wood suitable for use in rooms of marked personal character. We include two examples of furniture in this wood.

The natural waxed oak designs illustrated are of original character, and indicate a feeling of restraint and refinement. Their exceptionally fine workmanship (upon which these designs largely depend for effect) is only possible by using oak veneer mounted on mahogany. The dark line around the doors and drawers is of ebony.

Those who are tired of conventional mahogany bedroom furniture may be interested in the " flame " mahogany designs herewith. These designs were prepared specially to display effectively the very fine feather curls with which they are veneered. In colour this furniture is of the faded or brown mahogany tone and not the usual red.

We show an upholstered bed. This, of course, is intended to be covered with damask or other material to suit the particular room in which it is to be used. The sides have facings of burr walnut. This form of bed may also be used in divan form, or where an out-of-the-ordinary effect is desired.

Painted furniture is favoured by many. The examples given are constructed of mahogany in our usual first-class manner. The ornament is raised and decorated in colour or either silver or gold. The main surfaces are finished with cellulose paint and lacquer. The painted dressing table shown is slightly distorted in the photograph, having been taken at close range in order to show the ornamental pedestal tops. These tops are glass covered.

I was reading an article on lacquer work in a home journal recently giving hints for amateurs. In discussing the form of decoration for the particular article of furniture under consideration, the writer stated : " the style of ornament will, of course, be Chinese." This statement surely indicates a lack of imagination. The Chinese race has produced very fine lacquer work, and it is well that we should profit by their example and learn from them. There is no reason, however, why we should not interpret our ideas in a manner other than Chinese. If copies of Chinese furniture are desired, let us make them by all means, but if we wish to make English lacquered furniture let this be sincere English design.

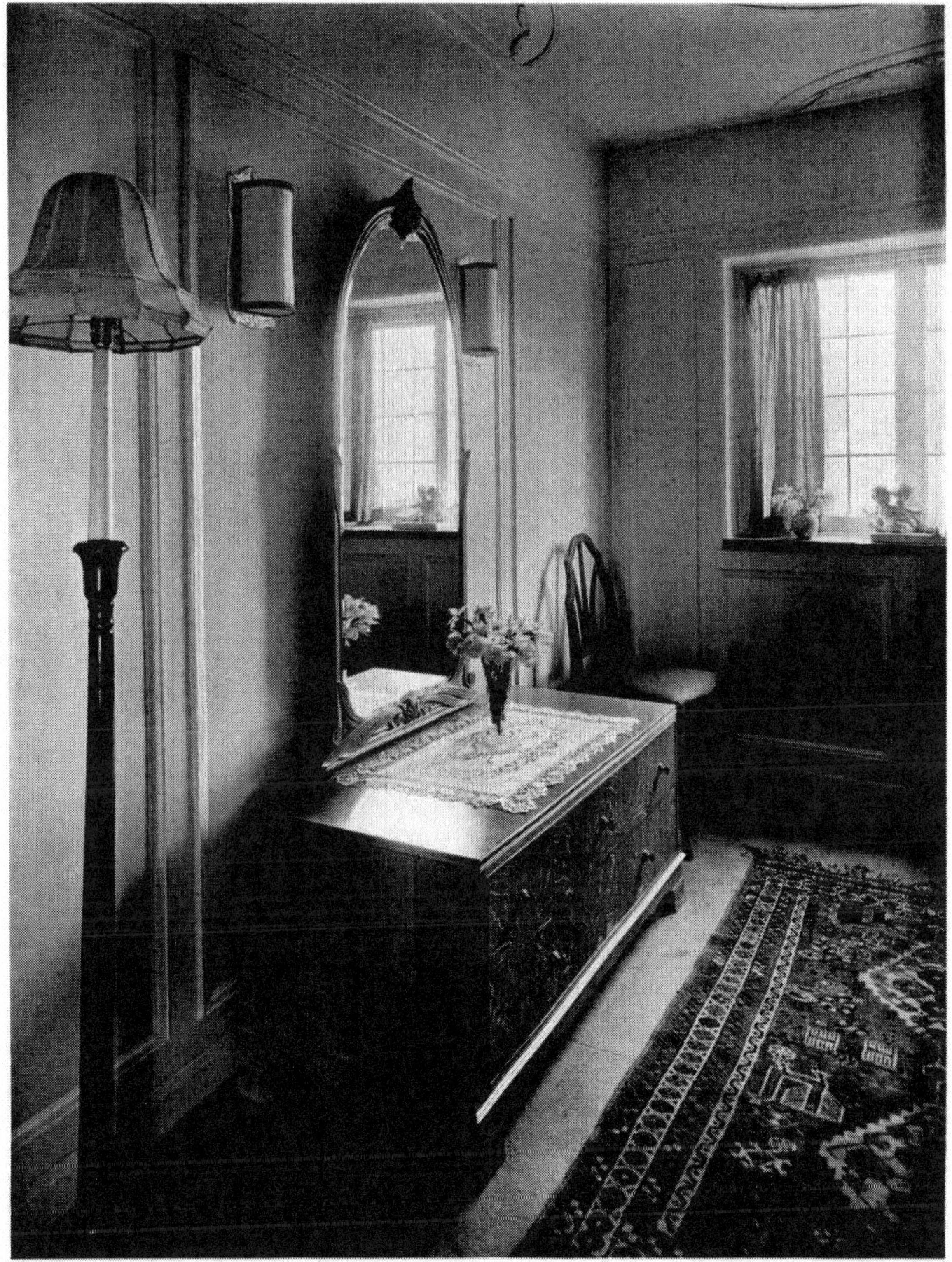

DRESSING ROOM DESIGNED BY MAURICE ADAMS

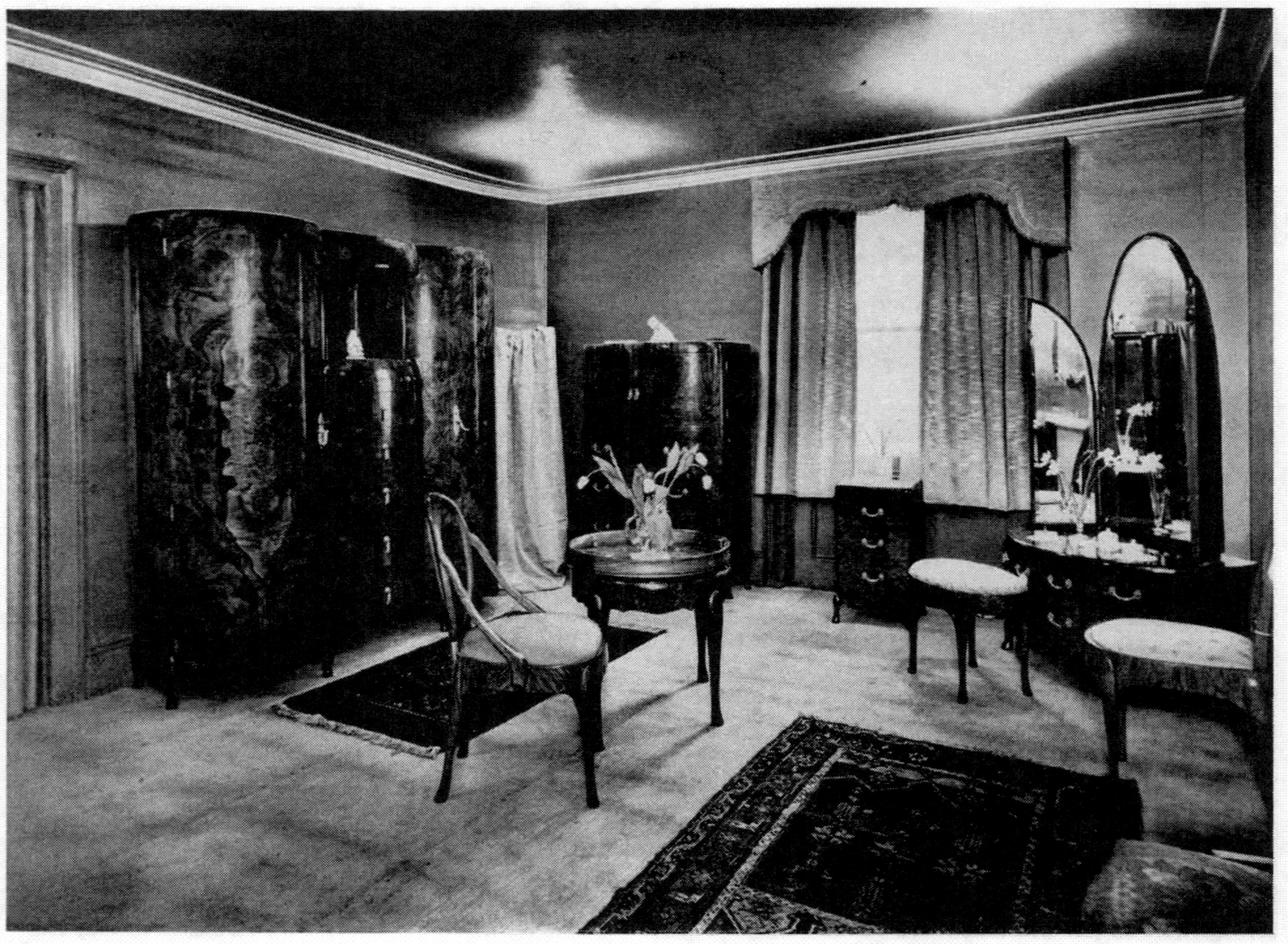

BEDROOM

DESIGNED BY MAURICE ADAMS

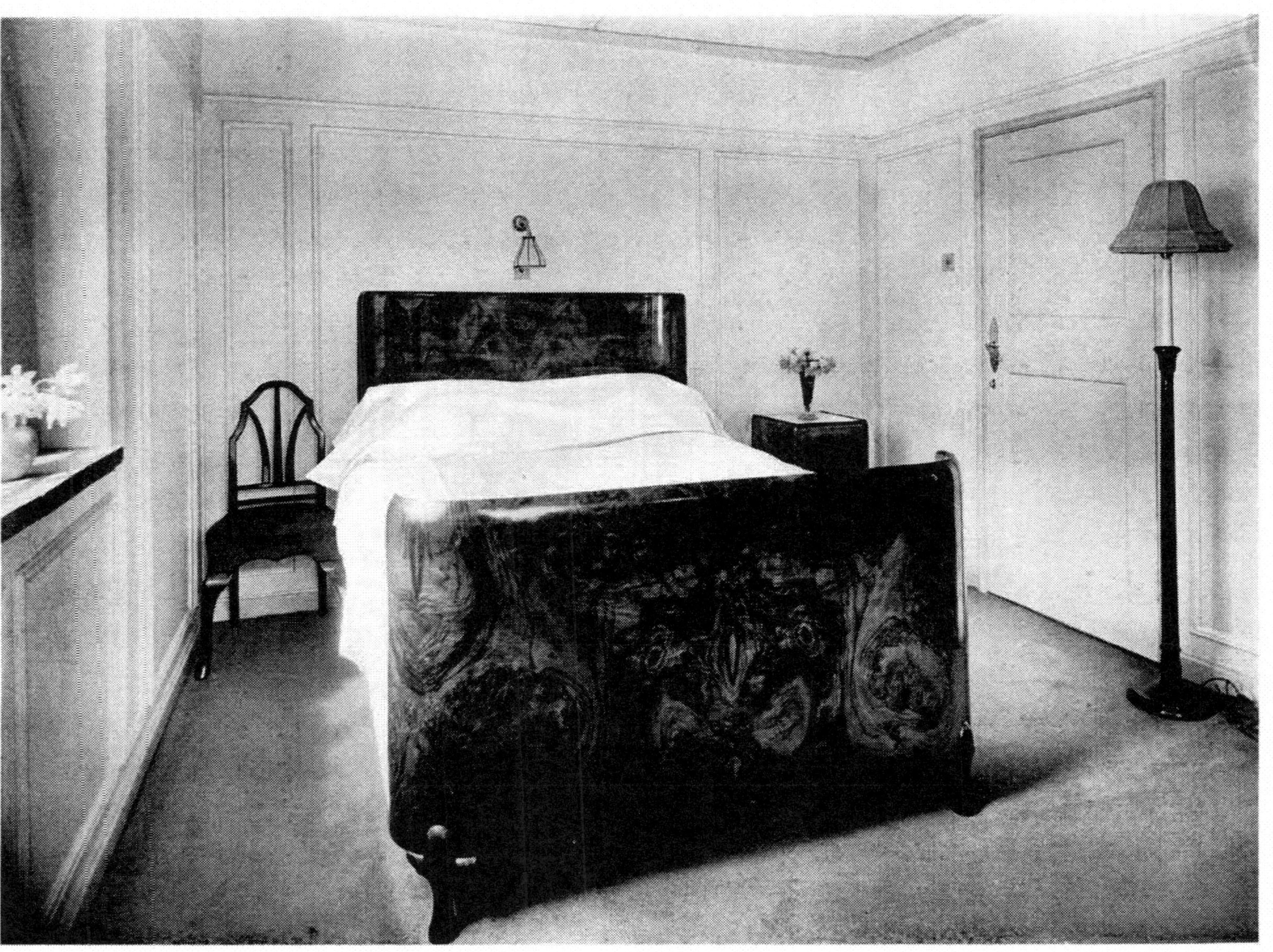

BEDROOM — DESIGNED BY MAURICE ADAMS

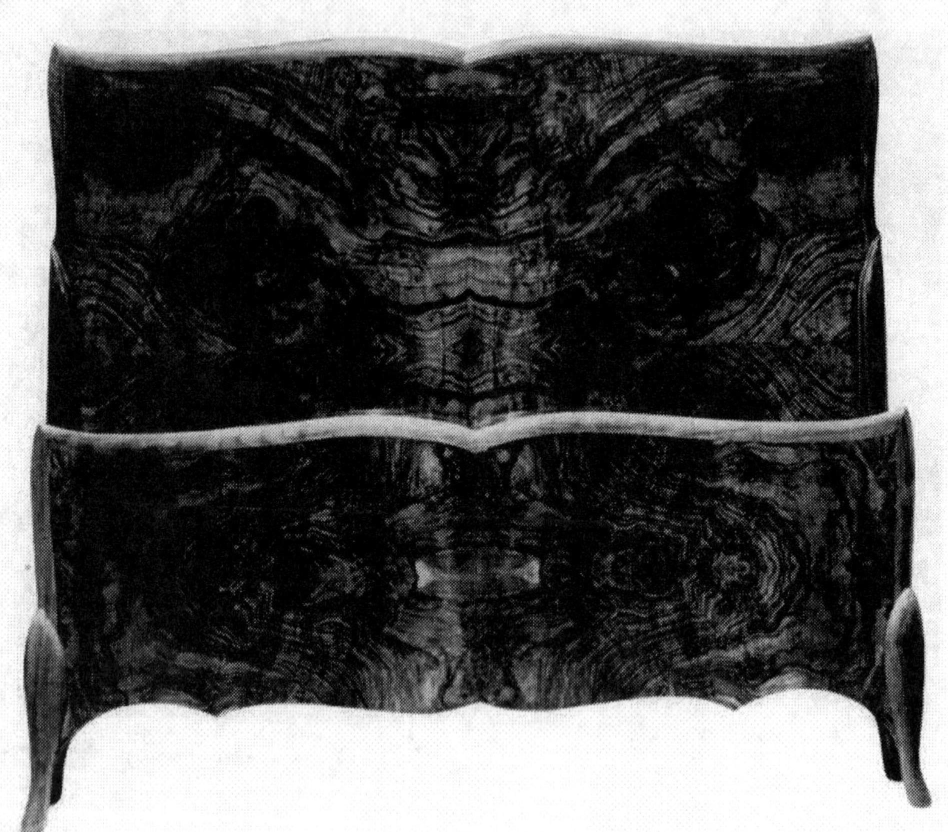

CORONET BED, NO. 665-C
BURR WALNUT

MAURICE ADAMS

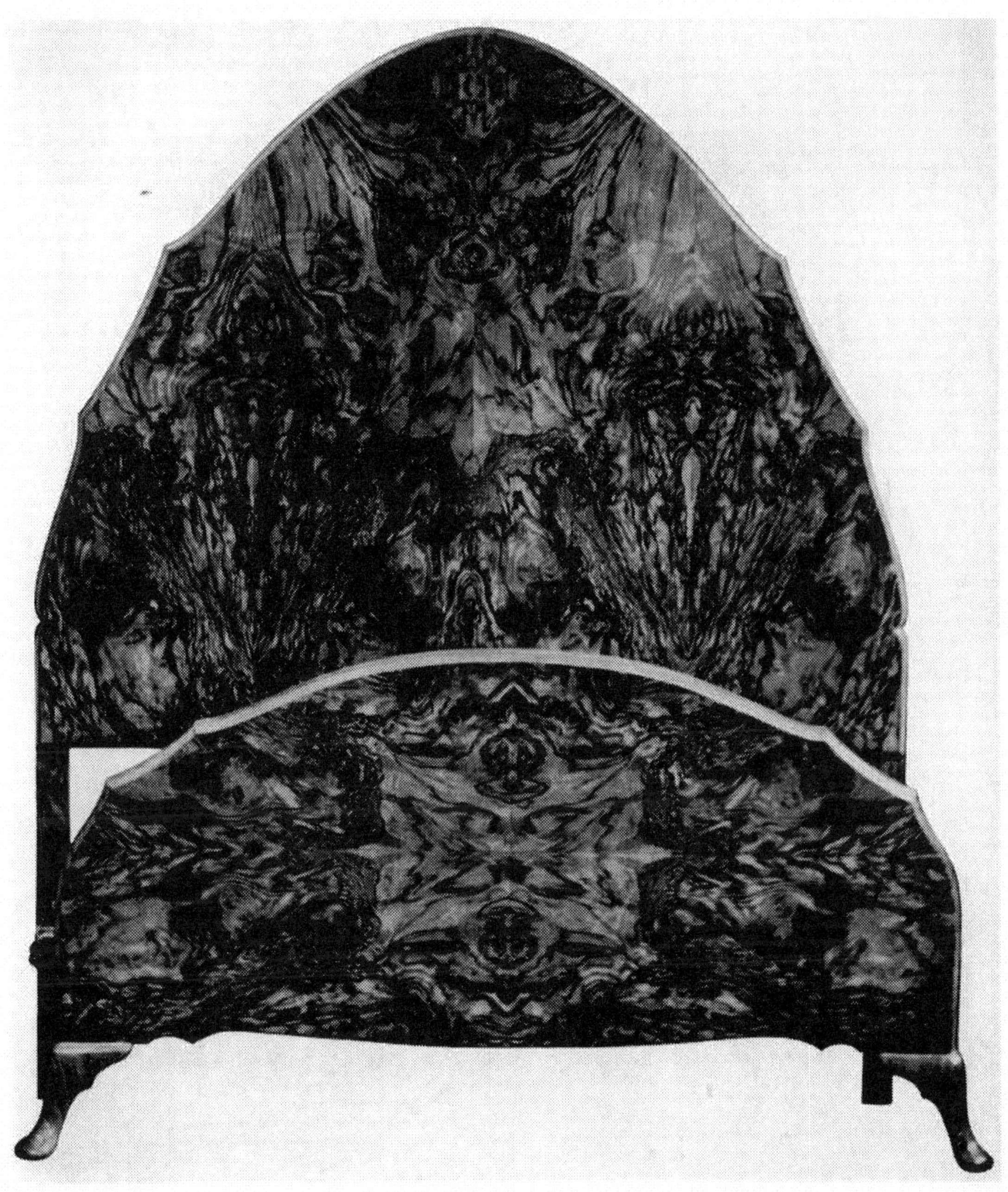

CONNAUGHT BED, NO. 355-C
BURR WALNUT

MAURICE ADAMS

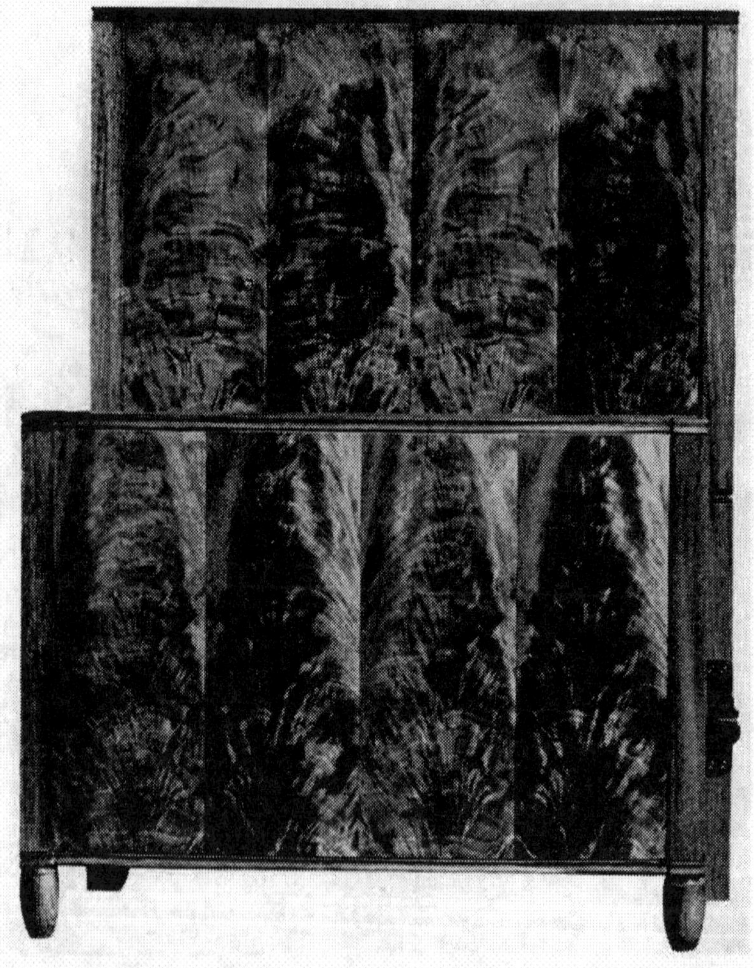

BED, NO. 428-C
FLAME MAHOGANY

MAURICE ADAMS

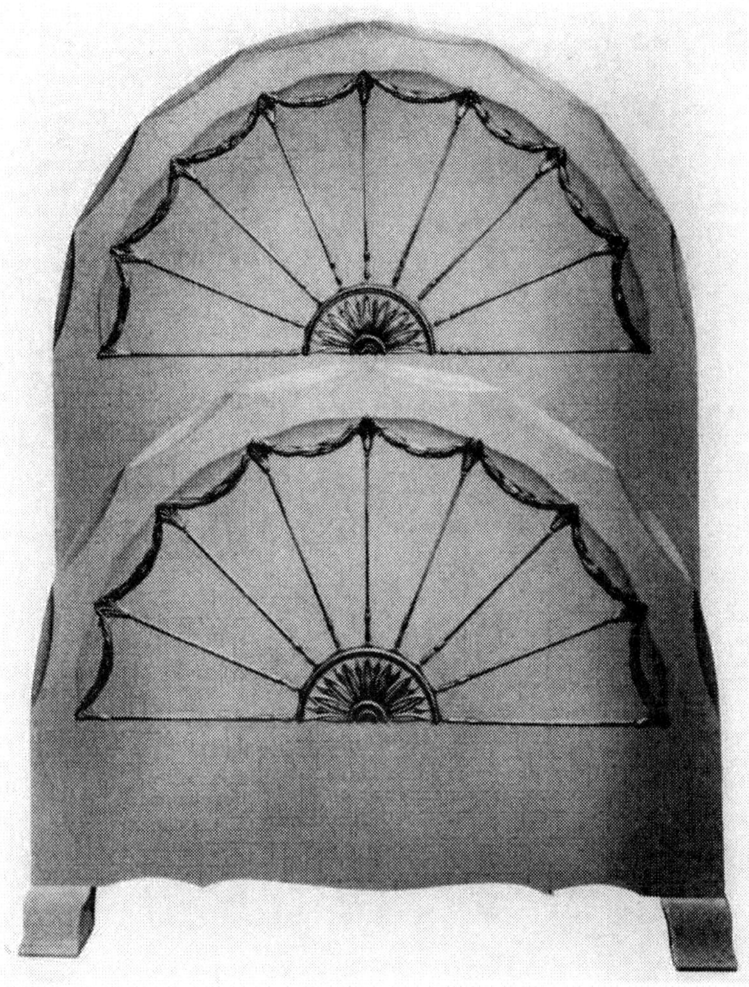

BED, NO. 711-C
PAINTED MAHOGANY

MAURICE ADAMS

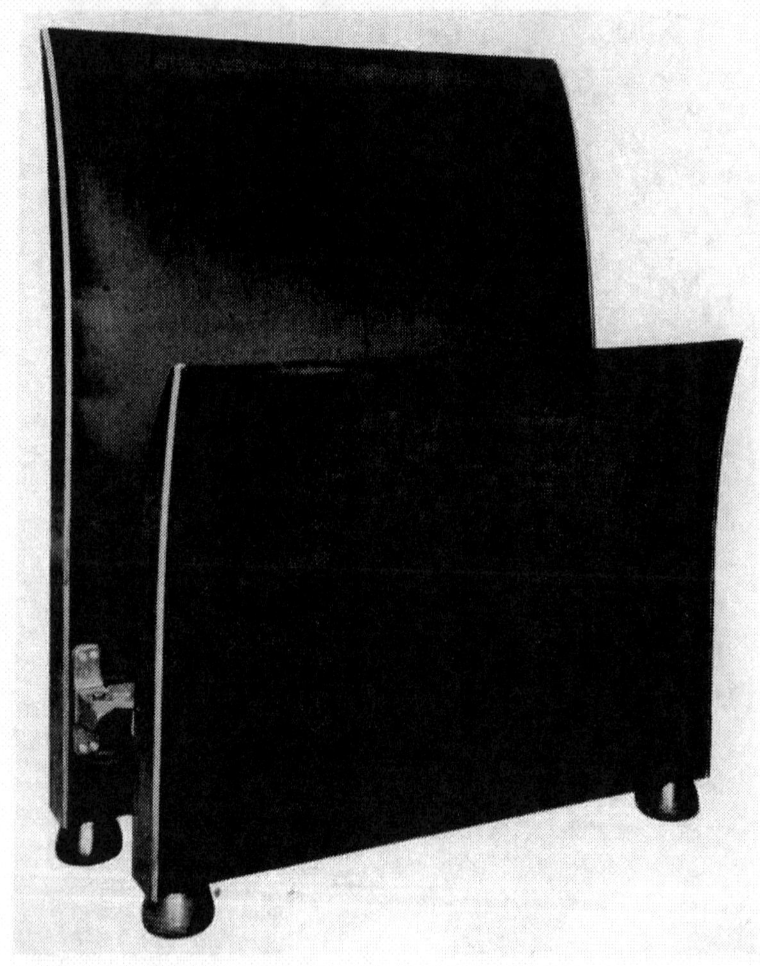

UPHOLSTERED BED, NO. 530-C MAURICE ADAMS

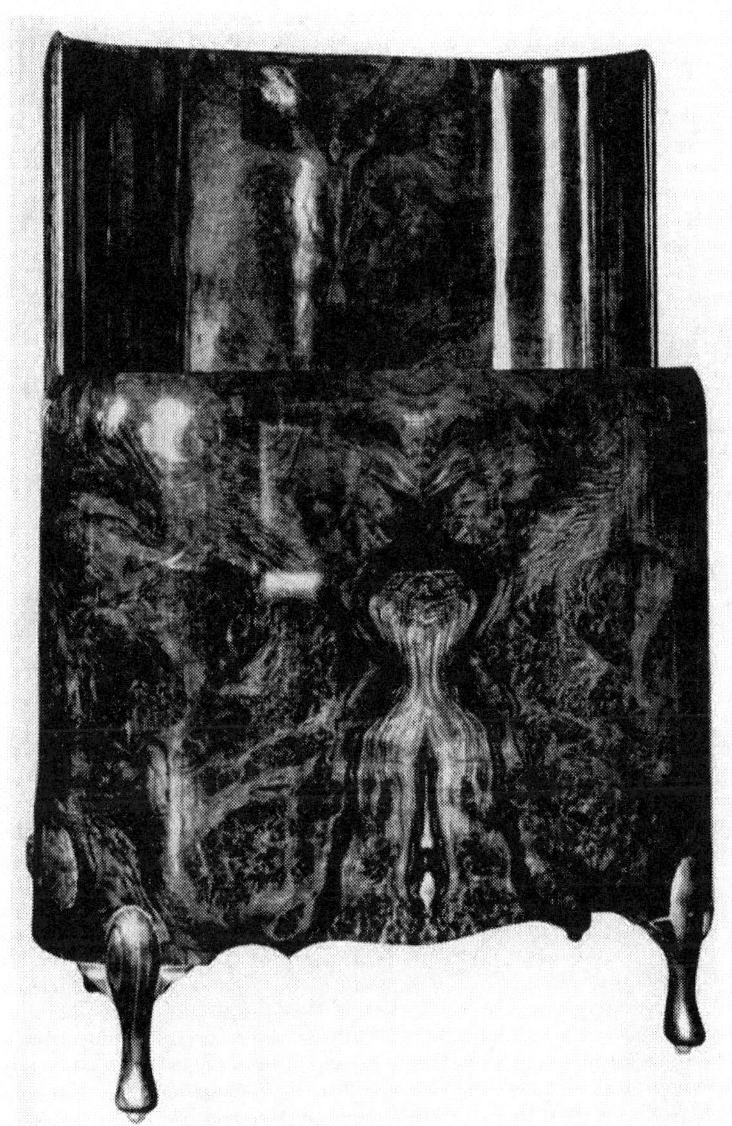

3 FT. GROSVENOR BED, NO. 459-C MAURICE ADAMS
BURR WALNUT

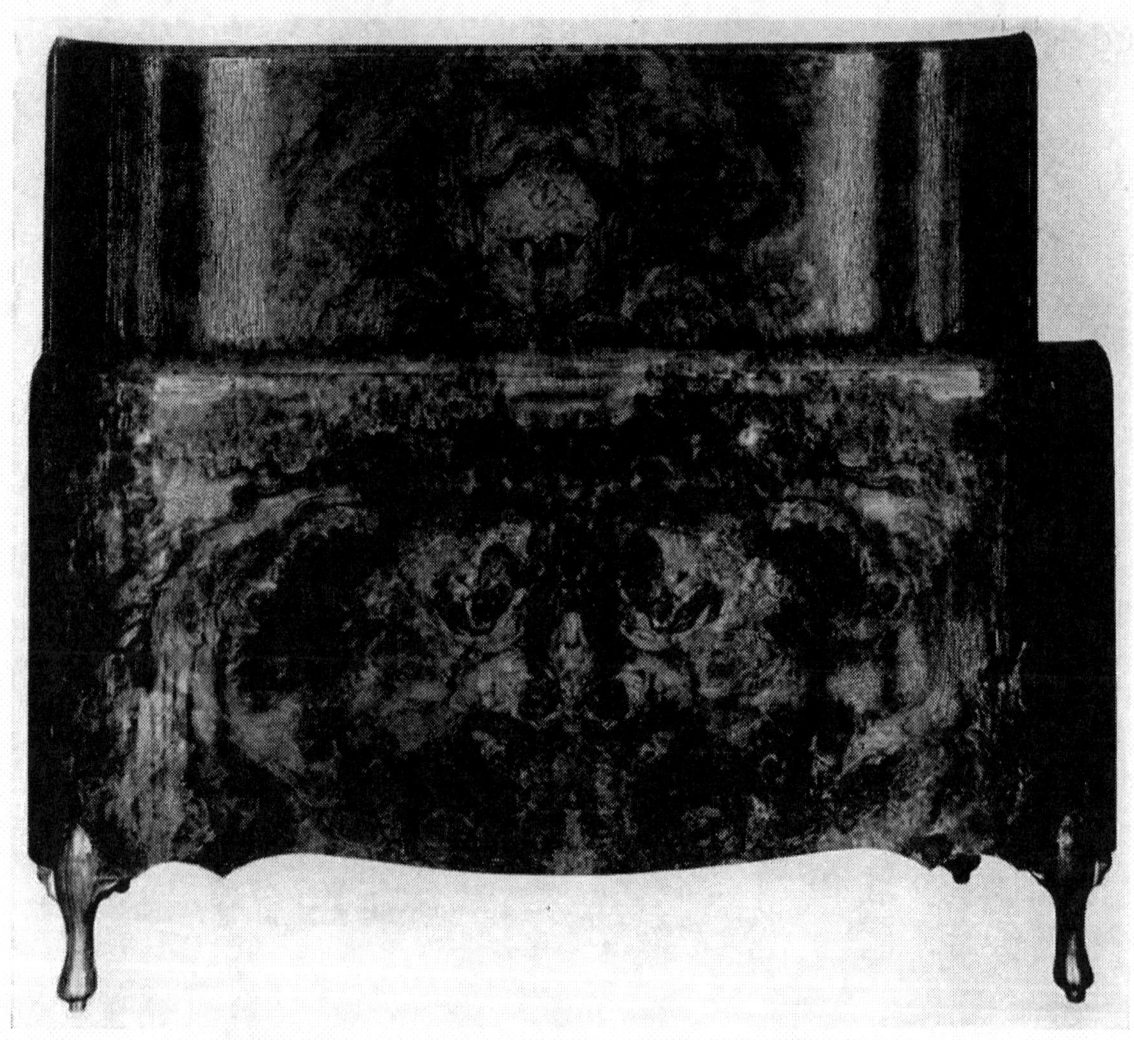

5 FT. GROSVENOR BED, NO. 459-C
BURR WALNUT

MAURICE ADAMS

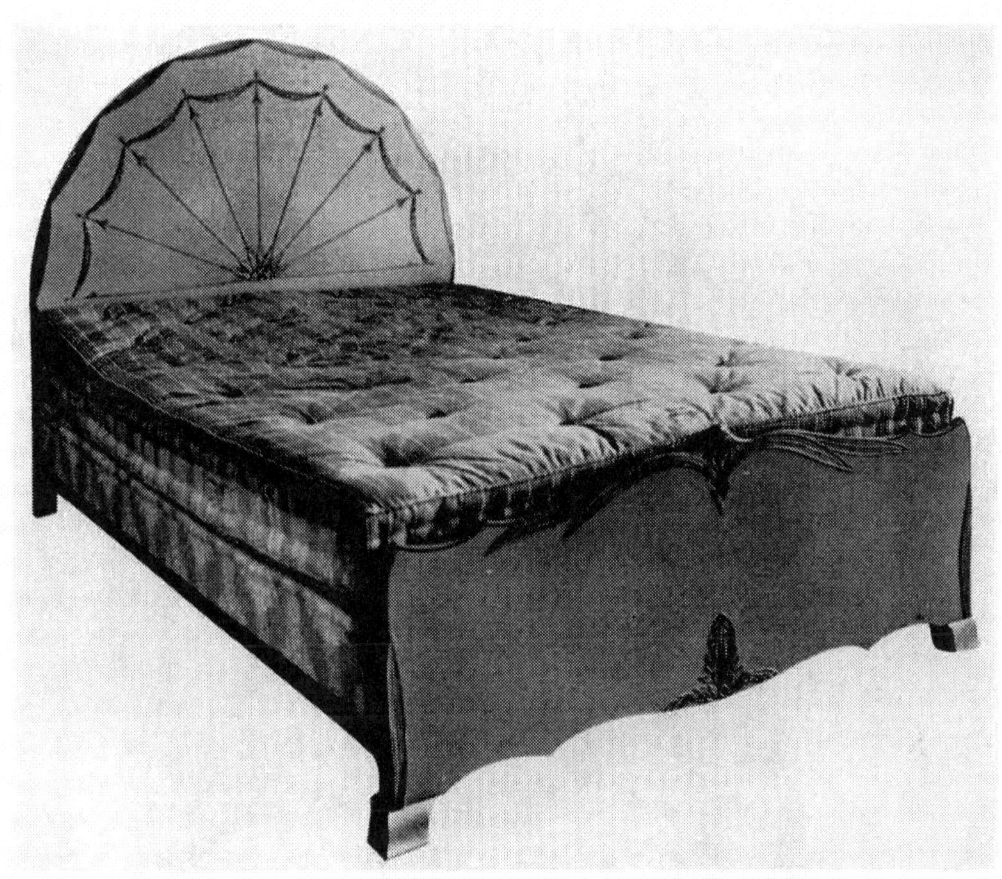

BED, NO. 556-C
PAINTED MAHOGANY

MAURICE ADAMS

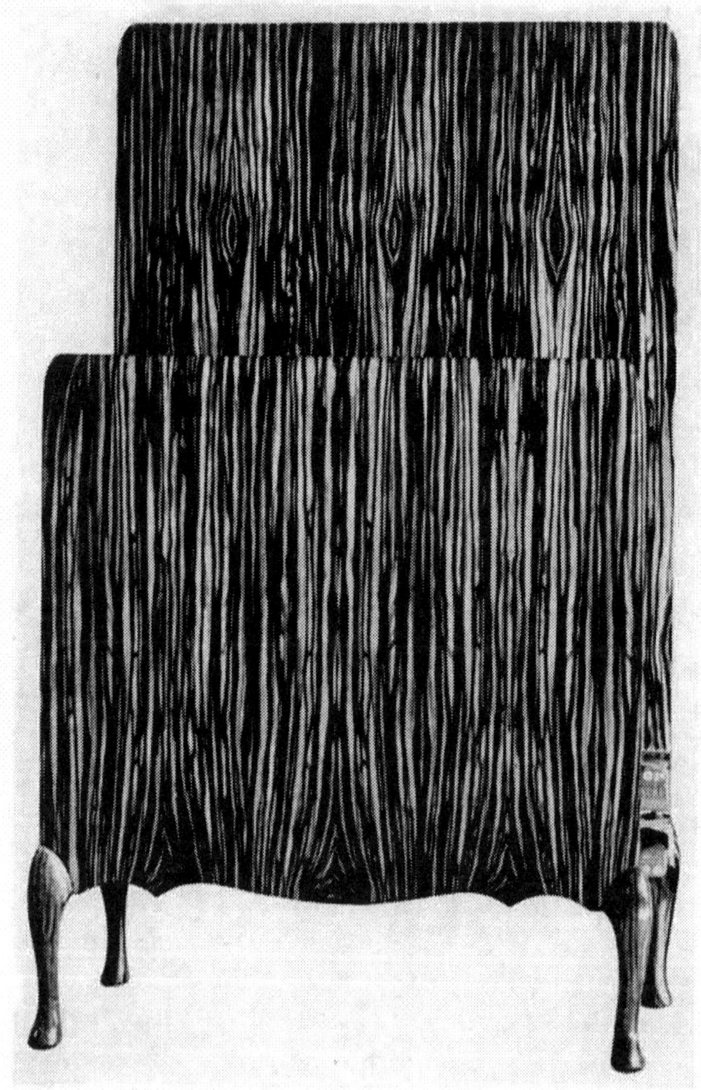

BED, NO. 473-C
COROMANDEL.

MAURICE ADAMS

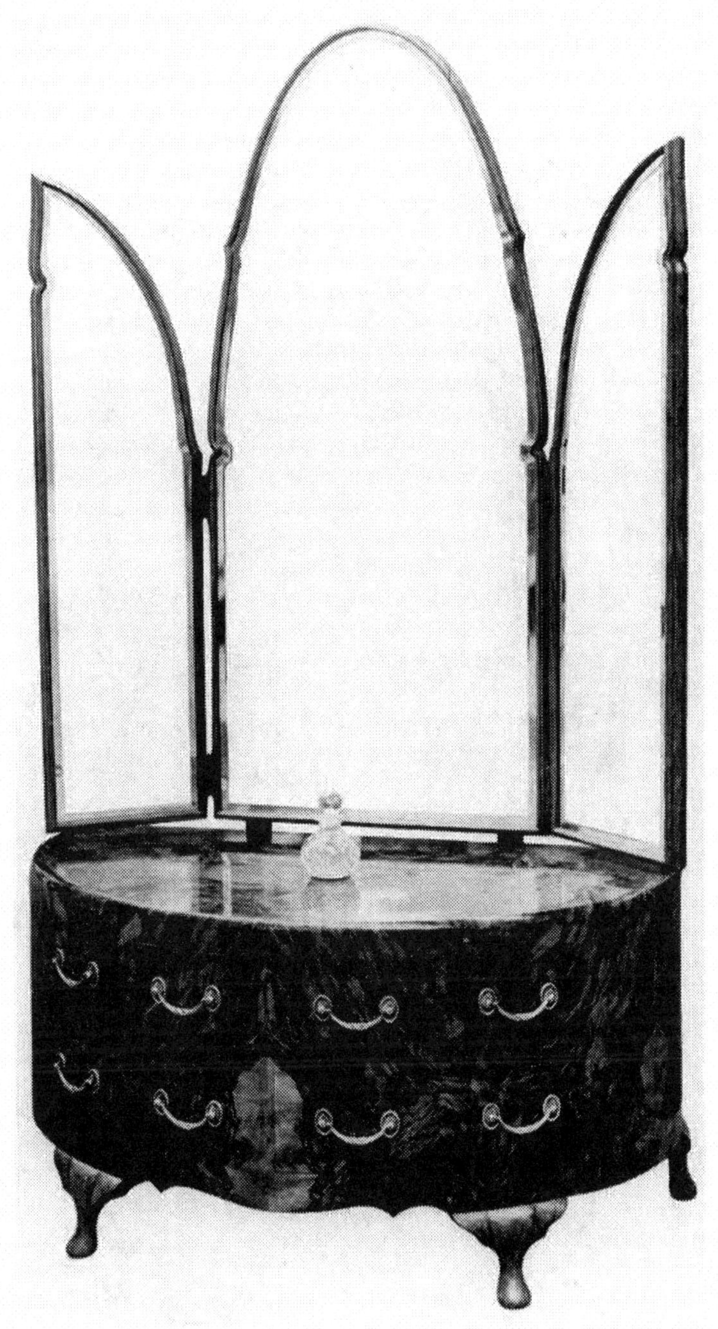

GROSVENOR WING DRESSING TABLE, NO. 398-C. MAURICE ADAMS
BURR WALNUT

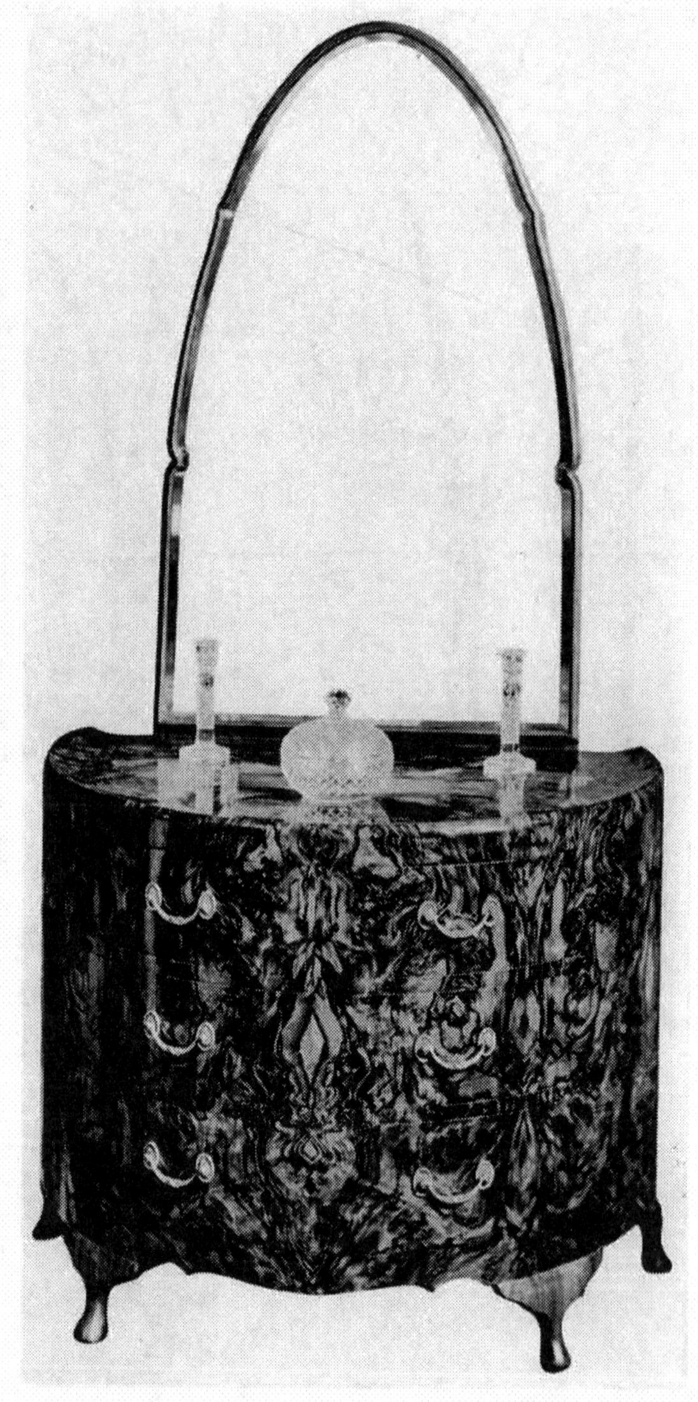

GROSVENOR DRESSING TABLE, NO. 386-C MAURICE ADAMS
BURR WALNUT

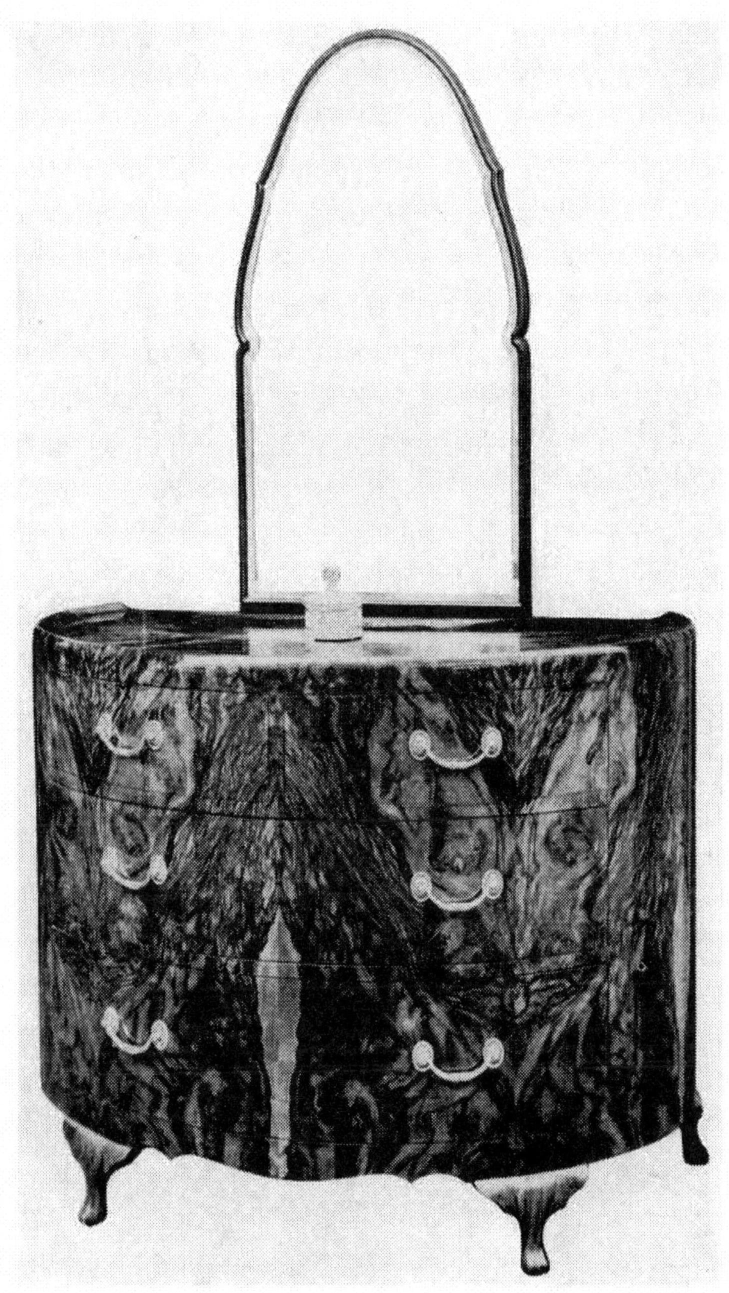

GROSVENOR DRESSING CHEST, NO. 399-C BURR WALNUT — MAURICE ADAMS

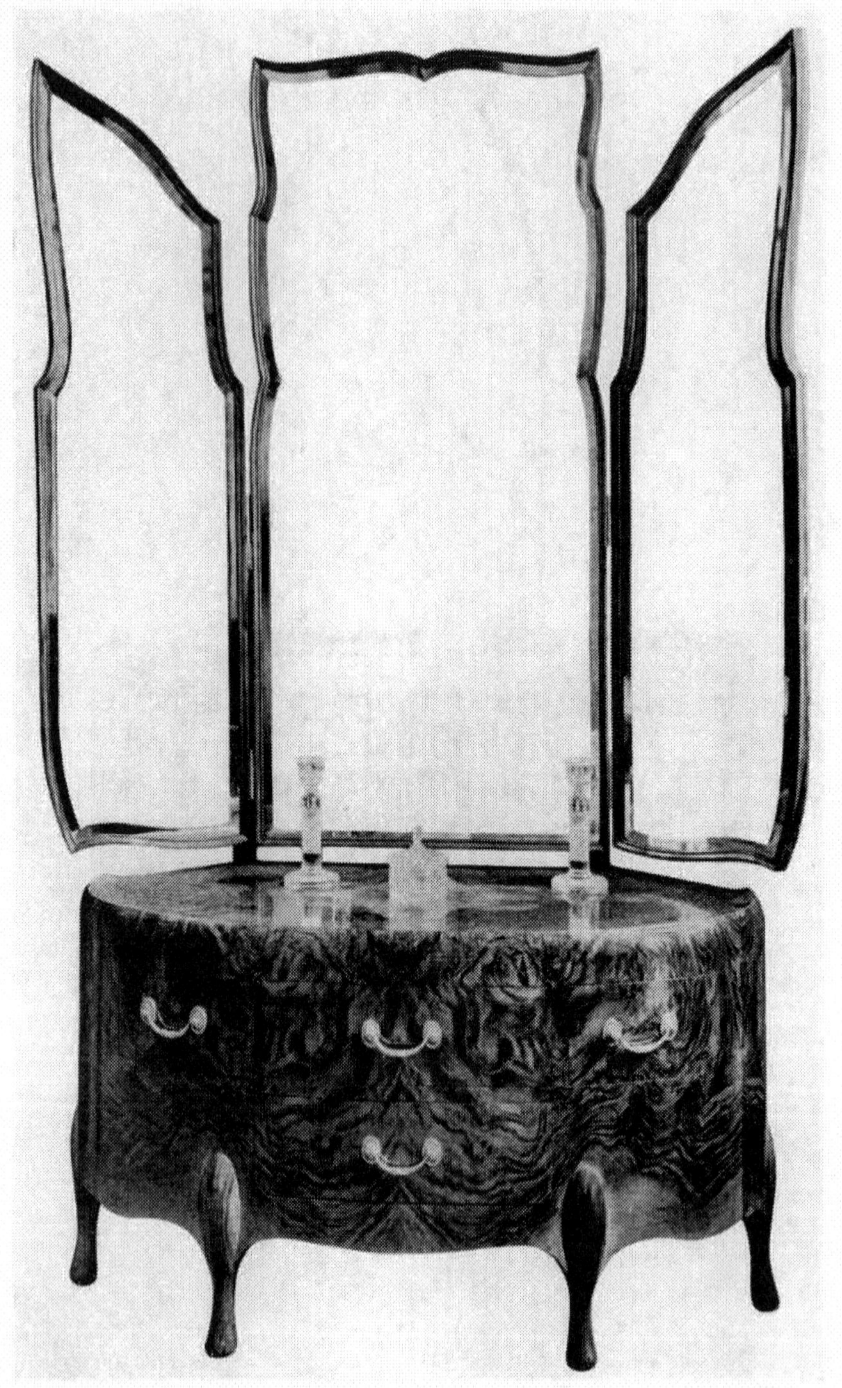

CORONET DRESSING TABLE, NO. 664-C
BURR WALNUT

MAURICE ADAMS

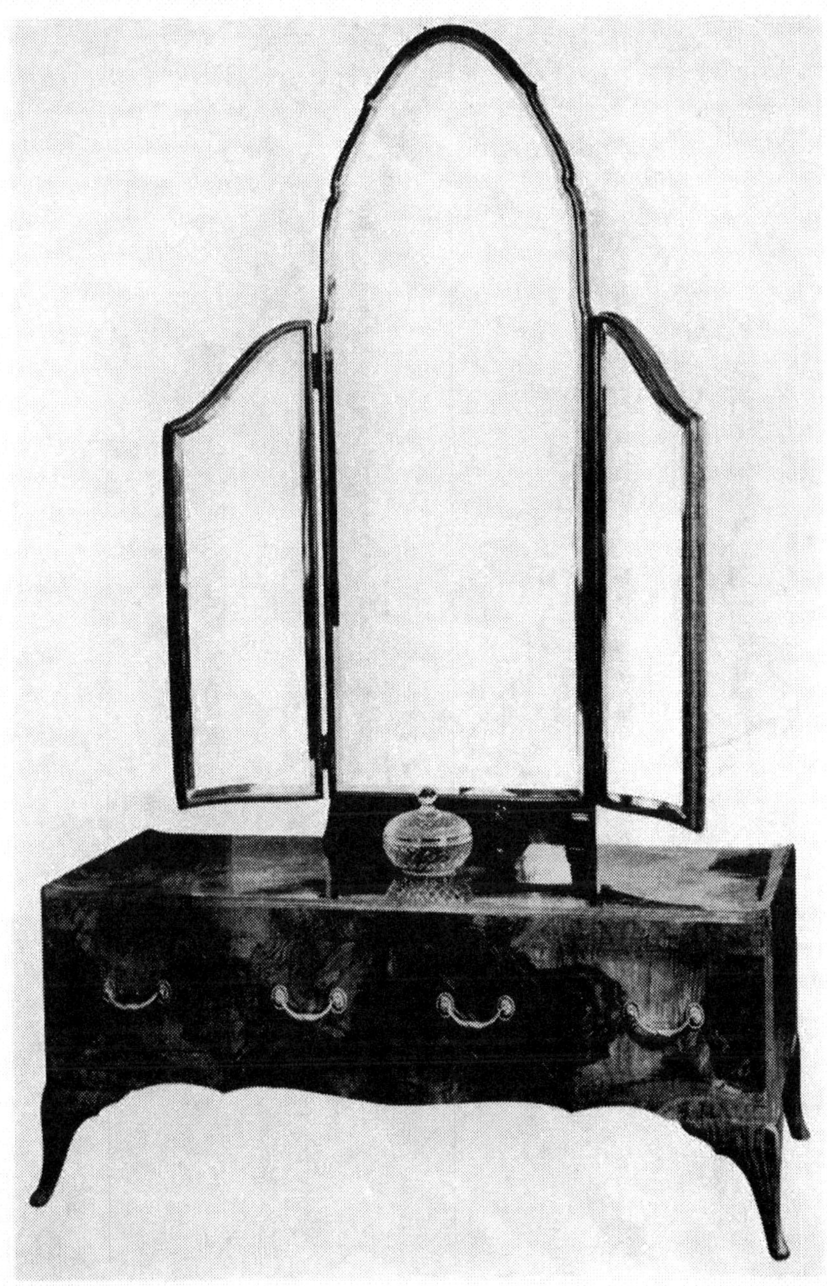

CONNAUGHT DRESSING TABLE, NO. 352-C — MAURICE ADAMS
BURR WALNUT

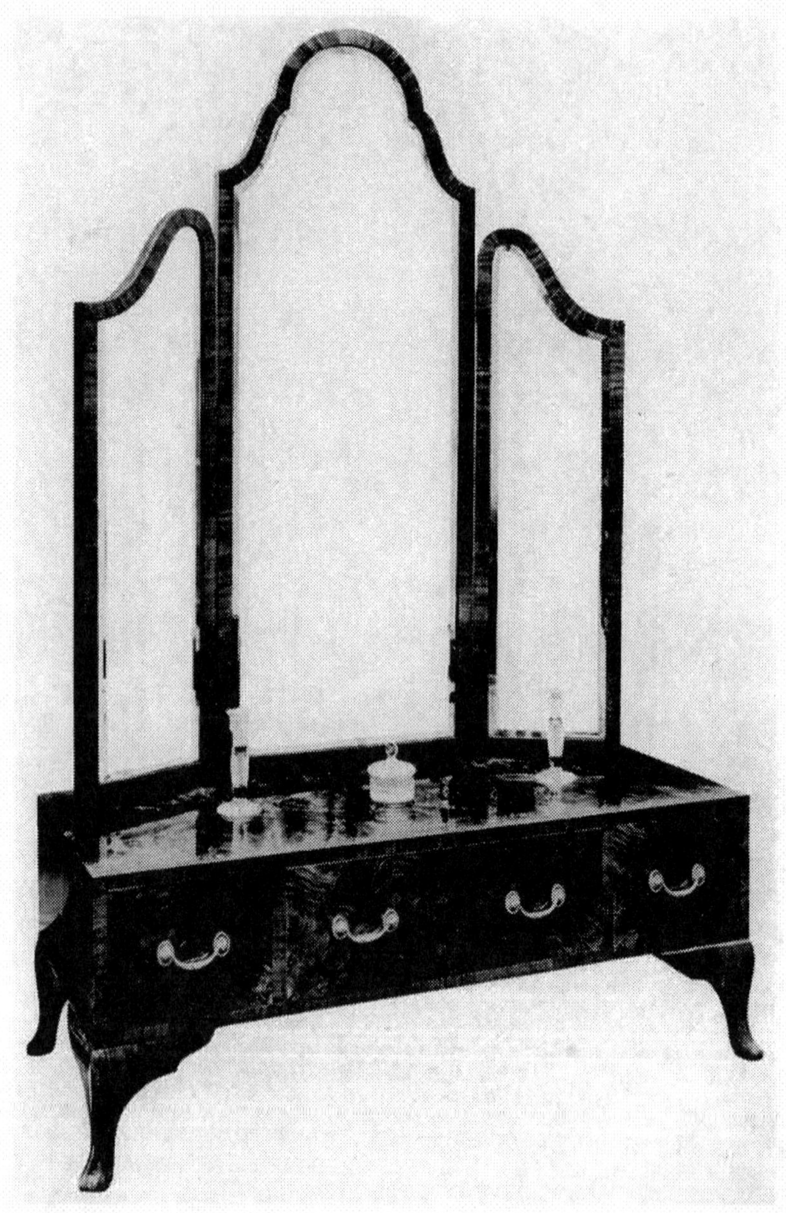

MARLBOROUGH DRESSING TABLE, NO. 331-C
BURR WALNUT

MAURICE ADAMS

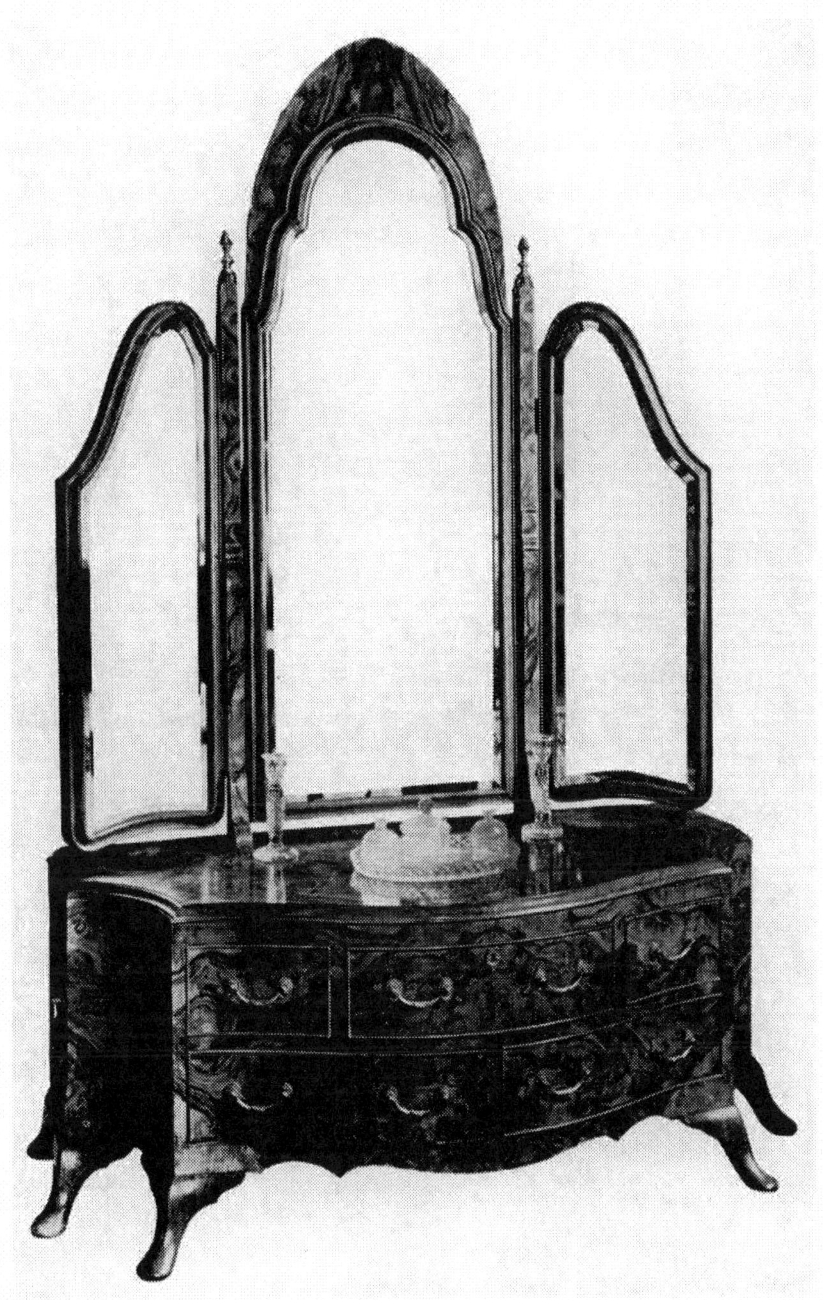

ALEXANDRA DRESSING TABLE, NO. 301-D
BURR WALNUT

MAURICE ADAMS

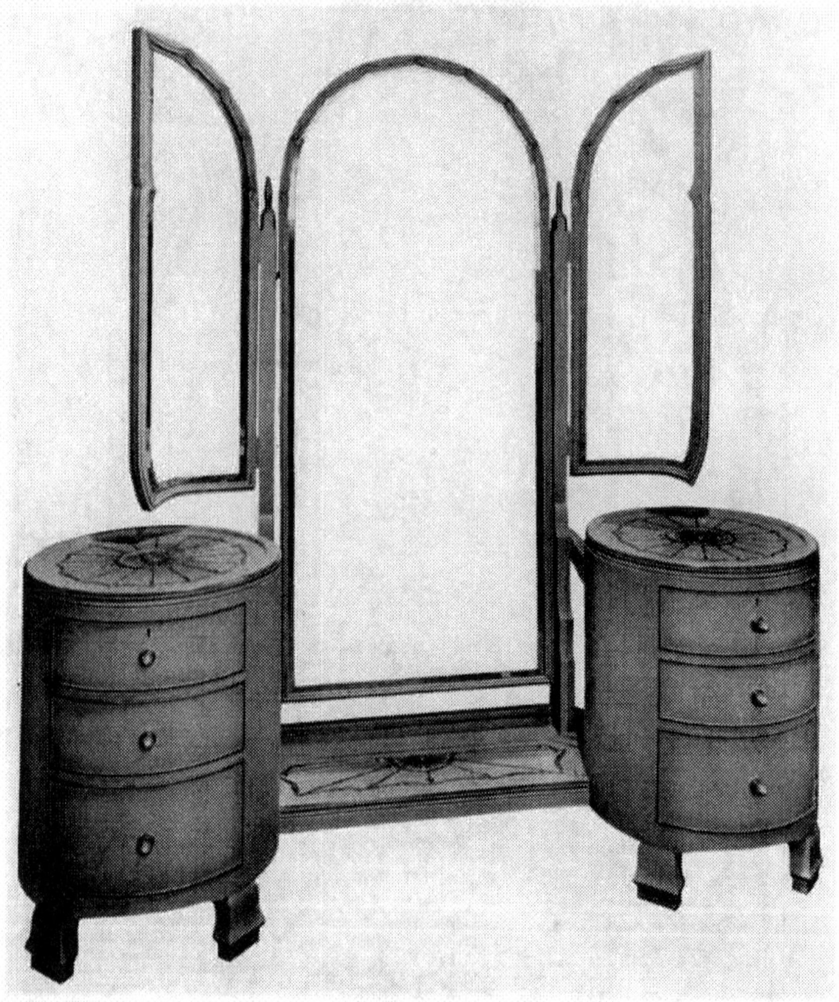

DRESSING TABLE, NO. 685-C
PAINTED MAHOGANY

MAURICE ADAMS

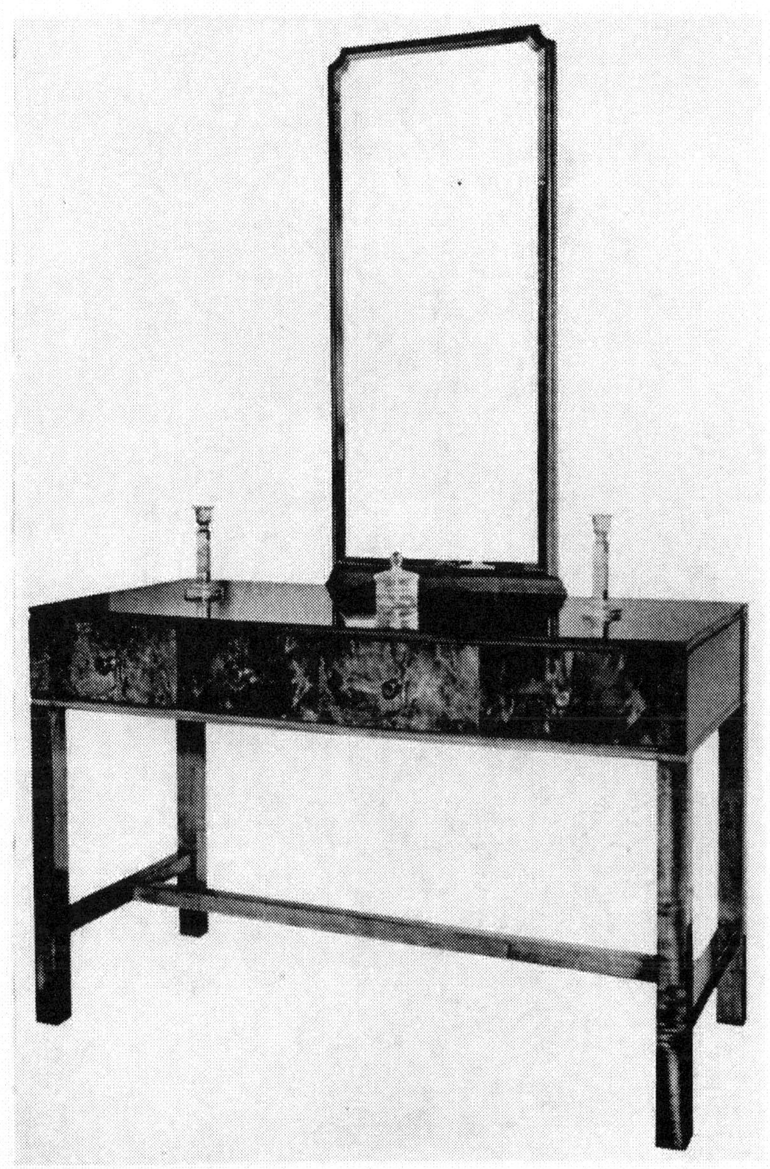

DRESSING TABLE, NO. 426-C
FLAME MAHOGANY

MAURICE ADAMS

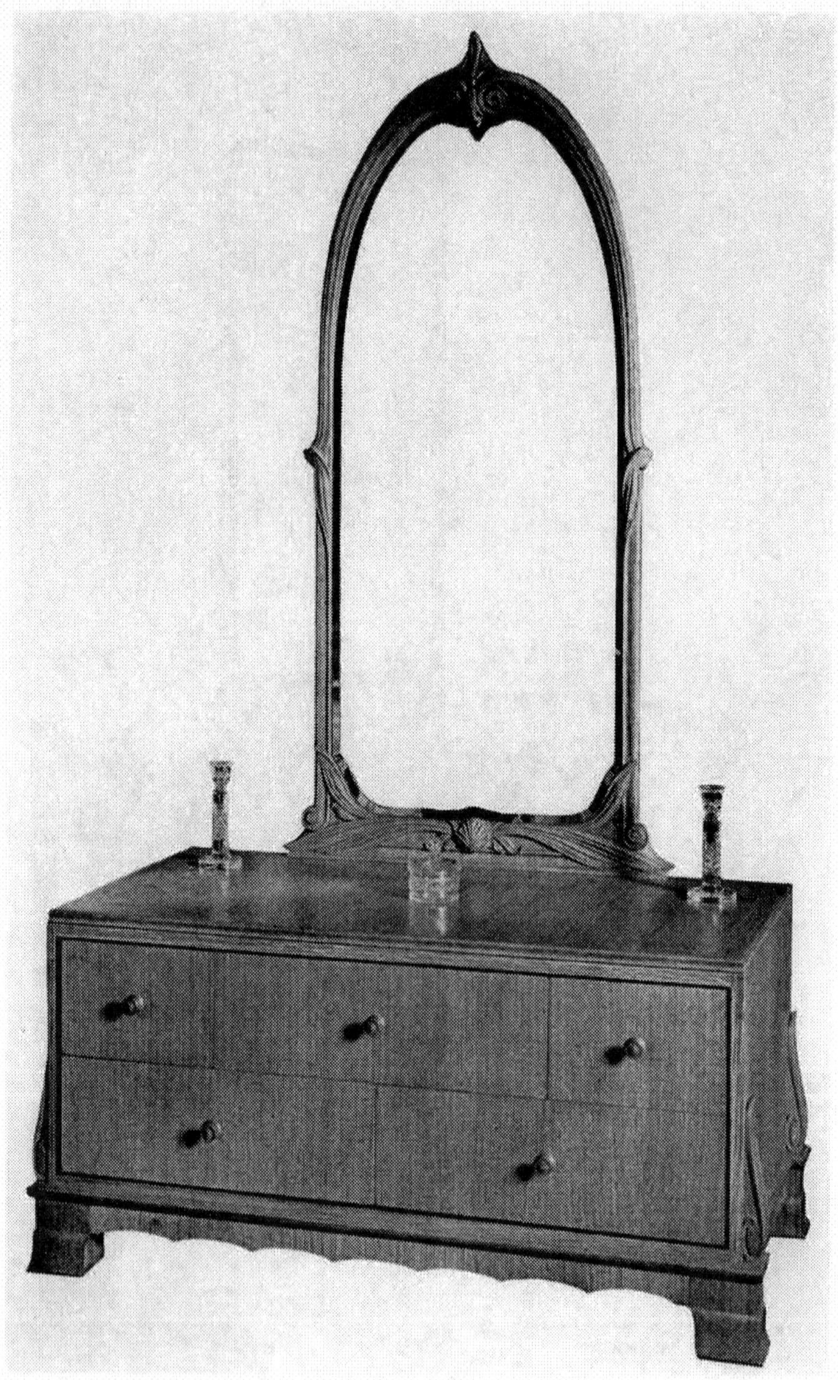

DRESSING TABLE, NO. 489-C
OAK

MAURICE ADAMS

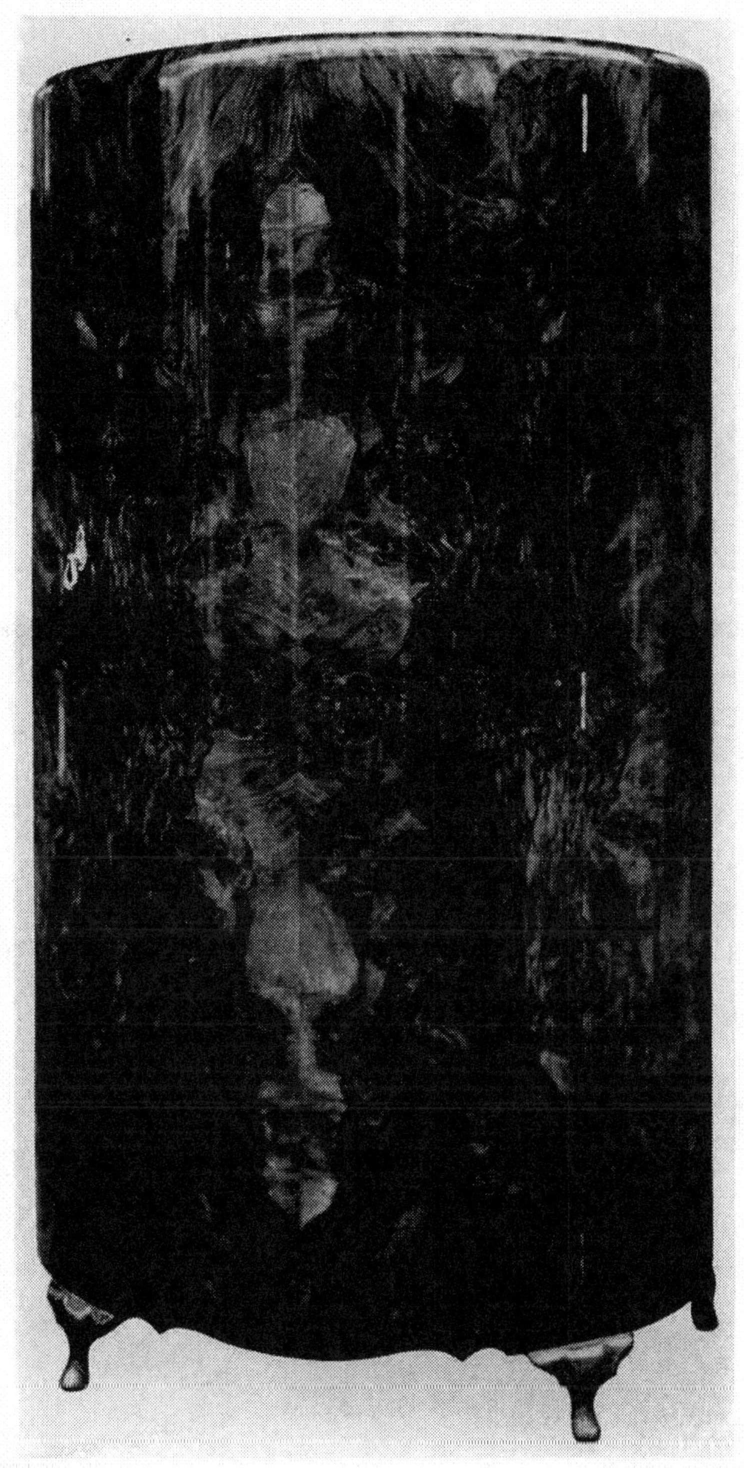

GROSVENOR WARDROBE, NO. 400-C — MAURICE ADAMS
BURR WALNUT

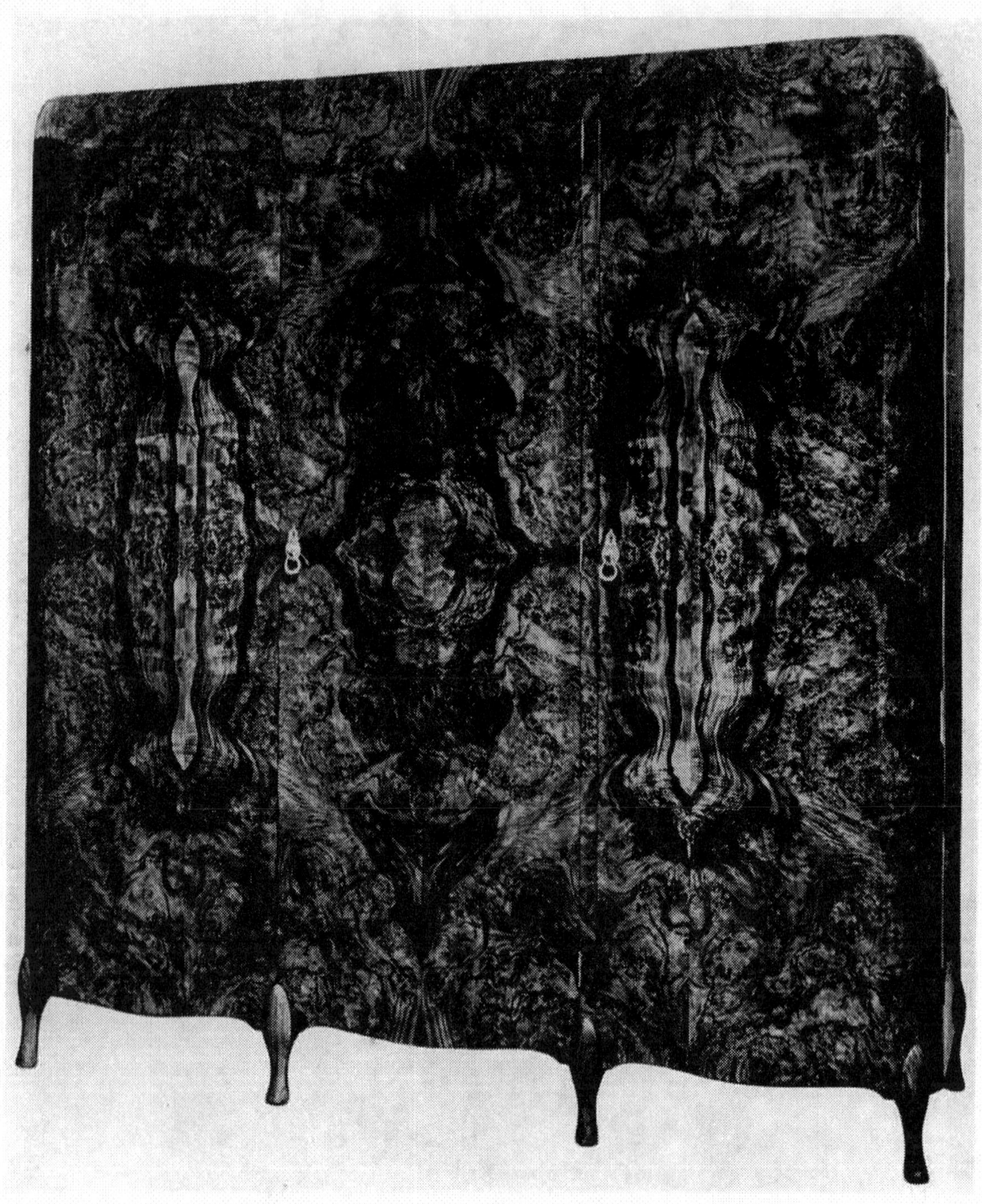

GROSVENOR WARDROBE, NO. 525-C
BURR WALNUT

MAURICE ADAMS

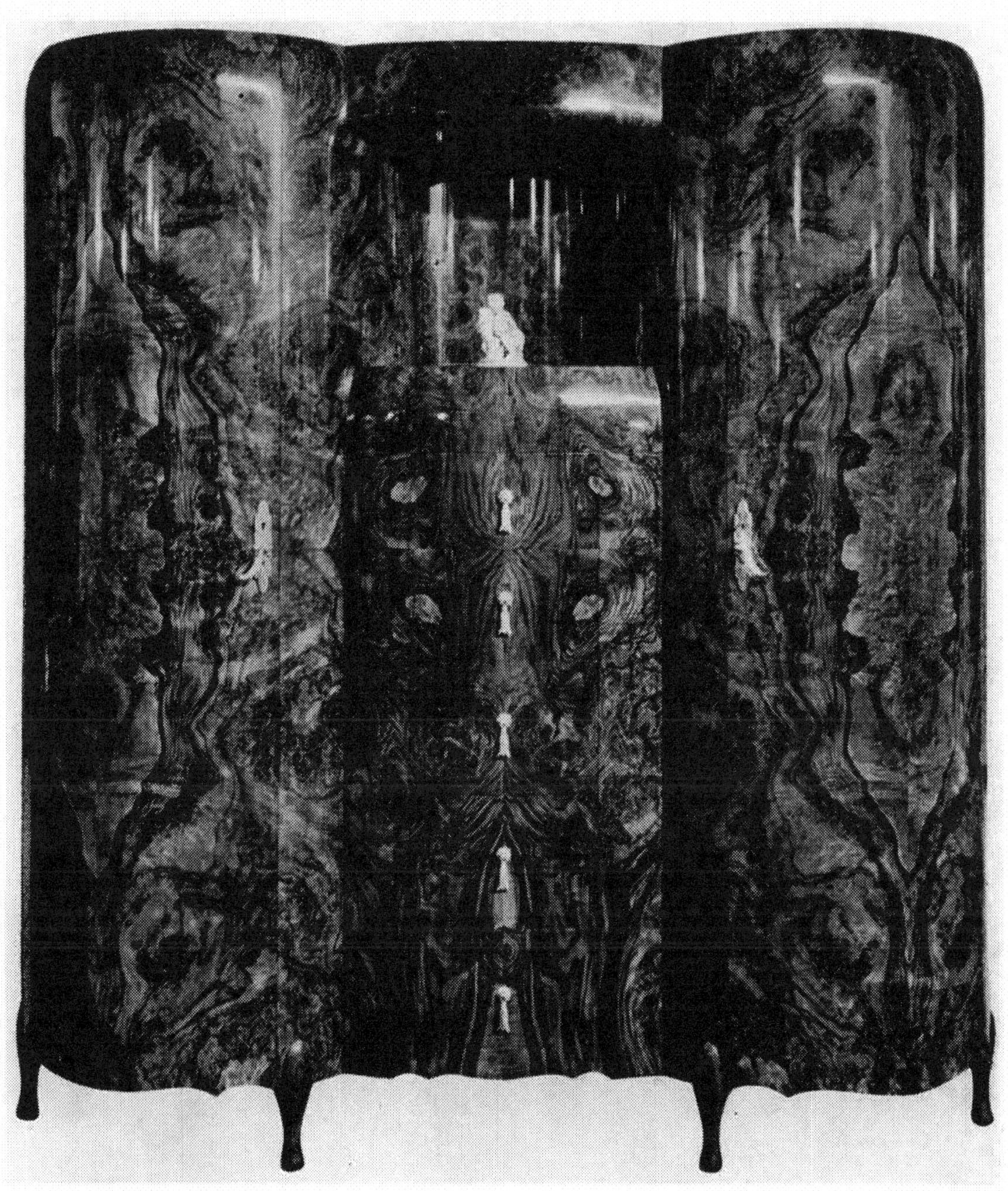

CARLTON WARDROBE, NO. 531-C
BURR WALNUT

MAURICE ADAMS

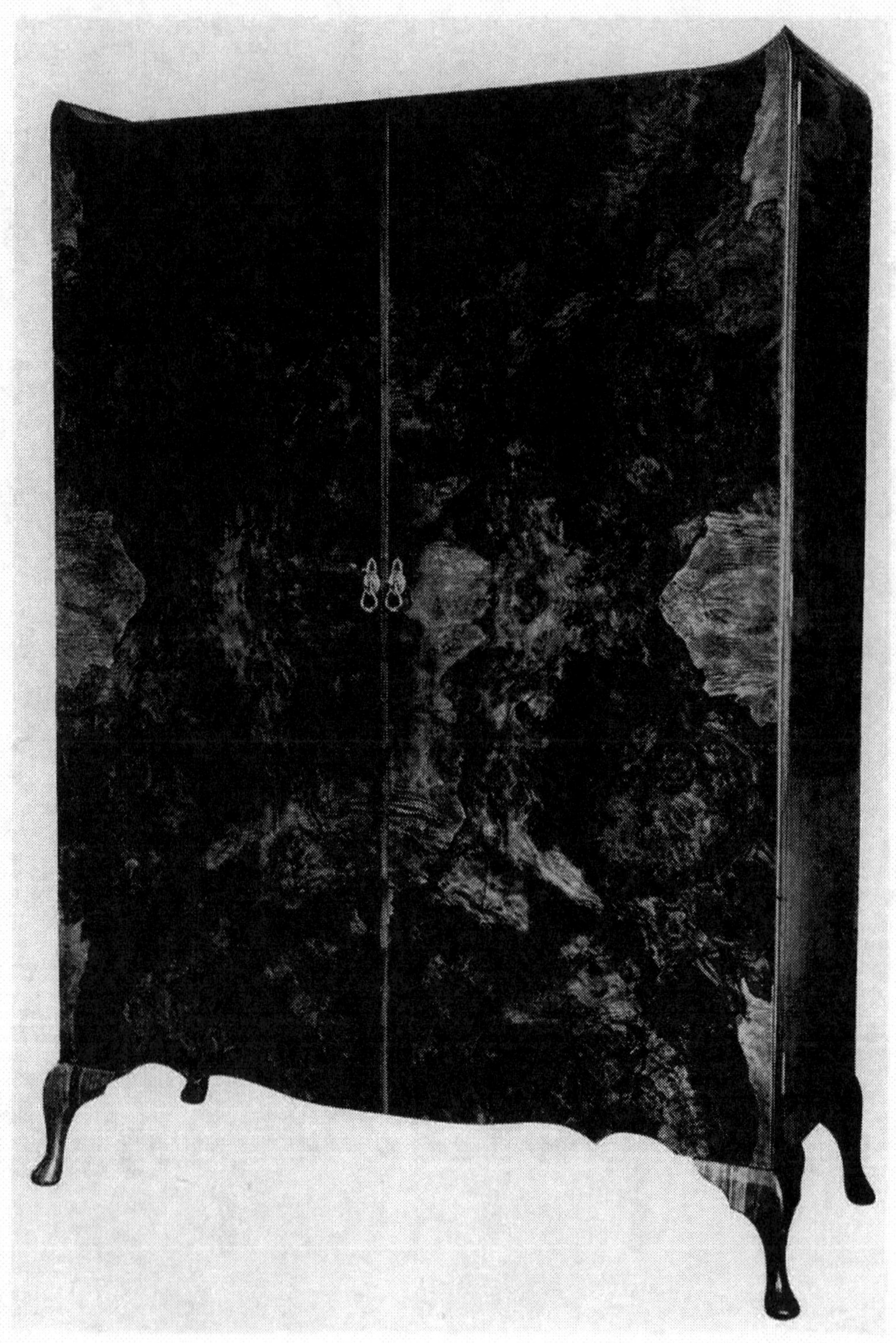

CONNAUGHT WARDROBE, NO. 387-C
BURR WALNUT

MAURICE ADAMS

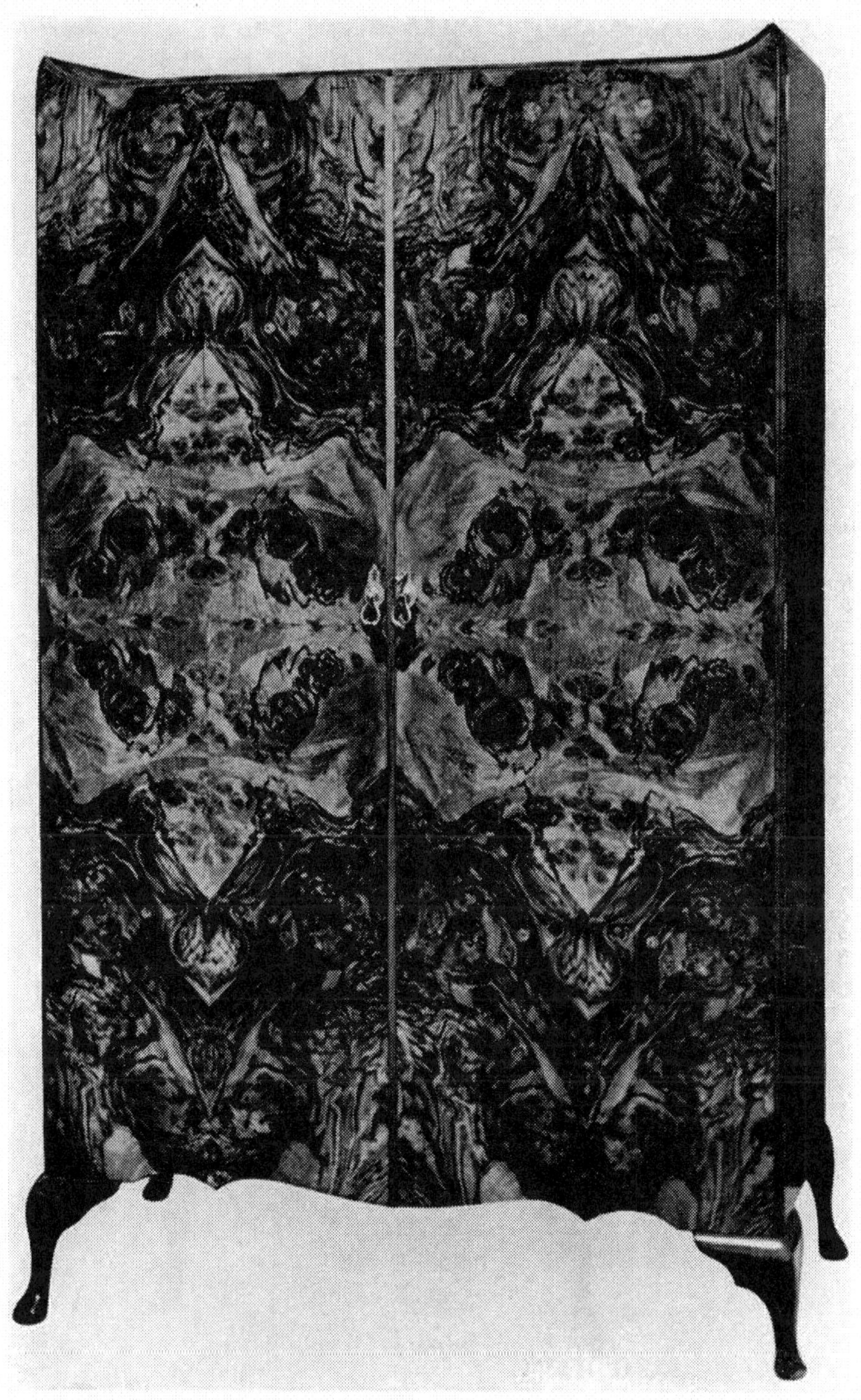

CONNAUGHT WARDROBE, NO. 387-C
BURR WALNUT

MAURICE ADAMS

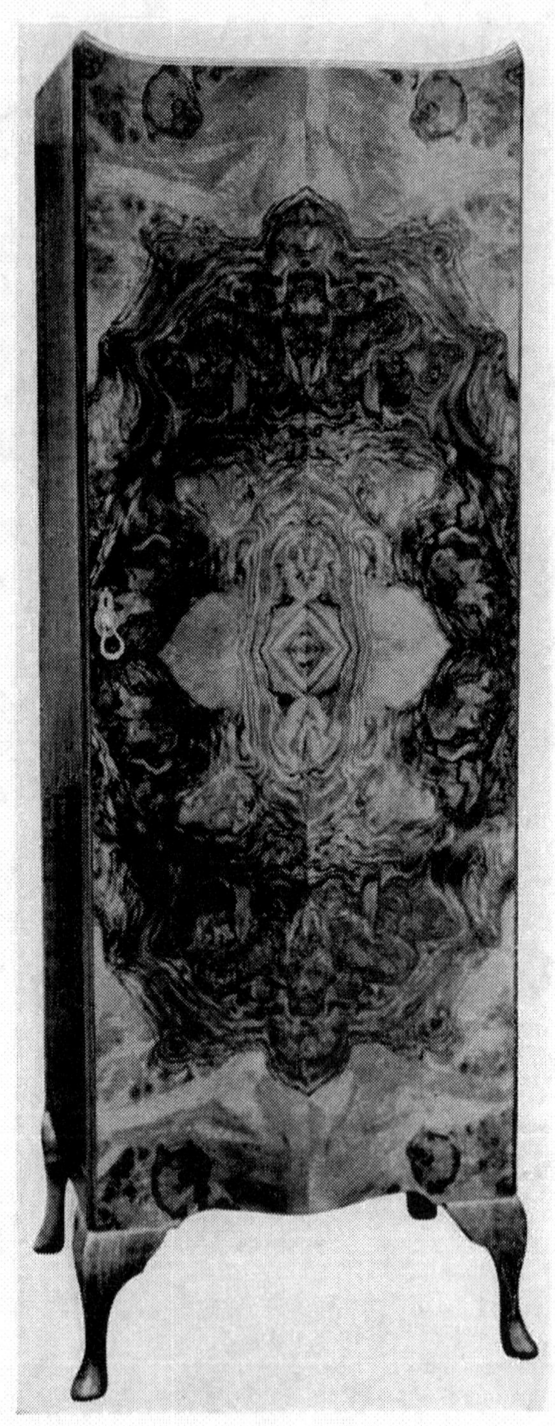

CONNAUGHT WARDROBE, NO. 388-C
BURR WALNUT

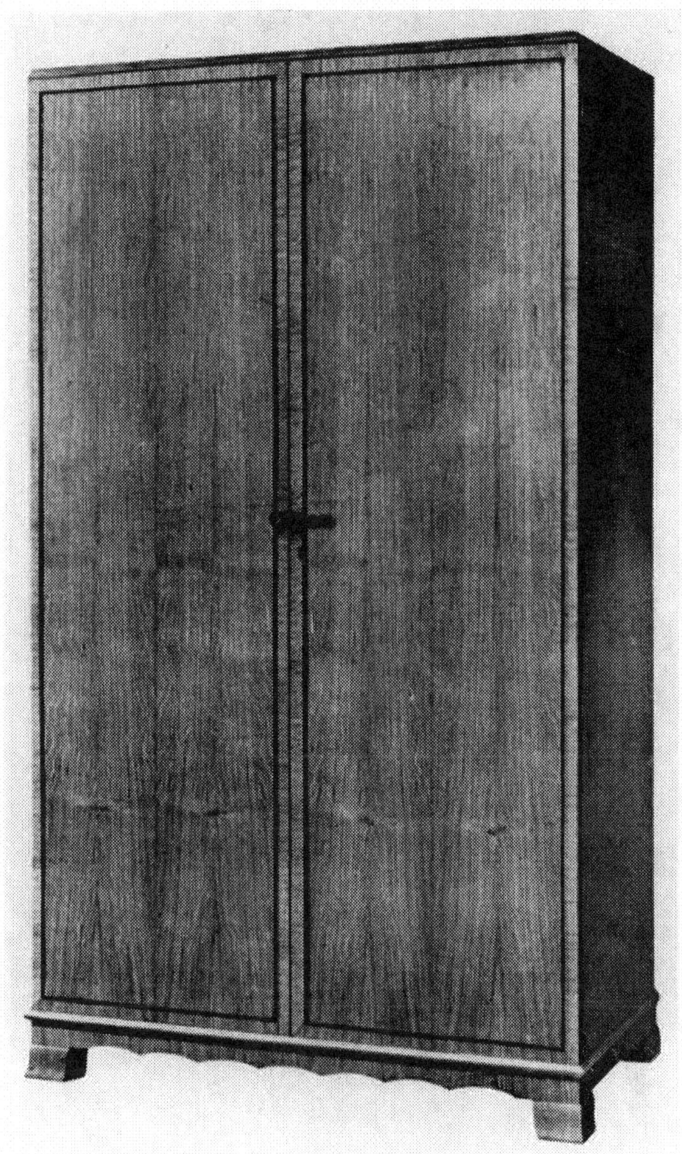

WARDROBE, NO. 422-C
OAK

MAURICE ADAMS

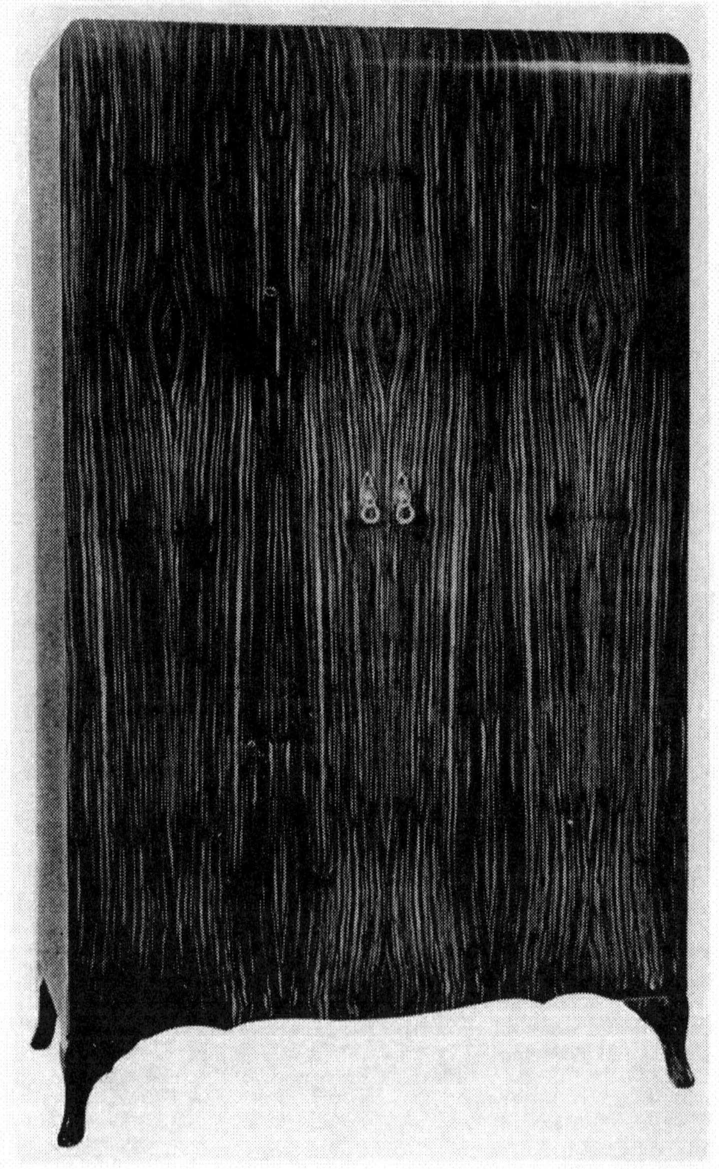

WARDROBE, NO. 421-C
COROMANDEL

MAURICE ADAMS

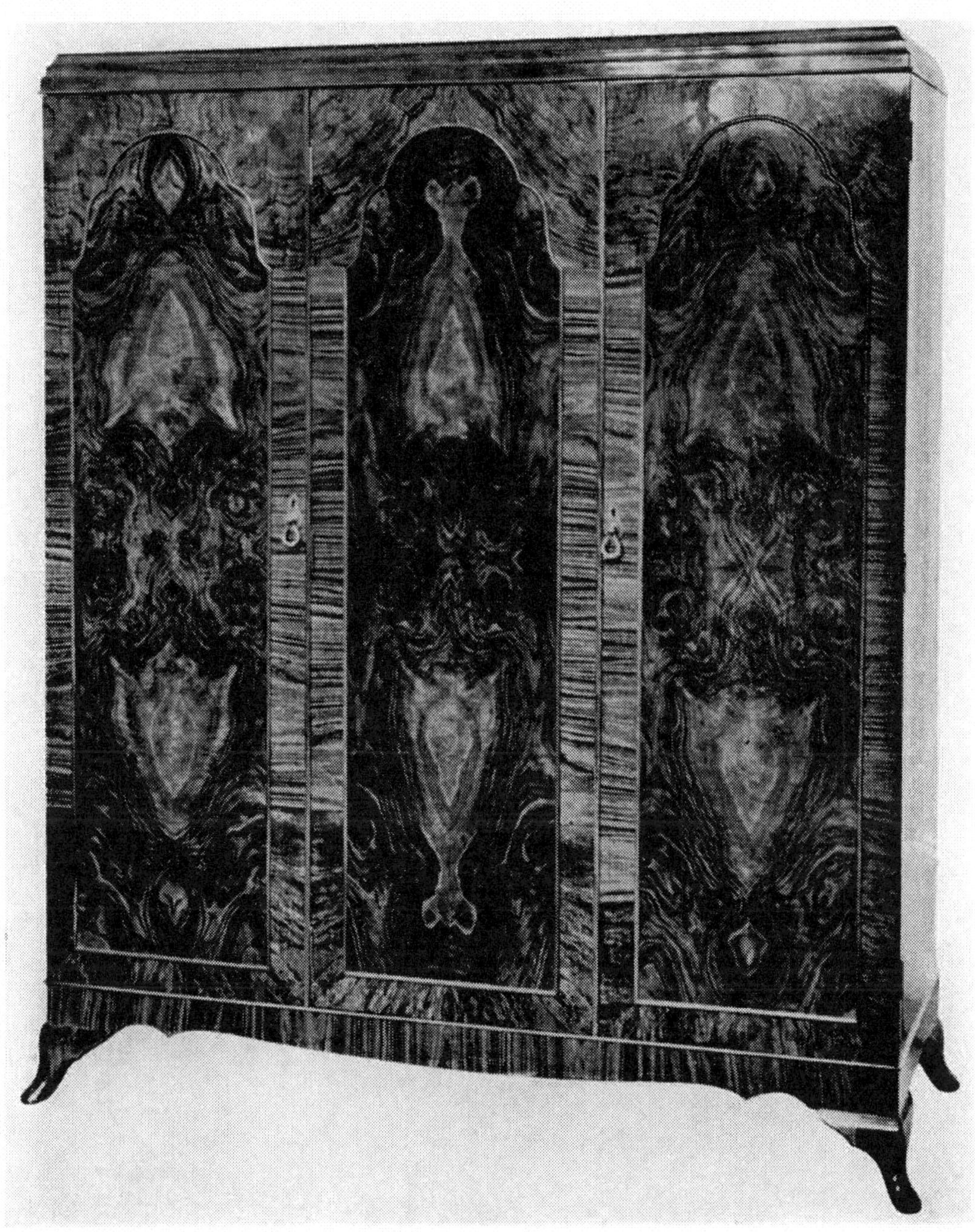

WARDROBE, NO. 364-C
BURR WALNUT

MAURICE ADAMS

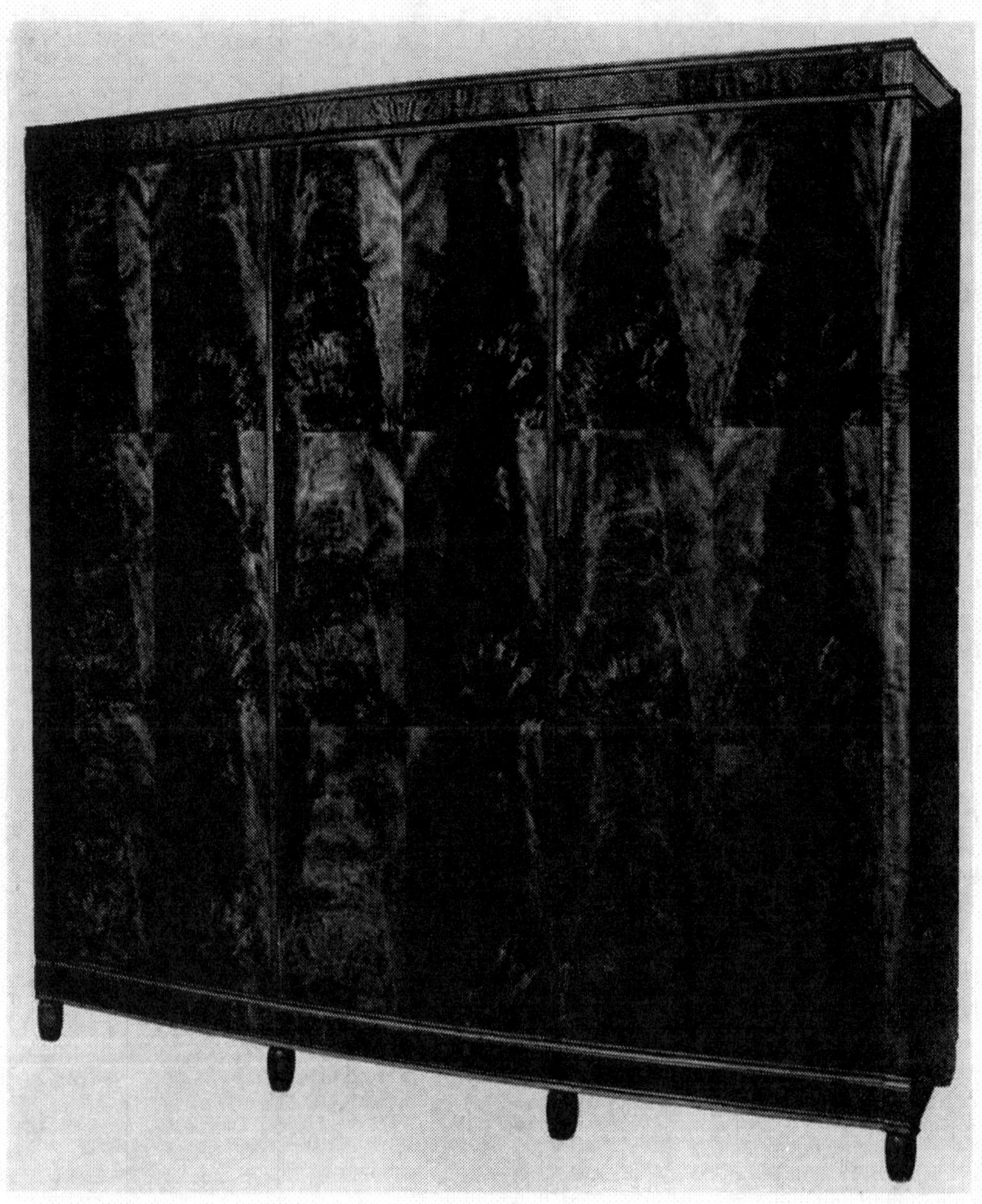

WARDROBE, NO. 427-C
FLAME MAHOGANY

MAURICE ADAMS

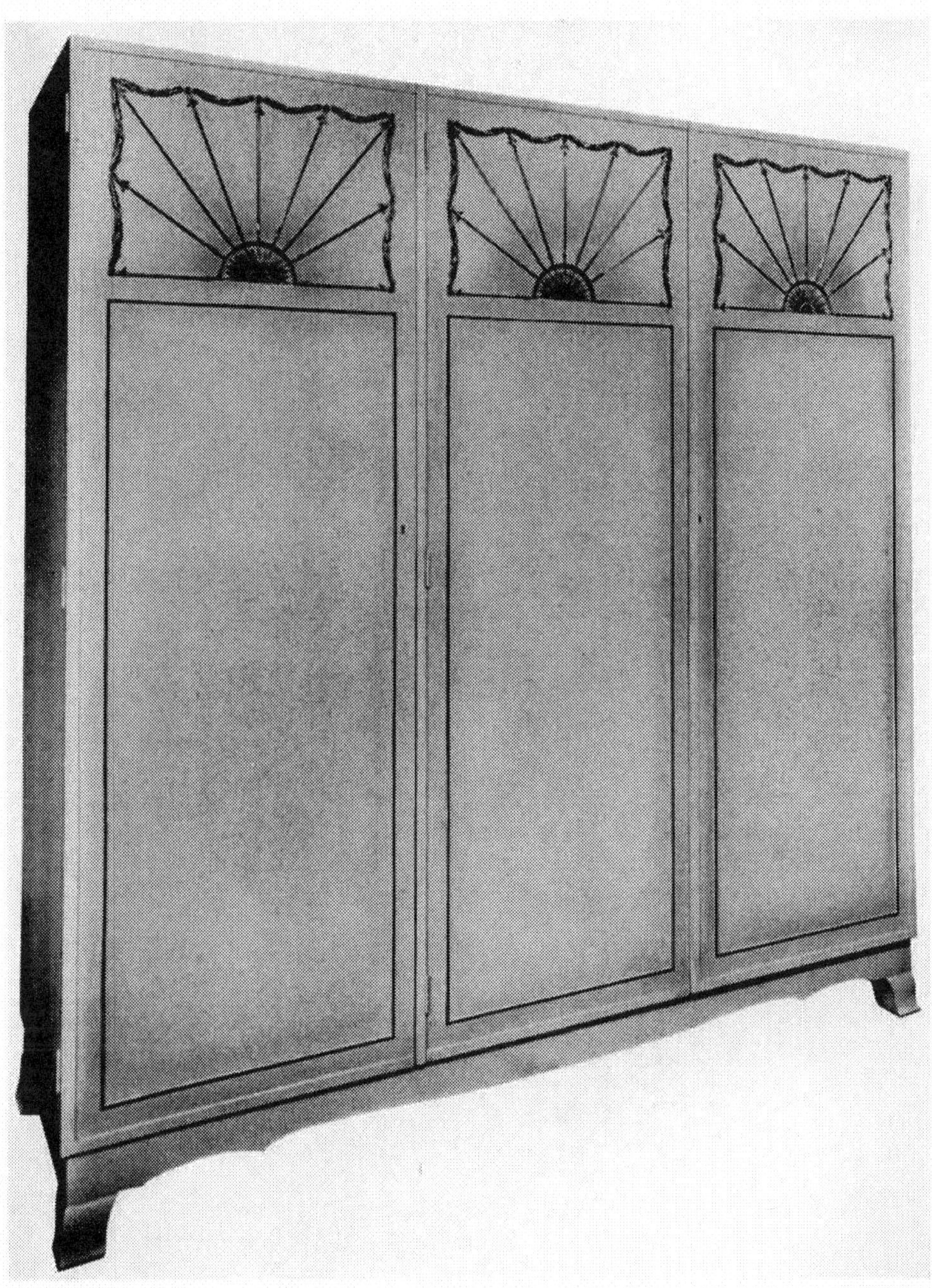

WARDROBE, NO. 686-C
PAINTED MAHOGANY

MAURICE ADAMS

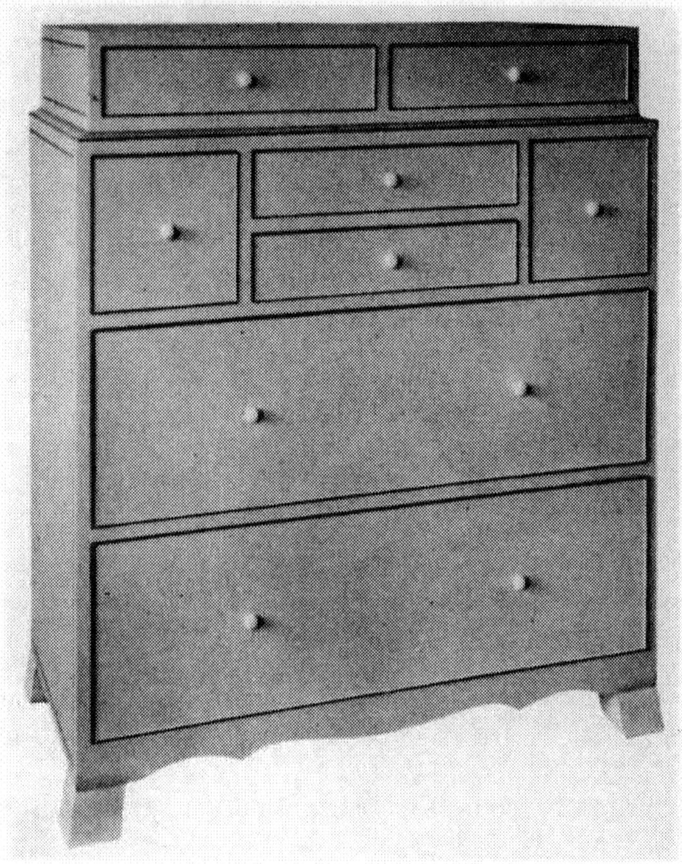

DRAWER CHEST, NO. 557-C
PAINTED MAHOGANY

MAURICE ADAMS

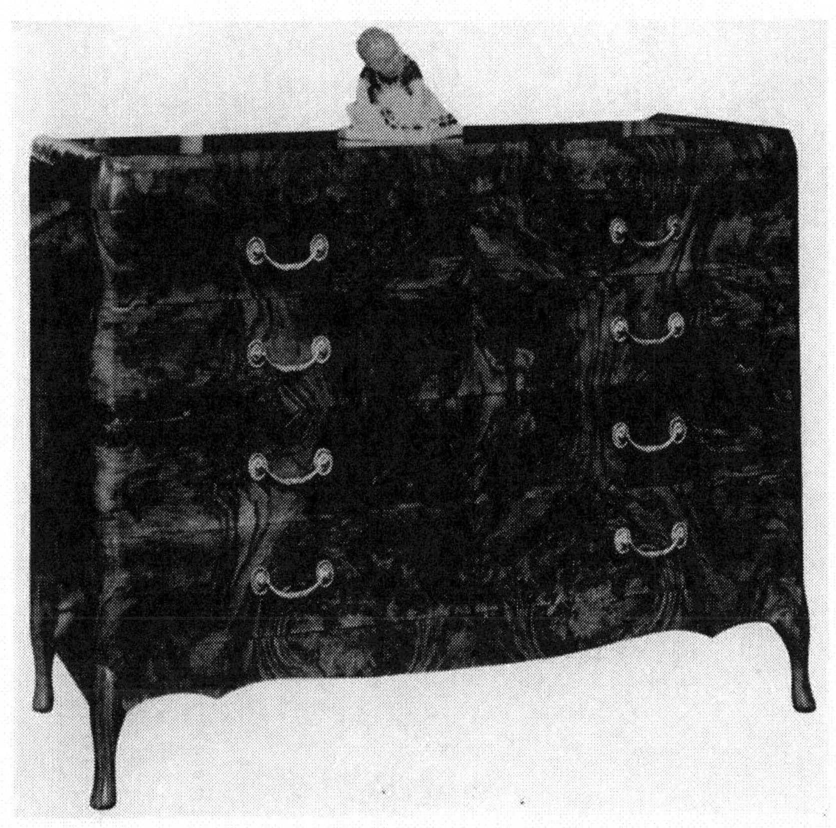

GROSVENOR CHEST, NO. 542-C
BURR WALNUT

MAURICE ADAMS

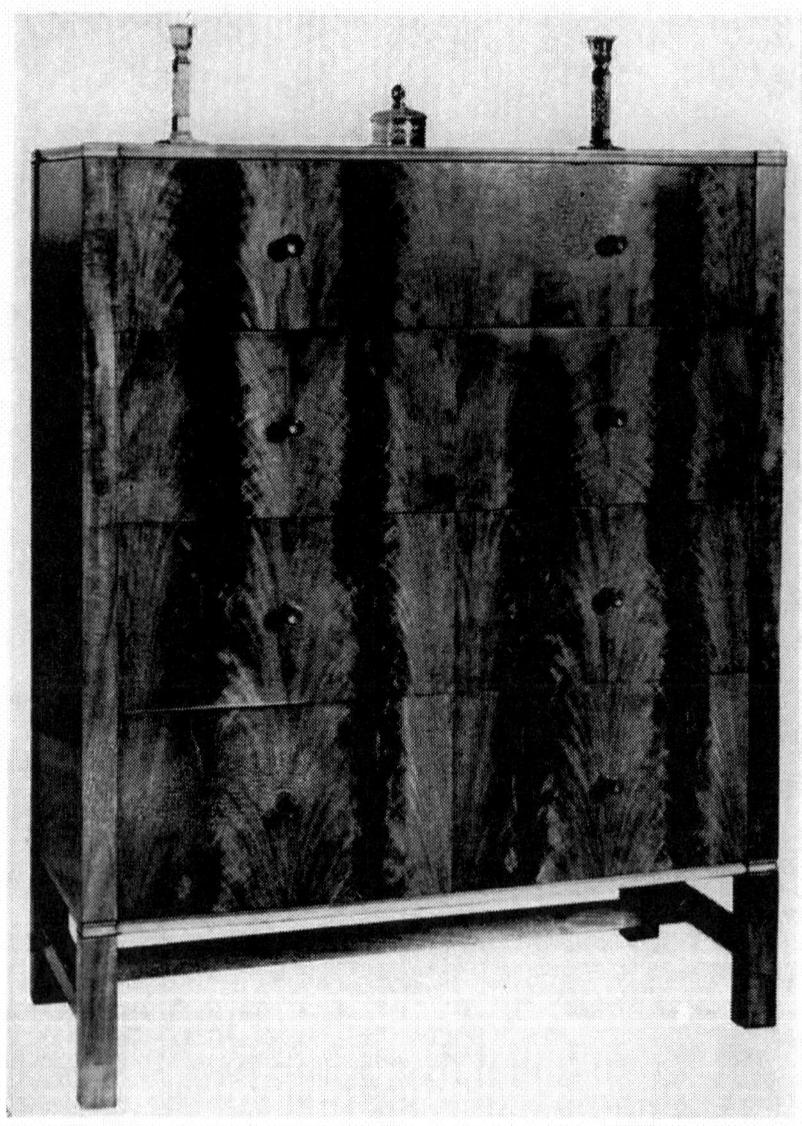

DRAWER CHEST, NO. 429-C — MAURICE ADAMS
FLAME MAHOGANY

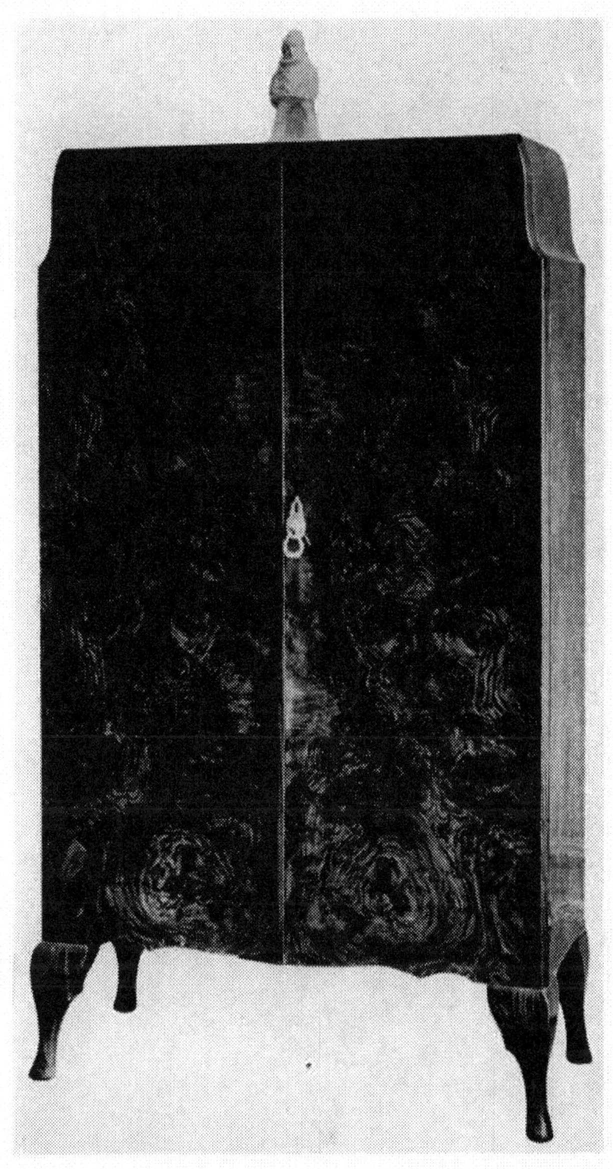

CONNAUGHT SHELF CUPBOARD, NO. 528-C
BURR WALNUT

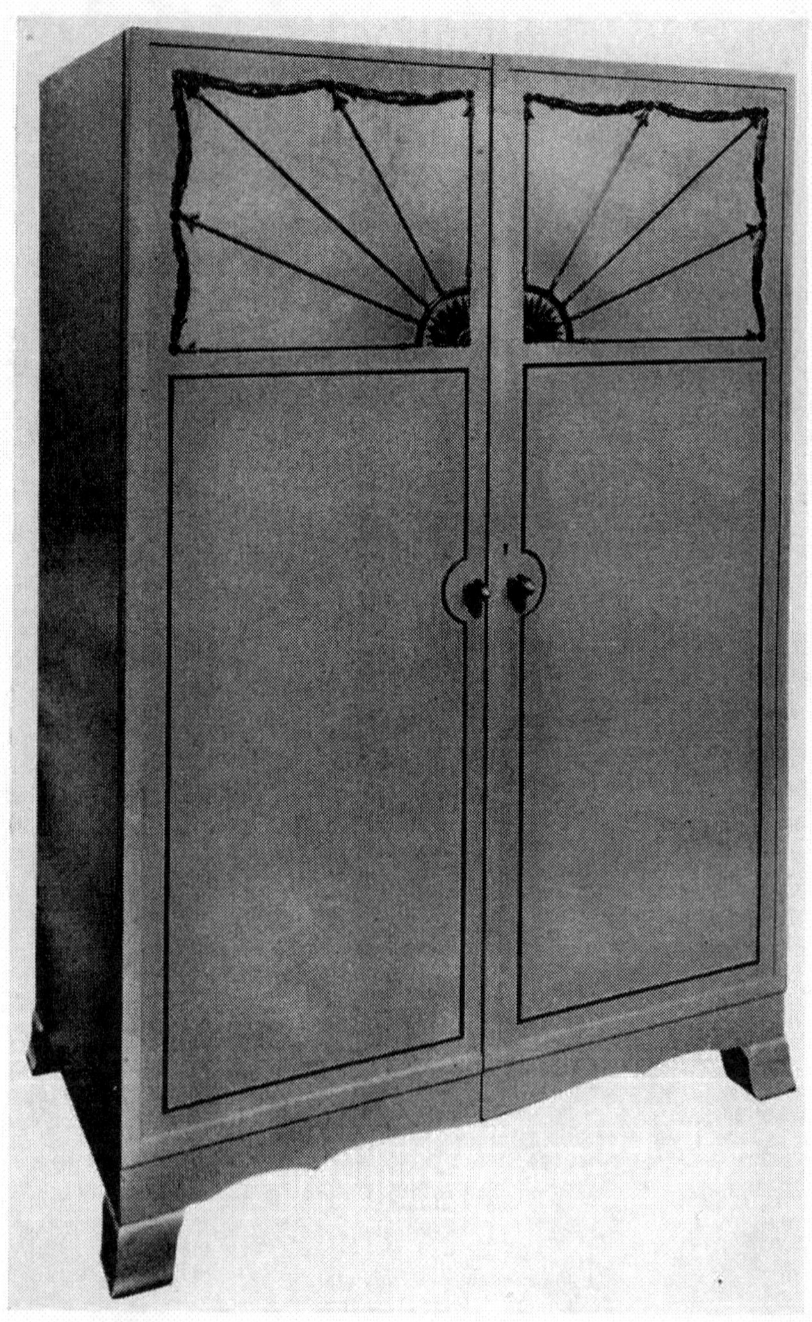

CUPBOARD, NO. 687-C
PAINTED MAHOGANY

MAURICE ADAMS

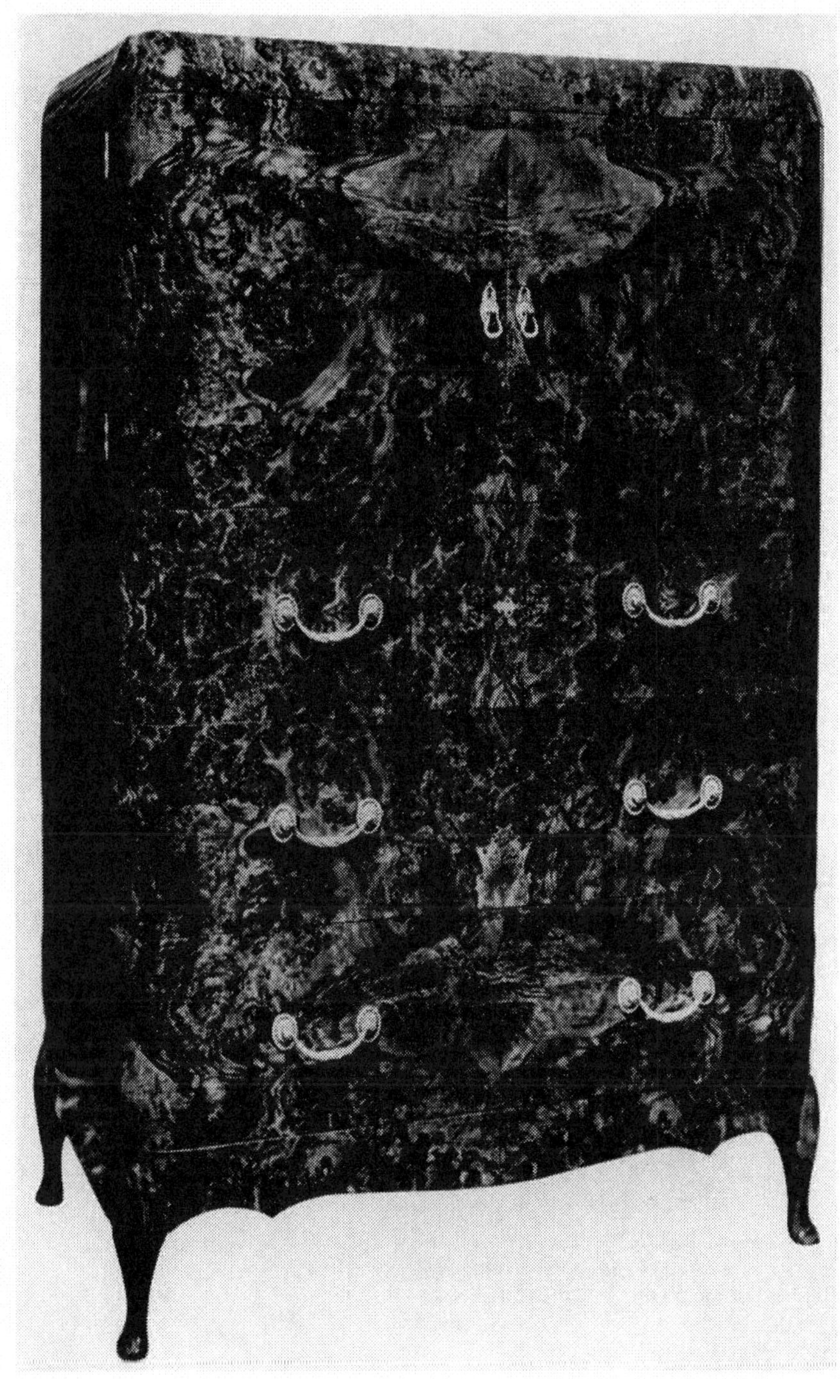

GROSVENOR CHEST CUPBOARD, NO. 526-C BURR WALNUT — MAURICE ADAMS

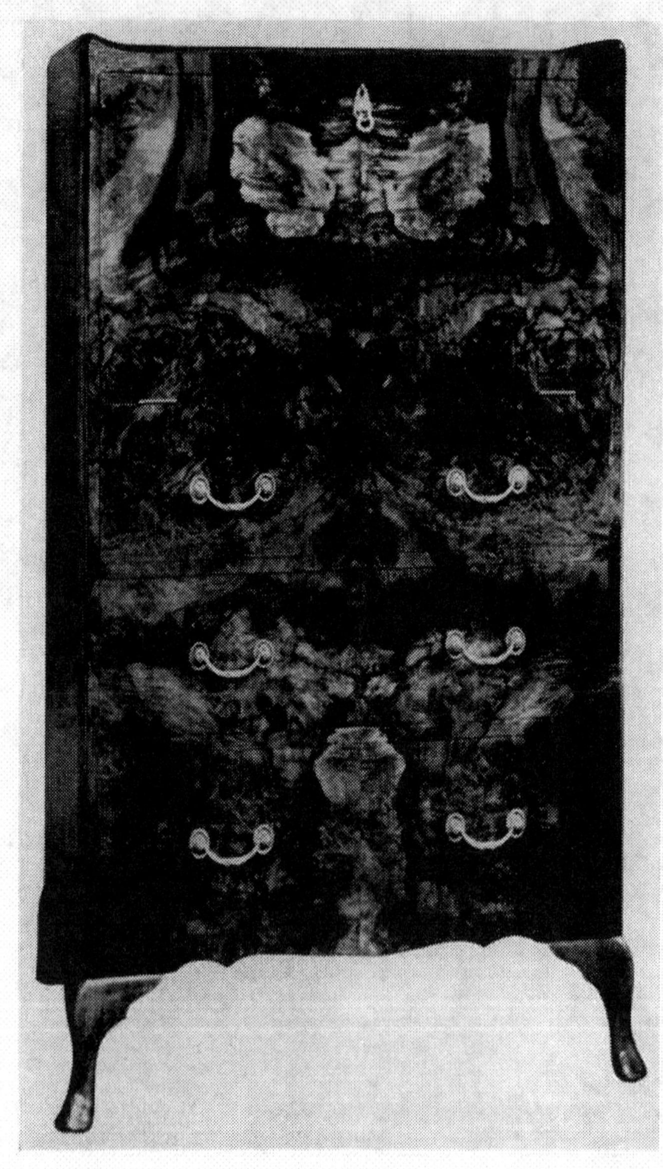

CONNAUGHT CHEST CUPBOARD, NO. 385-C
BURR WALNUT

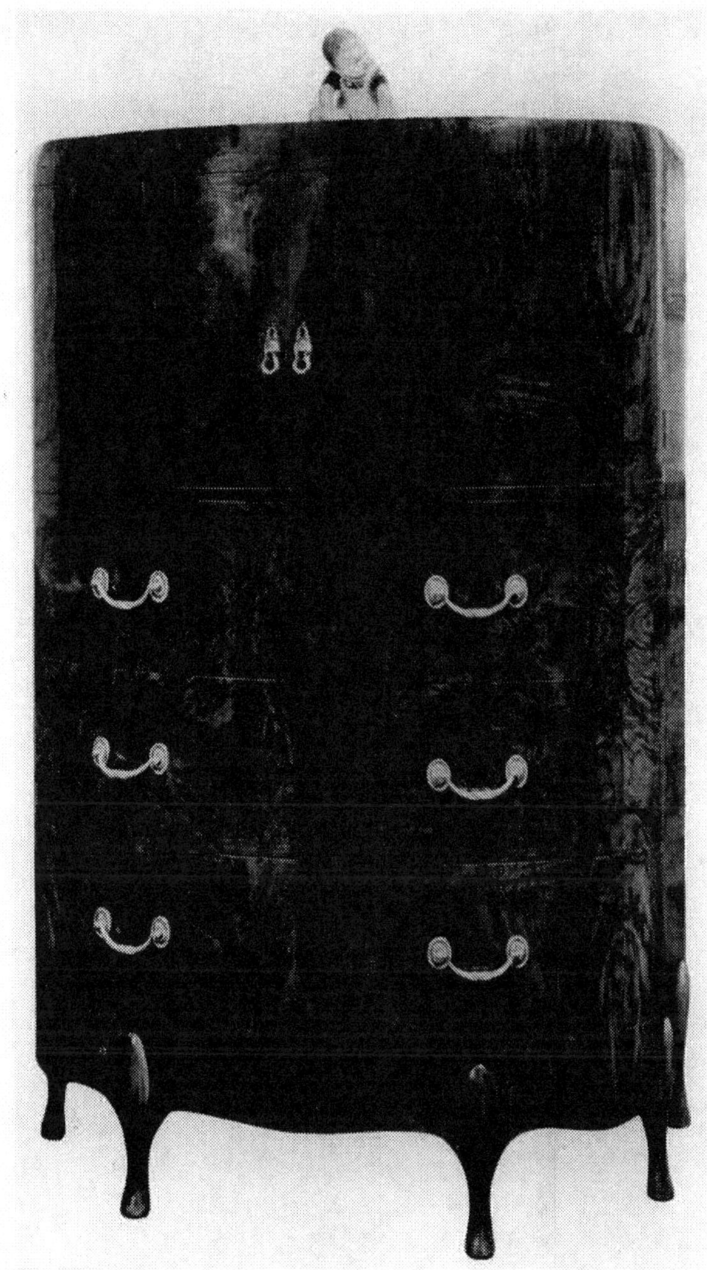

CORONET CHEST CUPBOARD, NO. 666-C
BURR WALNUT

MAURICE ADAMS

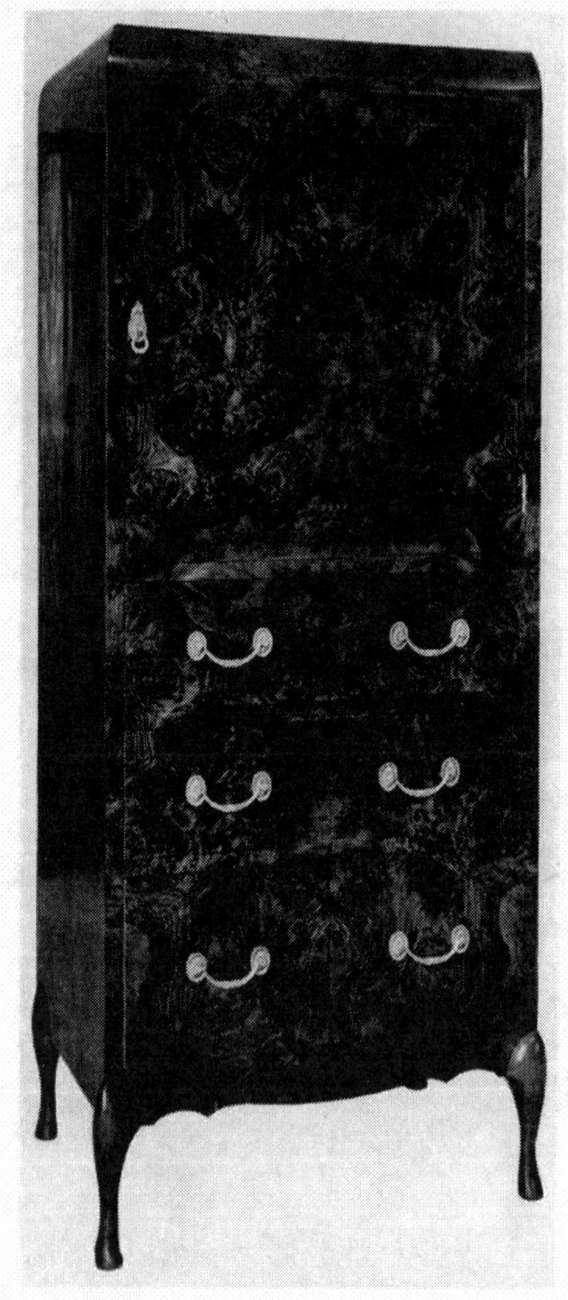

CHEST CUPBOARD, NO. 474-C — MAURICE ADAMS
BURR WALNUT

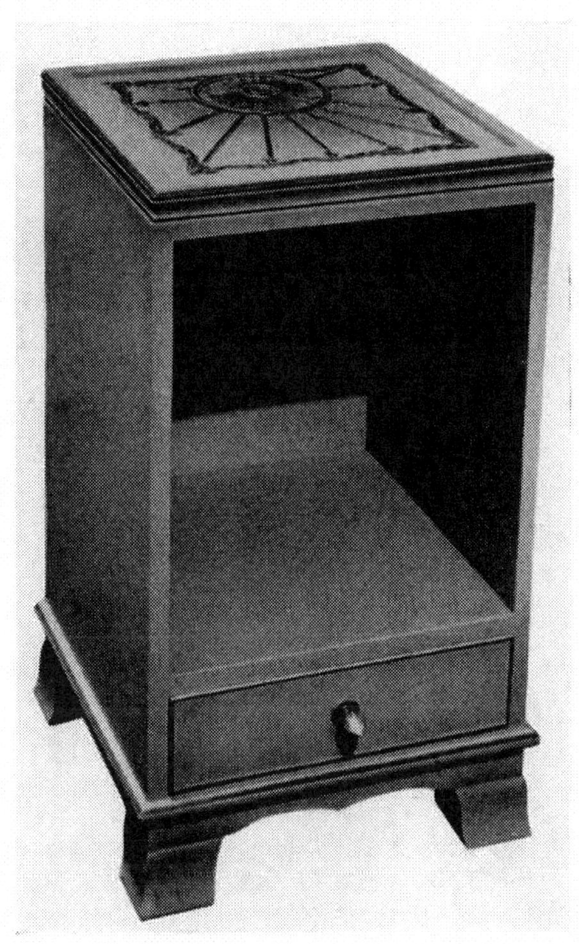

BEDSIDE TABLE, NO. 558-D
PAINTED MAHOGANY

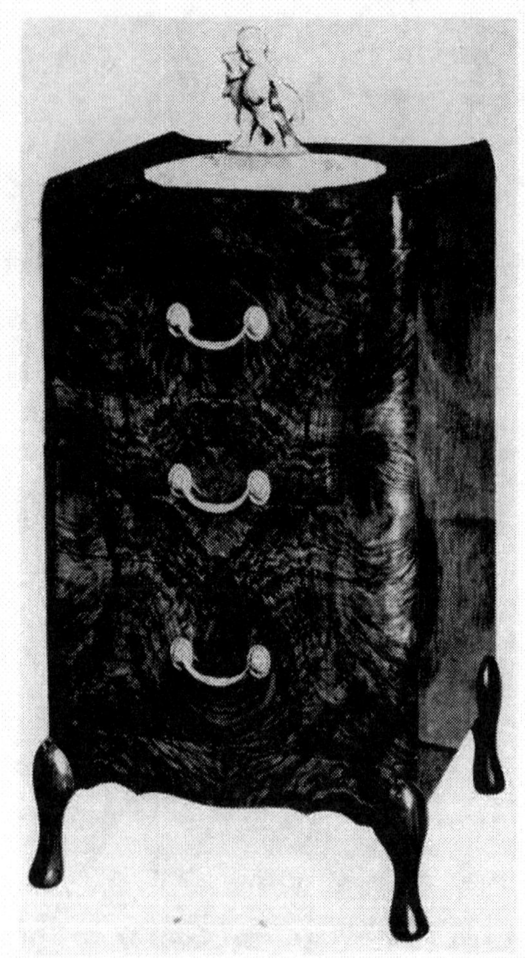

PEDESTAL CHEST NO. 527–C
BURR WALNUT

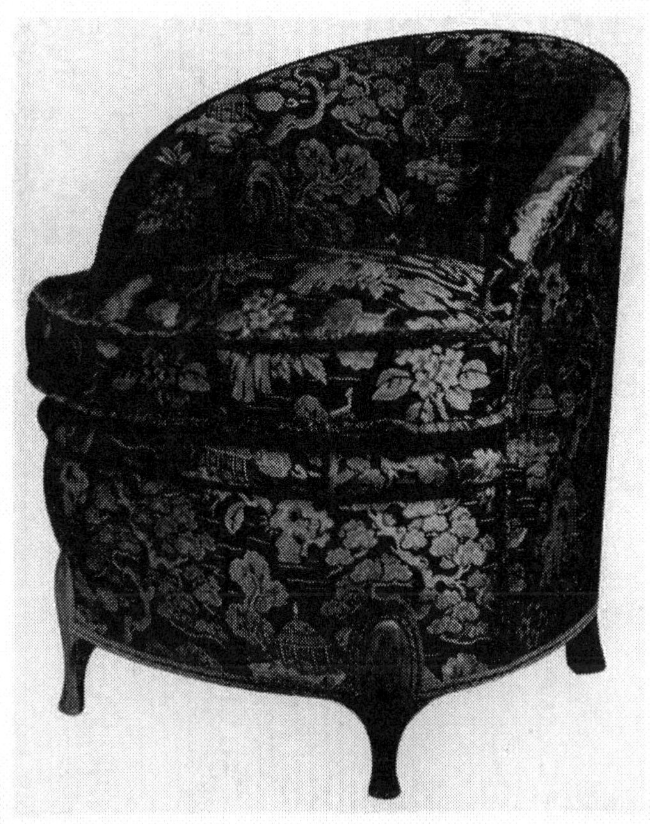

EASY CHAIR, NO. 729-C

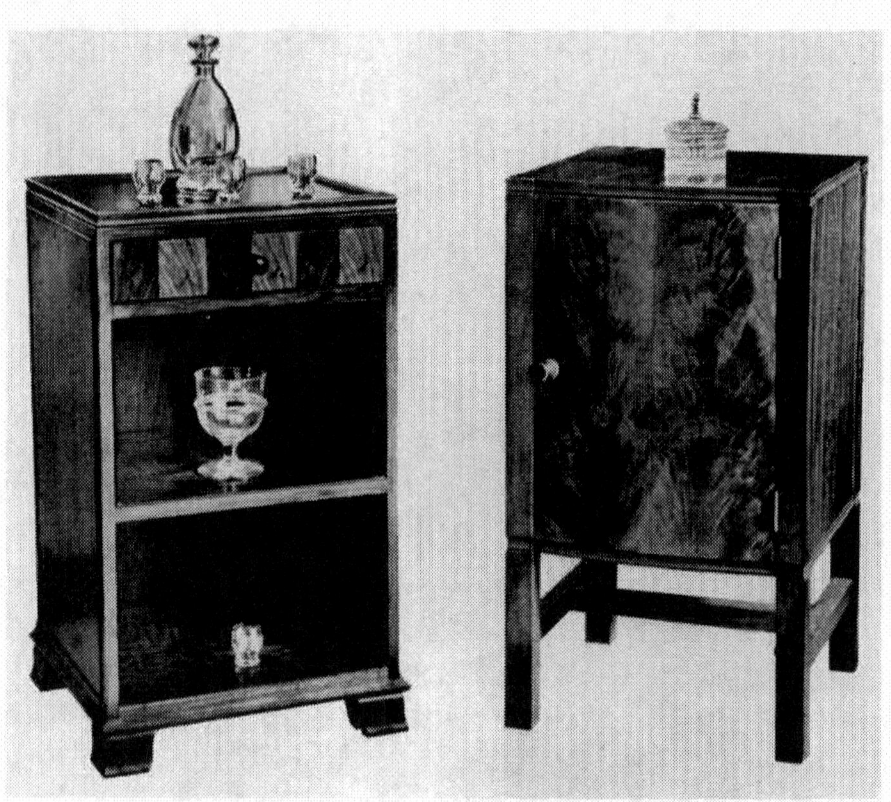

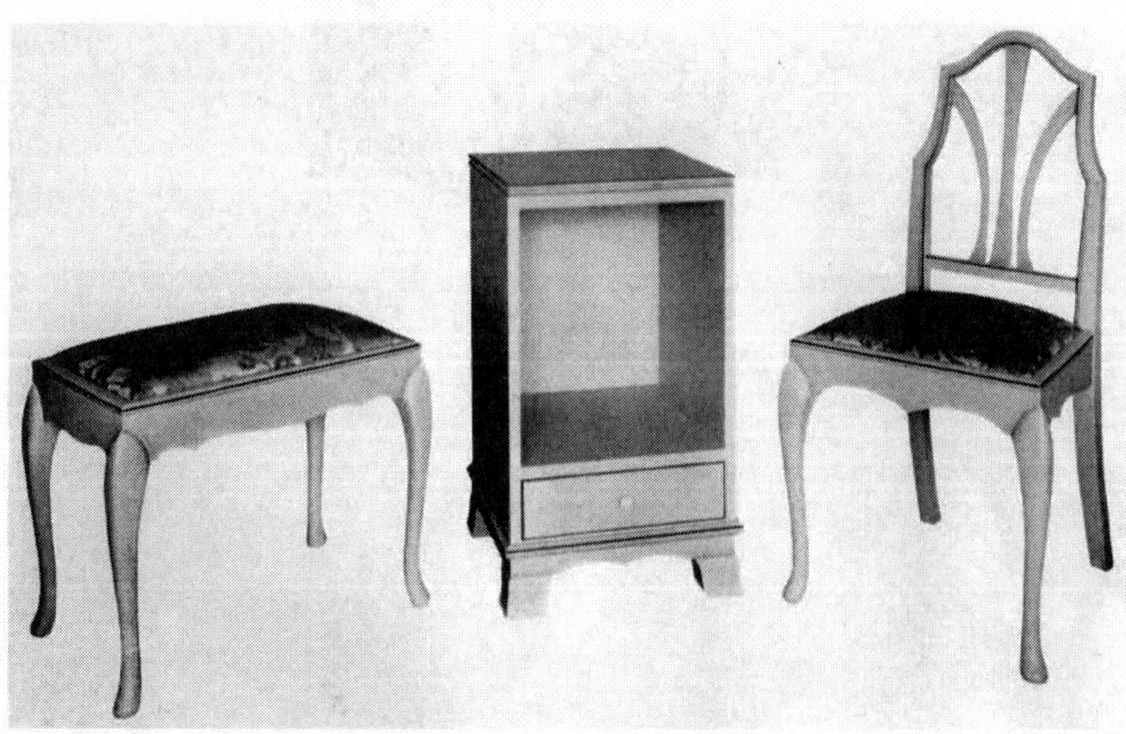

ABOVE—LEFT—WALNUT PEDESTAL, NO. 465-C ABOVE—RIGHT—MAHOGANY PEDESTAL, NO. 430-C
BELOW—PAINTED STOOL, NO. 433-C PEDESTAL, NO. 558-C CHAIR, NO. 633-D

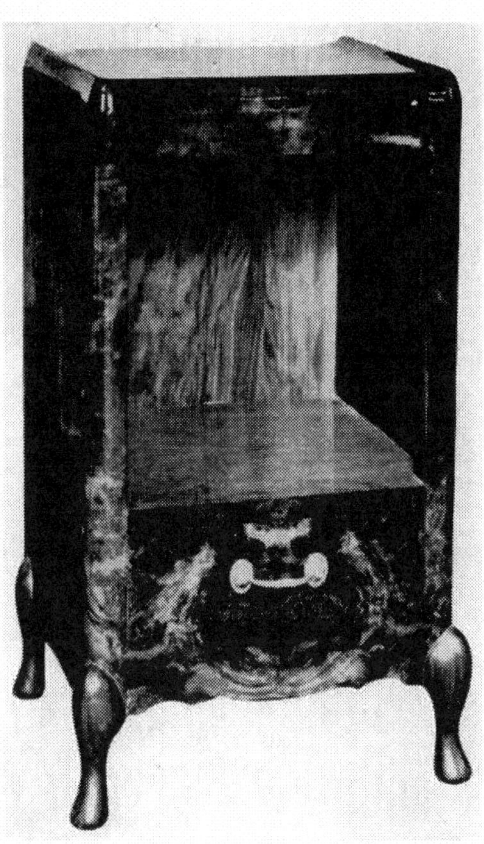

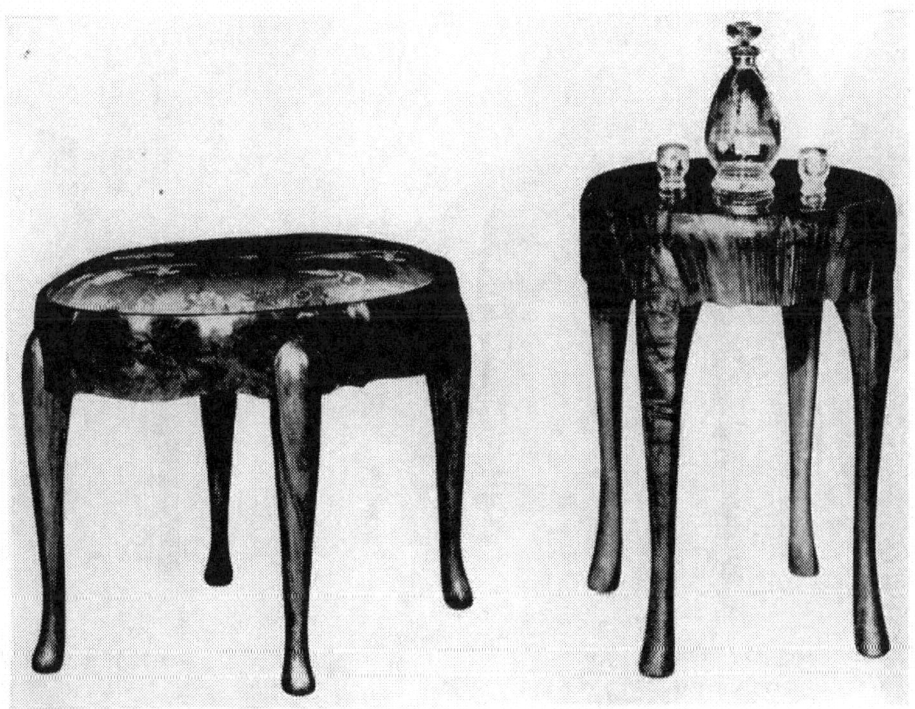

ABOVE—GROSVENOR BEDSIDE TABLE, NO. 470-C
BELOW—CORONET DRESSING STOOL, NO. 716-C
BURR WALNUT

COFFEE STOOL, NO. 483-C

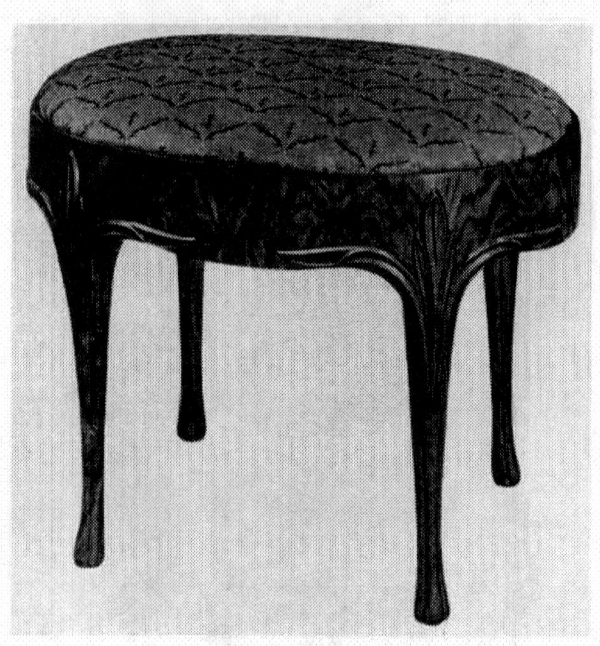

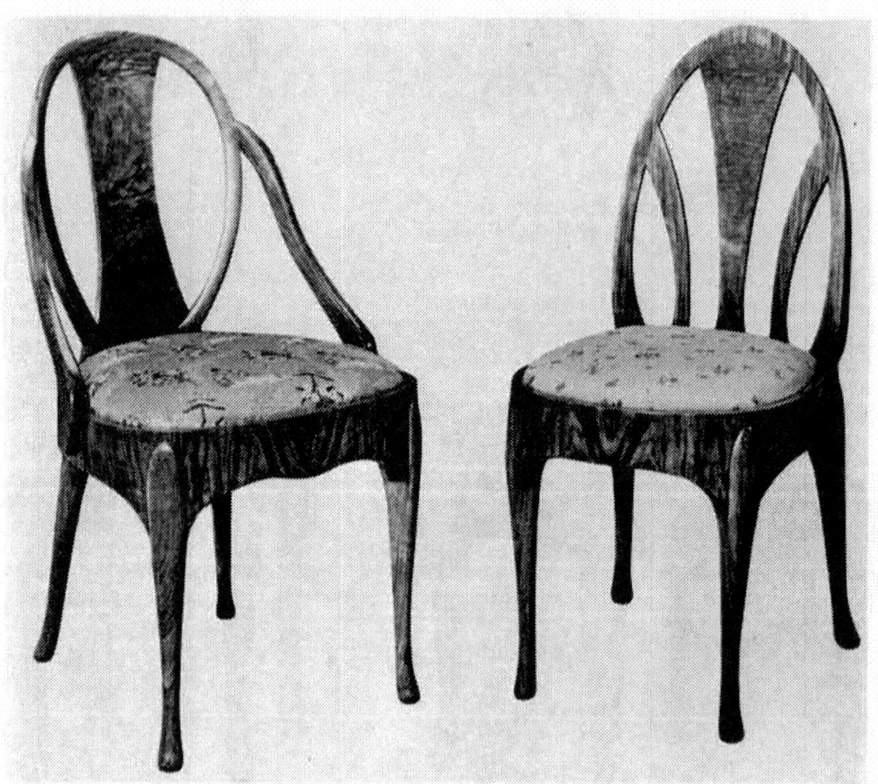

ABOVE—DRESSING STOOL, NO. 720-C
BELOW—CARLTON CHAIR, NO. 715-C

CHAIR, NO. 714-C

# DECORATIONS

OUR purpose here is not to furnish a text book for decorators—amateur or professional. Rather it is to offer suggestions and guidance to those contemplating the decoration of their house. While also we have no desire to belittle house decorators as a class, a good deal of subsequent disappointment may be avoided by the employer if, in the absence of personal decorative experience, he makes himself acquainted with modern decorative methods and gets to know about some of the difficulties and troubles which form a common experience of all those who have had to do with house decoration.

There are three primary considerations before success in decorations can be assured. The condition of the work to be decorated. The quality and suitability of the materials employed. The experience and skill of the operators.

We are dealing at the moment with practical considerations only, because the artistic preparation of the decorative scheme is, of course, entirely another matter.

No decorative work can be successful or permanent unless the surfaces to be decorated are in proper condition. In either new or old work the first thing to avoid is damp. Disappointment will follow if walls are painted or papered without being quite dry. In exposed positions trouble is frequently experienced, both in new as well as old houses, with damp around the window frames and cills. In old houses damp may be coming through the ceilings. If walls are damp, and expensive decorative work is contemplated, any damp plaster must be stripped from the brickwork, which should have two coats of waterproofing solution, be plastered with Pudloed cement finished with Keen's cement. If this is carefully done the damp trouble will be effectively cured. Any damp places beneath windows or where the plaster has crumbled, the same treatment should be followed. If necessary the window cills outside should be covered with lead which needs a good wide drip to throw off the water. Old brickwork should have the joints well raked out and be pointed with Portland cement. Damp walls should also be either coated with waterproofing solution or be faced with cement stucco outside. In all damp troubles, correct diagnosis as to the cause is essential before a cure is possible.

Defective damp courses may be cut out and made good, but this is a costly business. A waterproofed plaster described above is more reliable and cheaper in most cases.

Paint will not stand on new lime or cement plaster. Either a finishing coat of Keen's cement is necessary or a non-lime plaster must be used. With sirapite plaster the work may be painted or papered almost at once.

The durability of paint work depends upon effective preparation of the work to be painted, and the quality of the paint employed. All dirt must be removed from old work or the paint will not dry properly. The old paint must be slightly roughened to form key for the new paint or it will flake off. Oil paint consists of a base, medium, dryer and pigment. The base of the best paint is white lead and should be insisted upon for outside work. The medium or oil should be the best quality boiled linseed. The dryer is used to oxydize the oil, without which the paint will not dry. The pigment is to give colour only. Always insist upon the paint being supplied to specification or use a recognised brand from well-known paint manufacturers and insist on their own undercoat paint being used. Good paint will stand much longer and costs no more to apply than inferior paint. First quality paint and labour costs money. Competitive estimates cannot be rightly judged unless they be based upon the same specification. The decorator who intends to use the cheapest paint he can buy and employ odd men to carry out the work will, of course, quite easily be able to underquote his competitor who declines to do shoddy work, and bases his estimate on the use of first-class material and labour. The lower quotation may actually realize a larger profit to the contractor. The person who, in this way, obtains indiscriminate estimates and accepts the lowest price under the impression that he has made the best bargain, will be disillusioned when he finds that the work will require re-doing after twelve months.

Decorative paint work may be classified as plain work and shaded. Plain paint work is the common type. The colour is quite flat and even in tone. Providing the work be properly prepared and the paint of good quality, the minimum of skill is required for sound plain paint work. Shaded paint work requires first-class decorators and cannot be done by the ordinary house decorator. Effect is obtained not by flat coats of opaque colour but by partly removing the finishing coat so that the undercoat may show through. For this purpose a stippling brush, something like a flat hair brush, is used. The stippler is dabbed on to the wet finishing coat of paint, so that the brush hairs remove tiny blobs of paint and thus expose the undercoat.

There are several types of stipplers, coarse, fine and rubber. Rubber stipplers are used to give coarse effect. Much of the work now being done with coarse stipplers is in very bad taste. The most pleasing results are obtained by using fine hair stipplers and by shading the finishing colour, making this darker at the skirting and gradually fading away towards the ceiling. Mouldings to doors, etc., should be wiped while wet with a rag. This gives a shaded appearance. All stippled and wiped woodwork should have a final coat of thin varnish or glaze or it will not wear well.

Ceilings are best painted almost white or painted the same colour as the walls, using a much lighter shade. Alternatively they may be " clouded."

Varnish bought from houses of repute can always stand up to climatic conditions expected. Varnish should not be applied over a glossy surface that has not been rubbed down to provide a key. Varnish that remains " tacky " has been applied over an imperfectly cleaned surface or with a brush from which the oil has not been entirely removed. In these cases a thin coat of goldsize and turps. should be applied over which a new coat of varnish may be applied with confidence.

" Blooming " is due to deposit of moisture caused by unfavourable drying conditions. Sudden changes of temperature, bad ventilation, fumes from gas fires and draughts in corridors are factors liable to produce this defect. Work should, therefore, be carried out in a dry, well-ventilated atmosphere and where there is little chance of rapid change in temperature. A surface bloom may be removed by washing with water and then polishing with a small quantity of furniture polish. A permanent bloom must be rubbed down and a new coat applied.

Blistering is caused by the presence of moisture in a soft undercoat. This may be due to the wrong proportion of dryers or to condensation. Unseasoned and resinous wood, also poor turpentine substitute in the undercoat may also cause blistering. A too hurried application of the varnish over an imperfectly dried surface will also give rise to this trouble. Exposure to the sun is yet another cause. If a suitable hard undercoat is allowed to dry thoroughly, blistering should never occur in the finishing coat.

Cracking is caused by an excessively oily undercoating, or by the use of an insufficiently elastic varnish on the finishing coat. Inside varnish should dry in about 6 to 7 hours.

We are now supplying a transparent liquid preparation for rendering wall-paper washable. This penetrates the paper surface and establishes resistance to water and steam. Appearance of the paper is not affected.

Several materials of great value to the decorator are now available. Of these mention may be made of stone paint which gives the effect of stone. This material is supplied to represent Portland stone, lime stone, Bath stone, dark stone and light stone. This material may suitably be used in entrance halls, and in dining rooms. The surfaces may be jointed to represent joints of stone, but personally we prefer to use this material for its decorative value and not as actual imitation stone.

Another of these materials is Durotex, described as plastic paint. It is applied with a brush, like paint, to a thickness of one-sixteenth inch. For coarse effects it should be applied heavier. Various textures may be obtained by means of a wooden comb, or cloth pad.

Canvas is now supplied with waterproof backing. It may be hung like ordinary wall-paper. It has been used in several of the National Art galleries.

Grasscloth is the bark of the Japanese honeysuckle torn into fine strips, woven into 7½-yard lengths on old-fashioned hand looms by the cottagers of Japan, and mounted on plain or metallic paper. The glint of gold or silver showing through the dyed weaving provides a lovely and subtle decoration. It is supplied in 22 shades. Grasscloth is not effective unless well illuminated. It should, therefore, be used only in well-lighted rooms, and there should be plenty of artificial illumination at night. When used under proper conditions the effect is extremely beautiful.

Veneers of oak, walnut and mahogany are now supplied mounted on a flexible composition base. They may be hung like wall paper. Their flexibility makes it possible to cover curved walls. Used with judgment, these backed veneer are invaluable. We do not advocate the use of this material as an imitation of solid panelling, but as an "all-over" surface treatment.

Many things which at first acquaintance appear delightful and beautiful lose their charm after a longer acquaintance. This is often due to bad workmanship as well as material. Admiration soon fails where respect is lacking, and no one can respect shoddily executed work. If satisfaction with decorative work is to be permanent then we must consider quality and make quite sure that the work is properly carried out. Care, thought and understanding and correct choice of materials are needed. The workmen must be allowed time to prepare properly and for thorough drying of paints and rubbing down between the coats. Work carefully executed without haste is always more permanent. Delicate shades and beautiful surfaces cannot be got in a hurry but must be deliberately and skilfully built up. Old work must first be cleaned down, and crannies and worn patches must be stopped, also priming coats must be applied before any final colourings appear. All this is well worth while as without very careful preparation perfection is impossible.

Of white paint there are many forms. Plain white untinted by blue gives a chaste effect and is best left with a matte surface. This will prevent reflection which detracts from the pure white. Where a glossy white is desired this may have a touch of blue as tending to soften the reflections. Ivory white woodwork or walls may be obtained by means of white paint stippled with cream. Another near-white is obtained by stippling over pure white with the faintest of pinks. Yellow stippled over white gives a cream finish.

Rooms decorated in tones of blue are restful. The blue should have a touch of pink to soften the colour. For interior work greens should not be too bright or heavy. Either green or blue stippled over white give excellent results. Yellow is best for north aspect and will brighten even a gloomy room. Red is a difficult colour to use in paint. It is valuable to give sunshine where little exists. Black is useful as a contrast and should have high gloss. It may be used on woodwork in contrast with scarlet, orange or emerald green on the walls.

# MIRRORS

MIRRORS are a valuable form of wall decoration and tend to make small rooms look larger. When right in design and suitably placed they take away a cramped appearance from narrow halls and passages. Arranged to catch the light, a mirror will bring a touch of brightness into the gloomiest of rooms.

Usually when selecting a mirror for a particular position there will be three main considerations if the most suitable choice is to be made. Size, including proportions between height and width. "Weight" or thickness of the frame. Design, whether simple or elaborate.

No hard and fast rules can be laid down, but speaking generally, the smaller the mirror the heavier should be the frame and *vice versa*.

Suitability of proportion is very necessary and this will be governed by the space to be occupied. In some positions it may be desirable to make a sharp contrast as in the case of a low room where it is desired to increase the appearance of height. Here, a tall, narrow mirror would be the right proportion. But, as a general rule, the most suitable proportion for a mirror will be the same proportions as the space to be occupied.

Mirror No. 668 C. This is of original design and intentionally "different," having been designed purposely for use in entrance halls. Few necessary items of furniture being required for entrance halls, such pieces may, with advantage, be given a definite touch of individuality and distinction. This little mirror is of substantial appearance. The frame is of polished walnut, and the enrichments are finished with silver leaf.

Mirror No. 718 C. This is also suitable for use in a small hall. It is finished in silver leaf.

The two "cartouche" mirrors Nos. 424 D and 452 C are beautifully carved by hand in solid walnut. They are intended to be used over side cabinets, such as our Nos. 480 C, 425 C, 493 C and 424 C Grosvenor commodes. The two carved walnut mirrors Nos. 537 C and 536 C are designed for use over side cabinets or sideboards; over mantel-pieces and in similar positions.

# MIRRORS

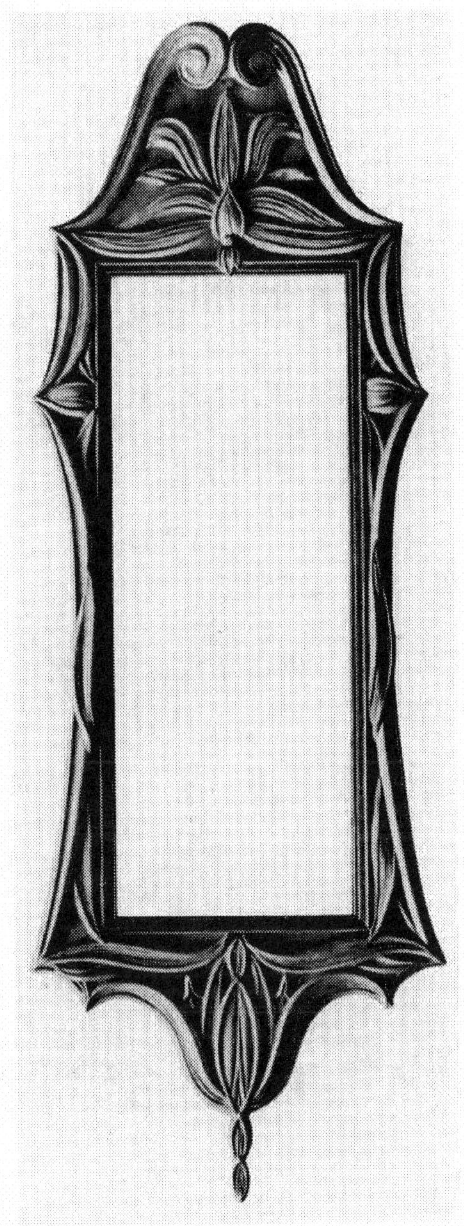

MIRROR, NO. 707-C
GOLD LEAF

MAURICE ADAMS

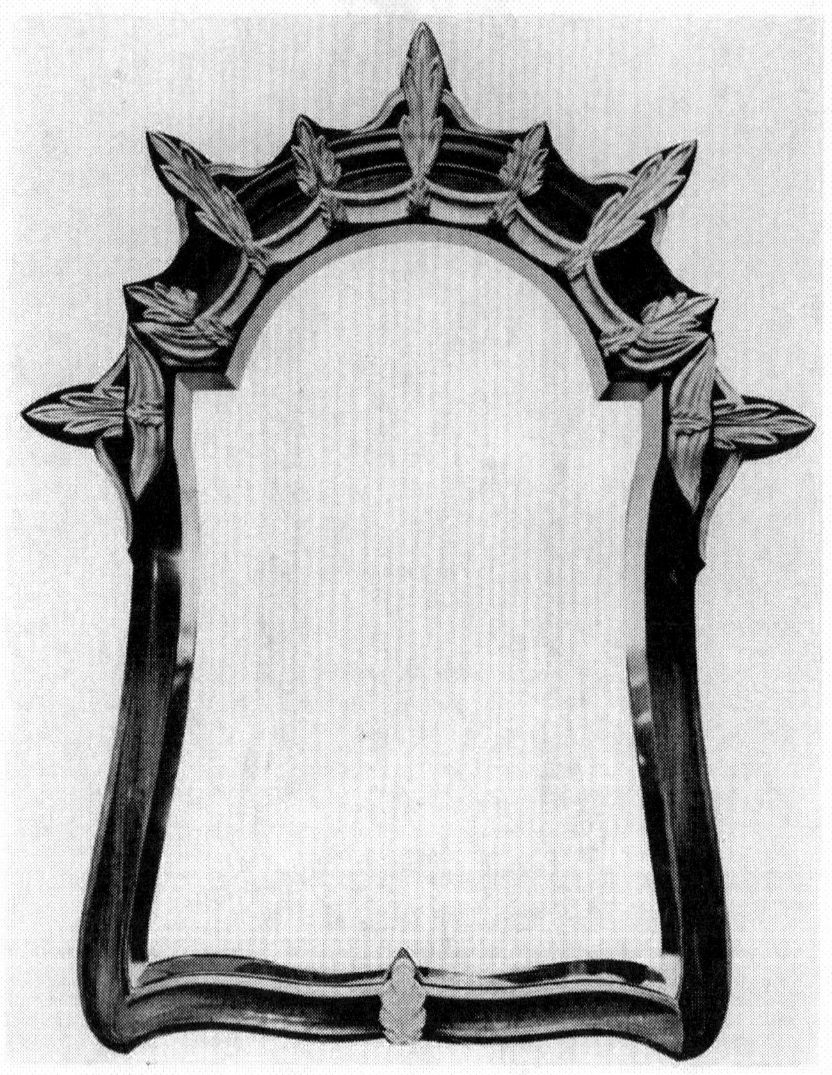

WALL MIRROR, NO. 668-C
WALNUT AND SILVER

MAURICE ADAMS

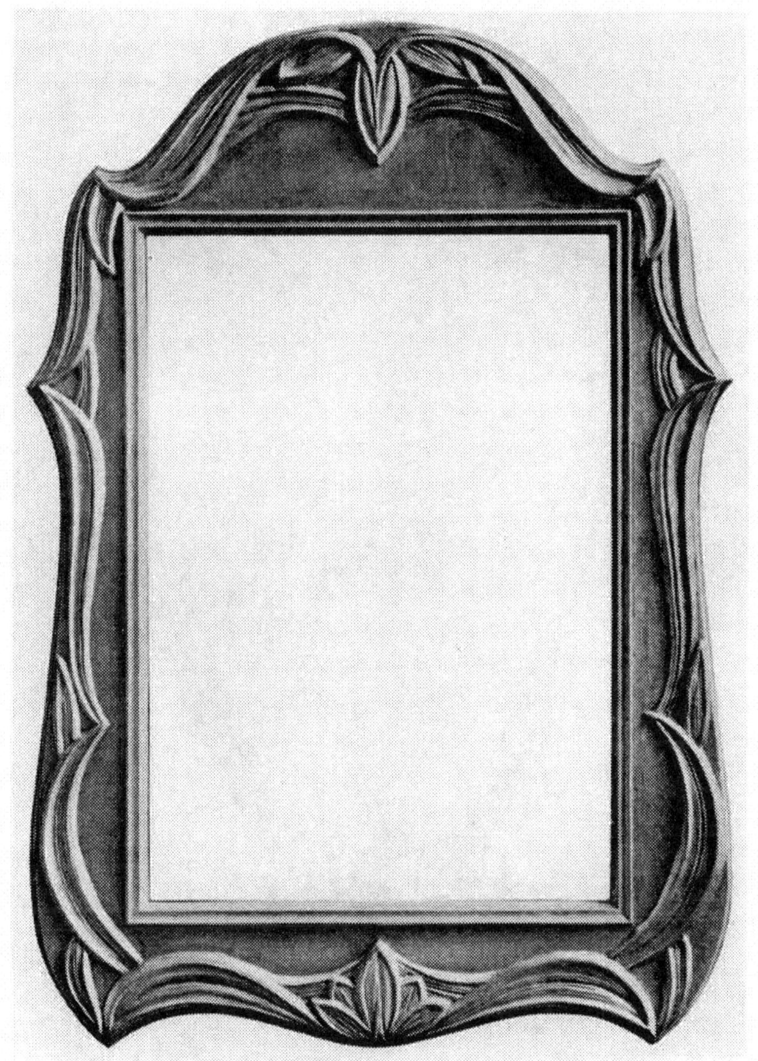

MIRROR, NO. 718-C
SILVER LEAF

MAURICE ADAMS

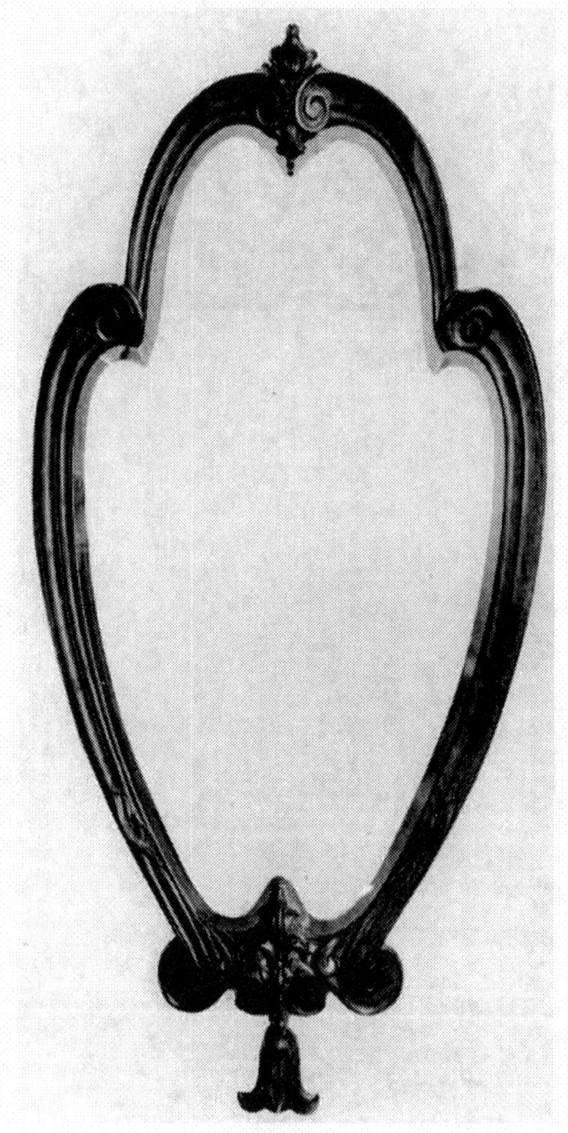

MIRROR, NO. 424-D
CARVED WALNUT

MAURICE ADAMS

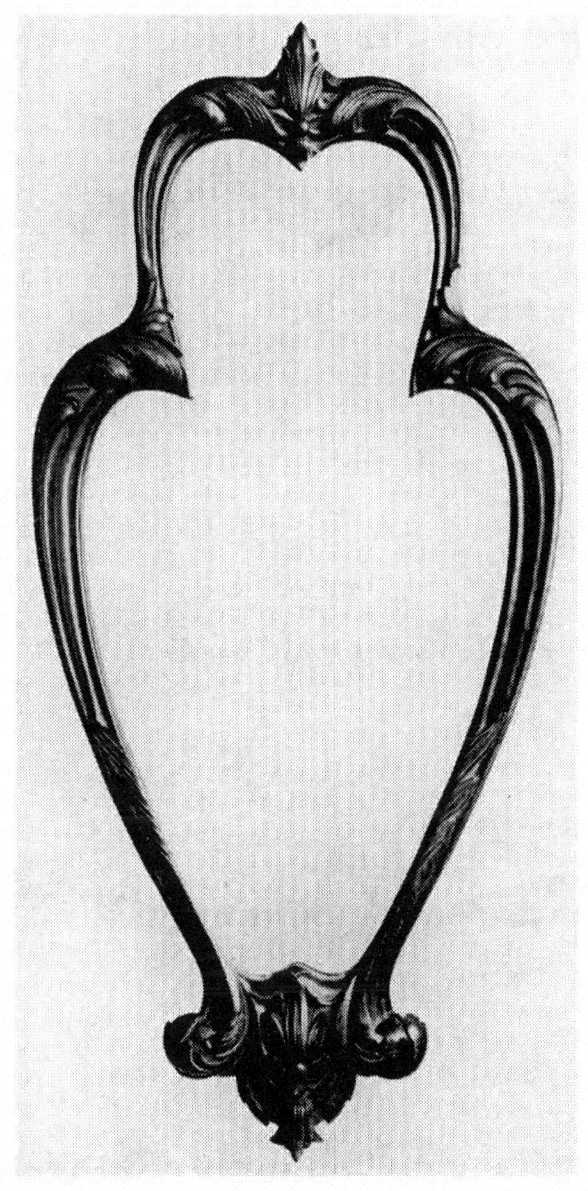

MIRROR, NO. 482-C
CARVED WALNUT

MAURICE ADAMS

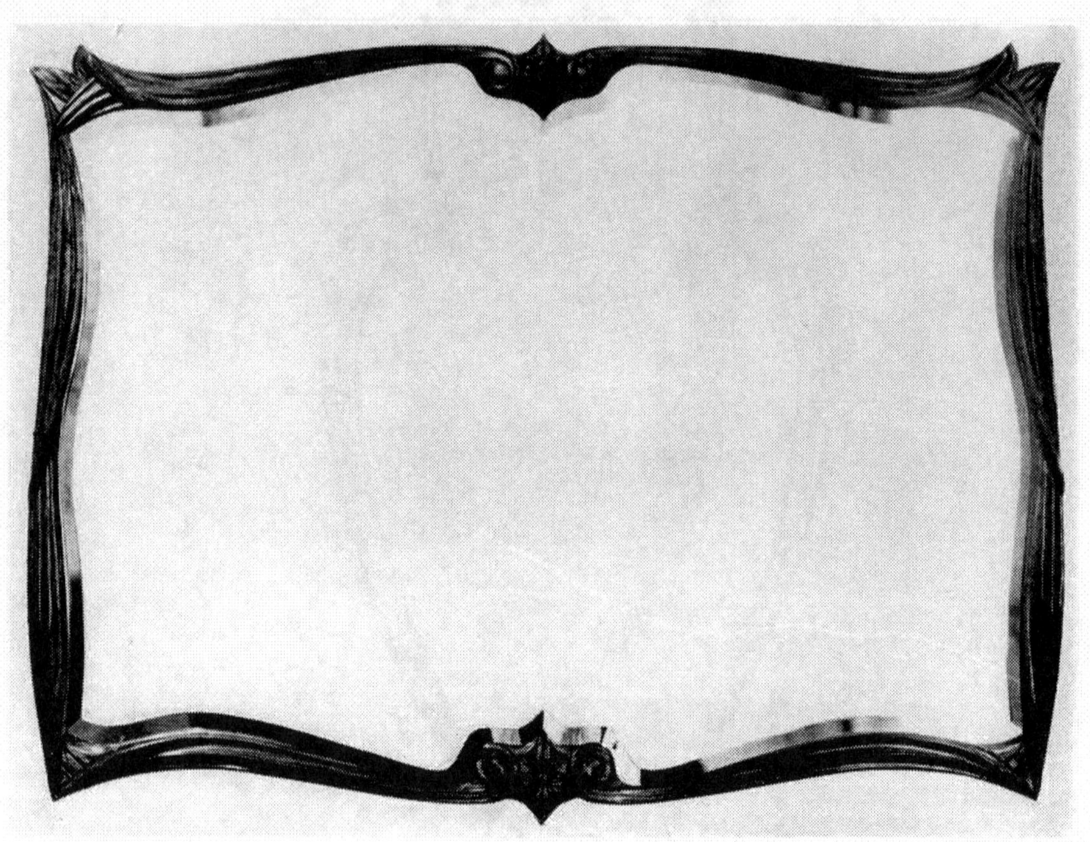

MIRROR, NO. 537-C
CARVED WALNUT

MAURICE ADAMS

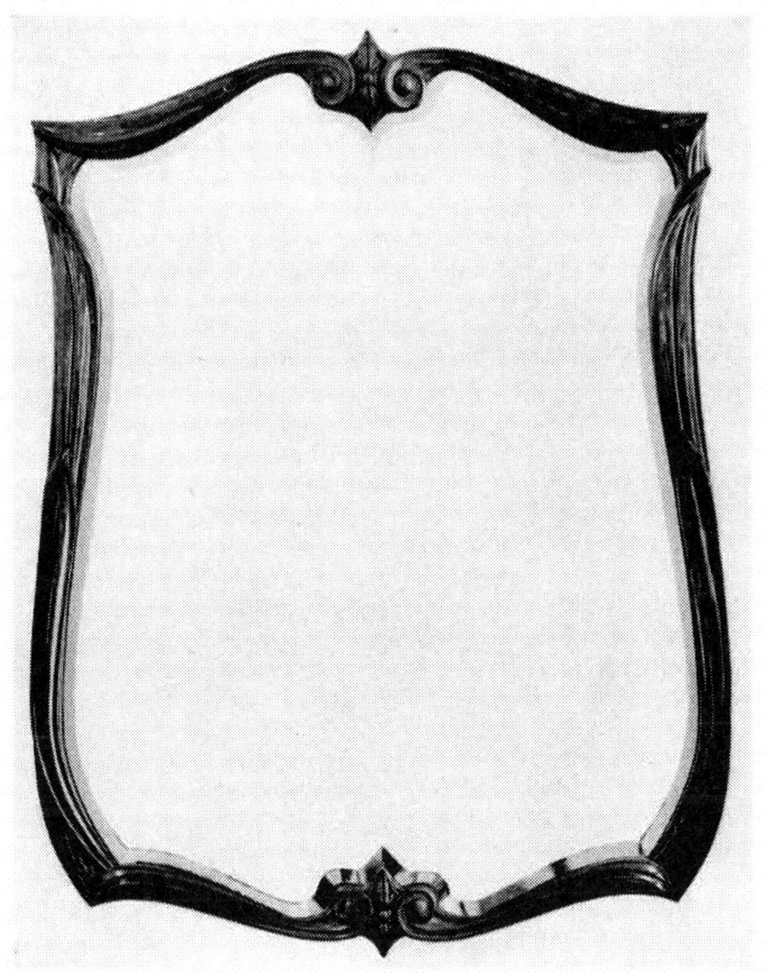

MIRROR, NO. 536-C
CARVED WALNUT

MAURICE ADAMS

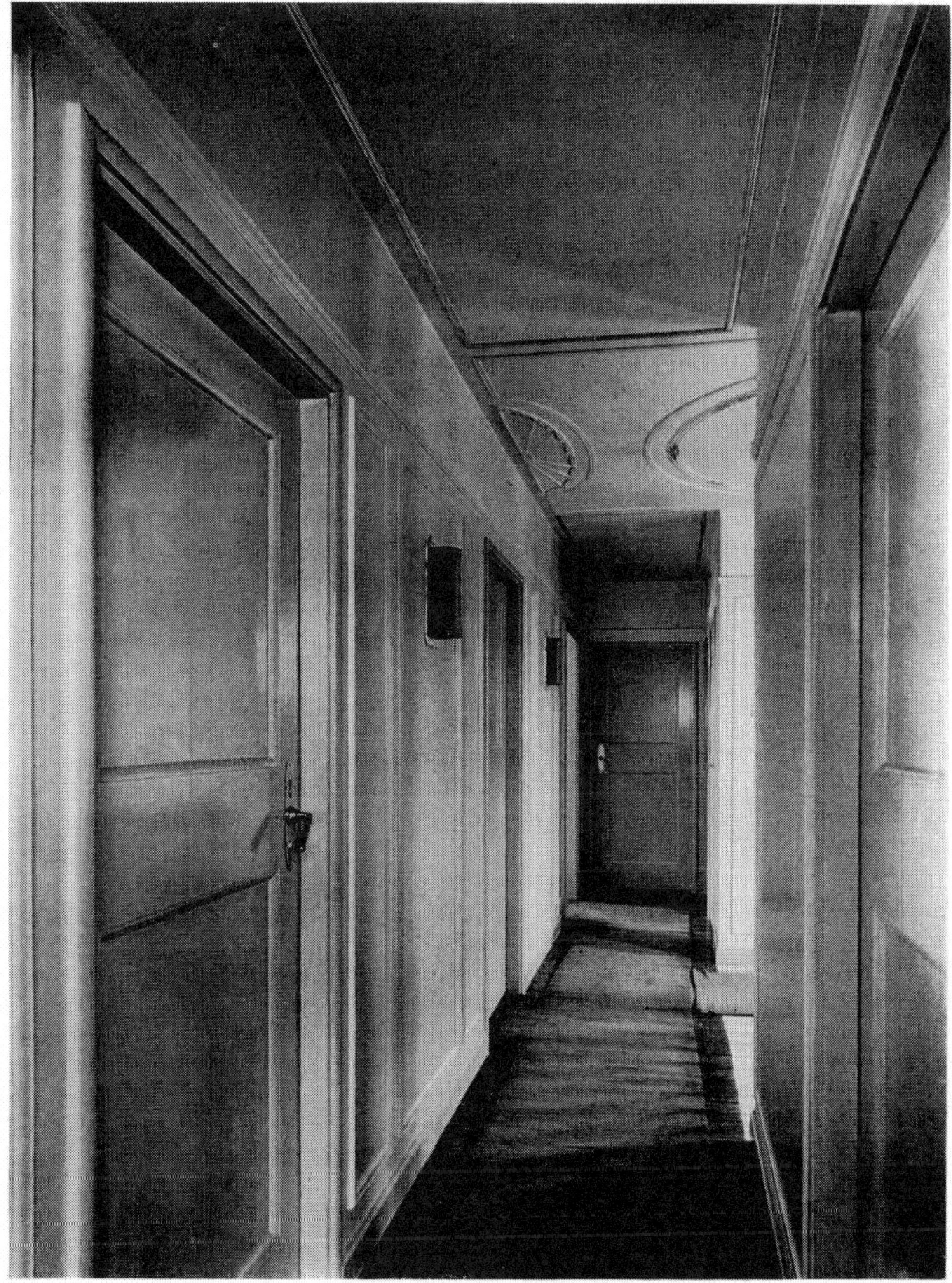

CORRIDOR DESIGNED BY MAURICE ADAMS

# ELECTRIC LIGHT FITTINGS

IN any artistic furnishing scheme it is essential that attention be paid to detail, yet most people consider that when they have selected the furniture, carpet, curtains and wall treatment, they have done all that is necessary to make their furnishing scheme complete and an artistic whole. To replace such items as hideous light switches, light fittings and door handles is regarded as extravagant and unnecessary. Yet several times the cost will readily be spent on sundry " ornaments " without the slightest hesitation.

Many people's homes are veritable warehouses of superfluous and undesirable oddments. In the aggregate they have cost a vast amount of money, and every week they take up a vast amount of somebody's time in cleaning and dusting. When furnishing for the first time or when refurnishing, make a firm rule not to become a collector of superfluous furnishing oddments. You will make your home much more healthy, less ugly if not more beautiful, and will save almost enough to retire on in your old age.

Make a second rule that everything in your home must have beauty. Not some things only, but everything. Take right away those hideous switches, light fittings, ceiling roses, door handles and similar items and replace with beautifully designed and made fittings. This is not extravagance but true economy. Let every fitting be an ornament in itself and less further " ornaments " for the room will be necessary. There is absolutely no reason whatever why such fittings should be ugly.

Examine the photographs of these Maurice Adams' fittings and you will profit thereby. A vast amount of care has been taken over their design and manufacture. They express the amount of thought that brought about their creation.

Lamp No. 606 C (page 178). This is of solid bronze, very finely detailed and beautifully finished. It was designed to flank an entrance door which it enriches and beautifies. Lamps of this quality stamp the house as built or occupied by someone of culture and good taste.

Light fittings Nos. 495 C, 498 C, 490 C, 523 C, 496 C, and 507 C. These are hand-made and finished antique silver. The ornament is finely detailed and beautifully finished by hand.

Light fittings Nos. 671 C, 559 C and 706 C, are made of mahogany, ornamented with carton pierre and finished with silver leaf. The shades are of silk fringed with braid. These fittings are decorative and have the advantage of low cost. They may suitably be employed where the metal fittings would be too expensive.

Light fittings Nos. 637 C, 632 C and 641 C. These are of silk, beautifully made by hand and lined with white or cream silk. They are inexpensive and effective.

No. 726 C is an example of a lantern suitable for entrance or porch. Except for the supporting frames and copper leaf-shaped ornaments, it is made entirely of glass.

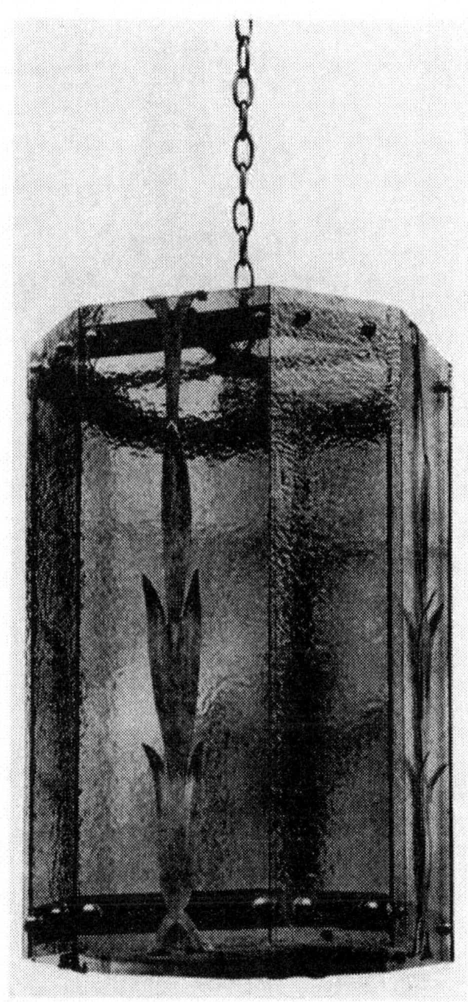

LANTERN, NO. 726-C
COPPER AND GLASS

MAURICE ADAMS

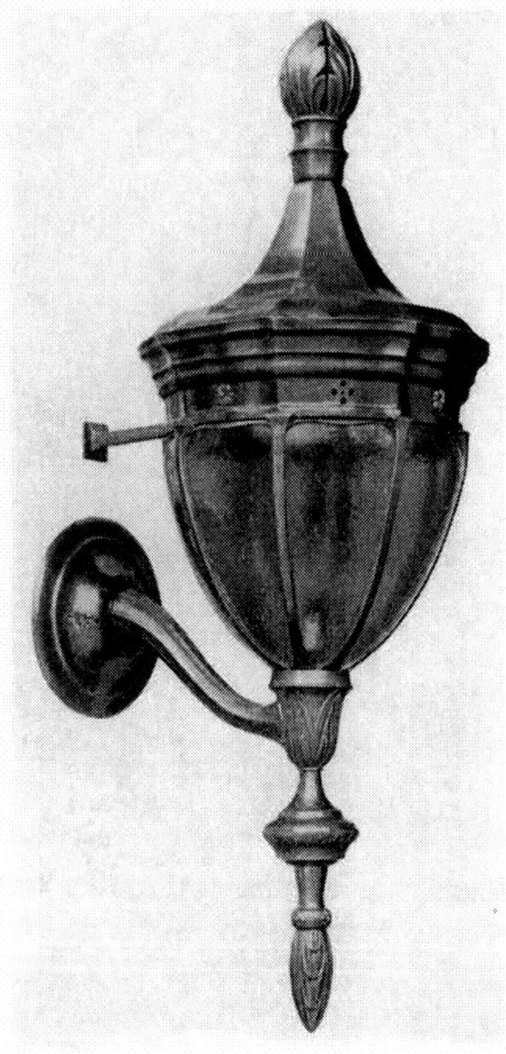

ENTRANCE LAMP, NO. 606-C MAURICE ADAMS
BRONZE

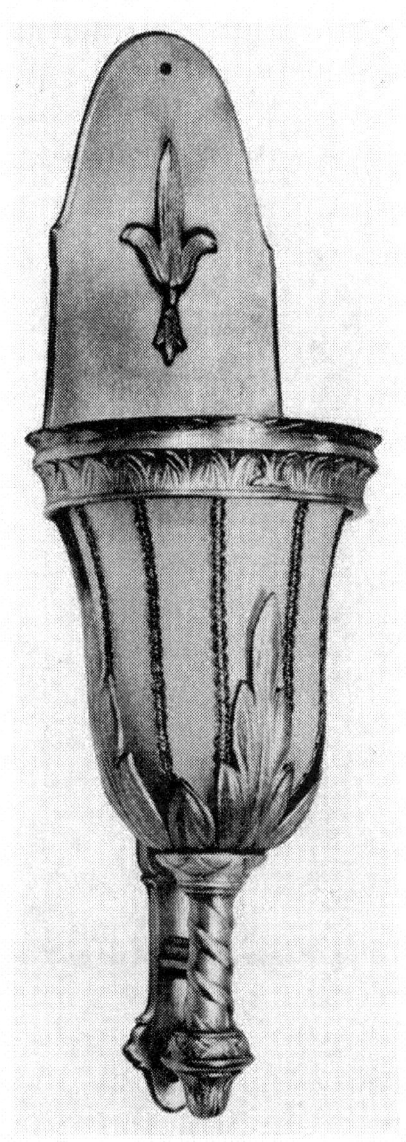

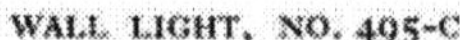

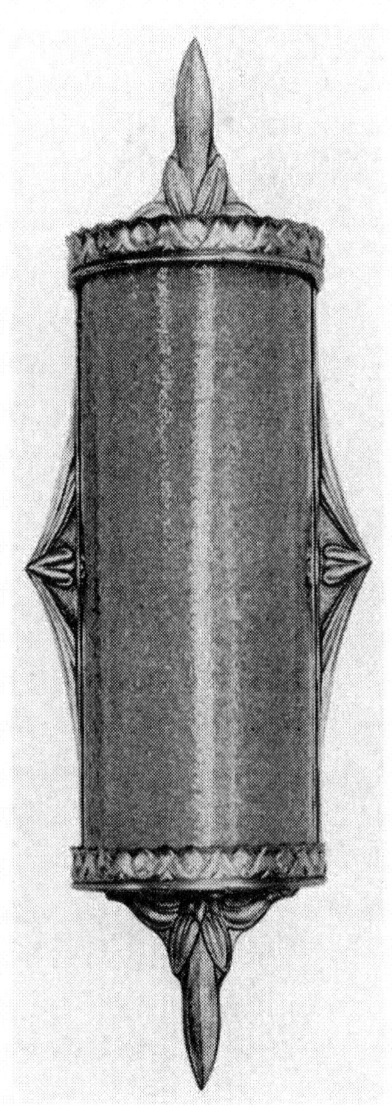

WALL LIGHT, NO. 495-C

WALL LIGHT, NO. 498-C

SILVERED BRASS

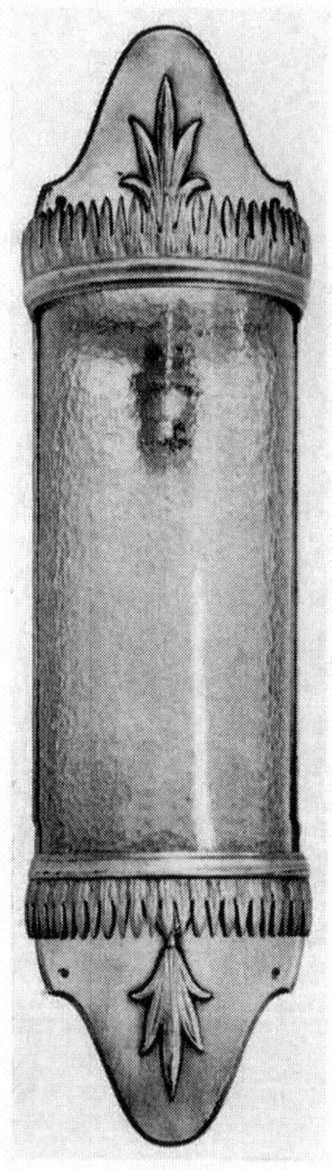

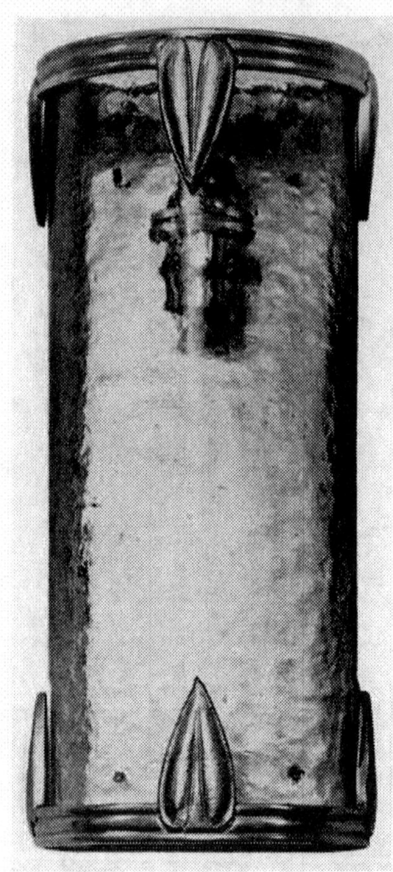

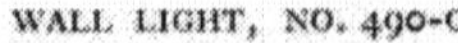
WALL LIGHT, NO. 490-C

WALL LIGHT, NO. 523-C

SILVERED BRASS

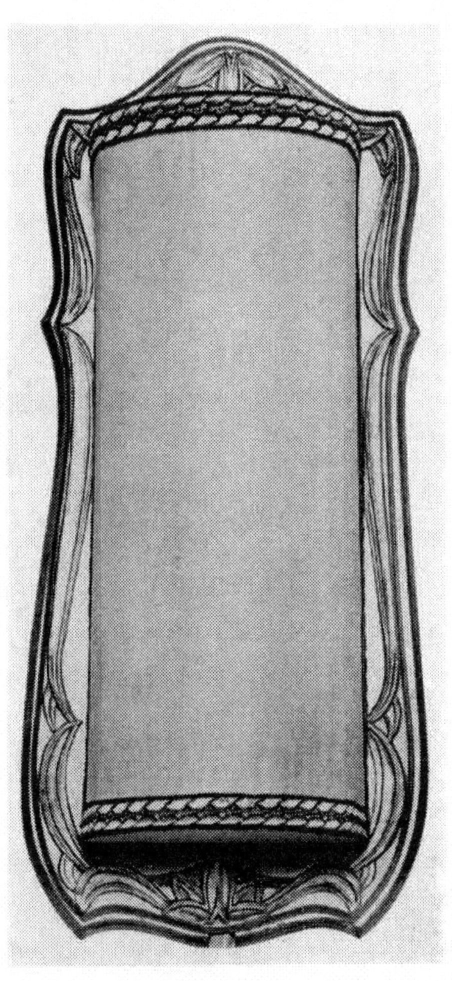

WALL LIGHT, NO. 671

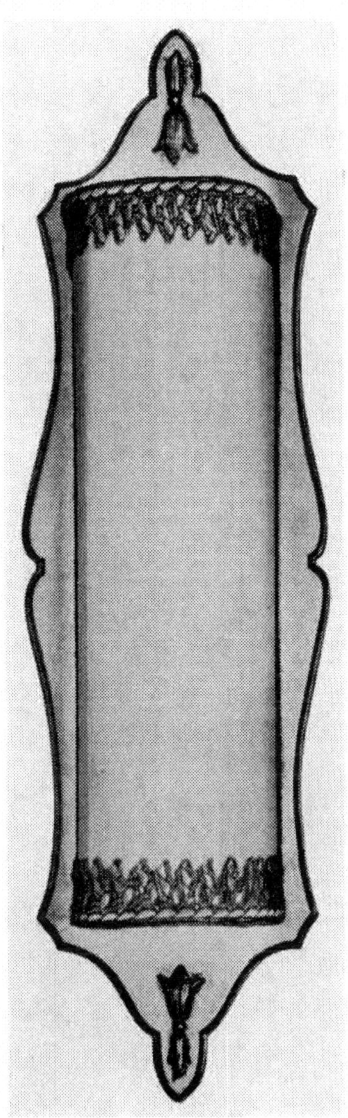

WALL LIGHT, NO. 559-C

SILVERED WOOD

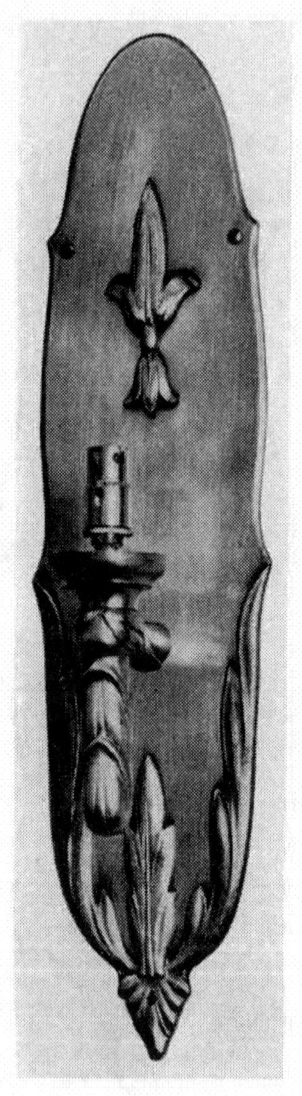

WALL LIGHT, NO. 496-C

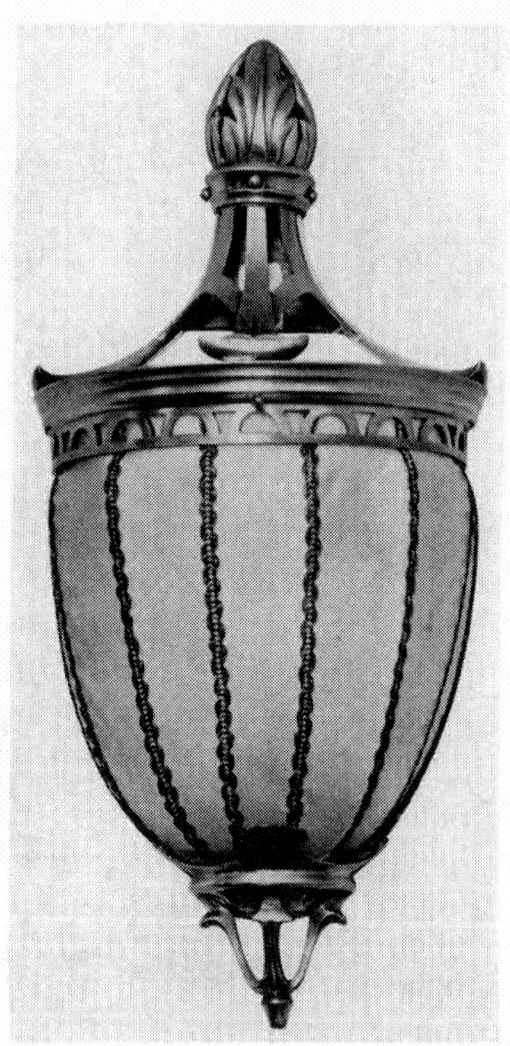

WALL LIGHT, NO. 507-C

SILVERED BRASS

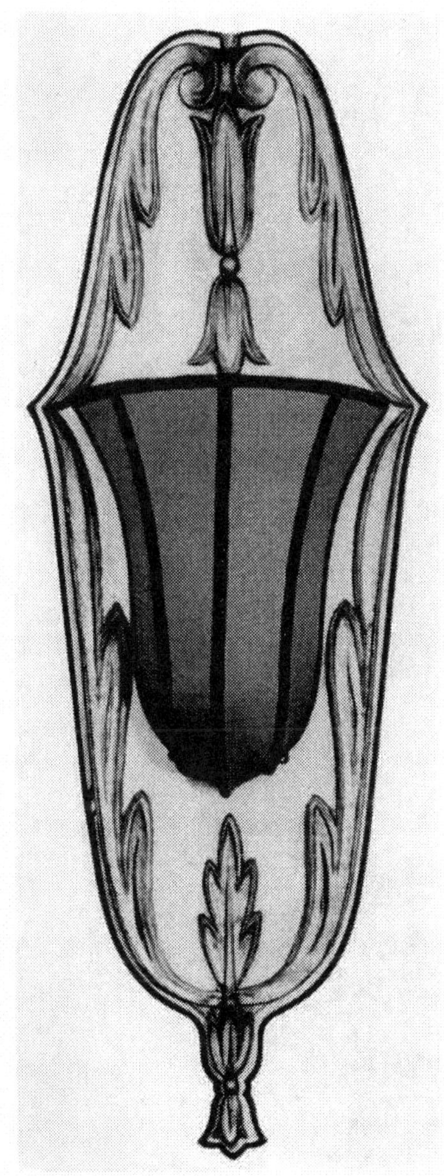

WALL LIGHT, NO. 706-C

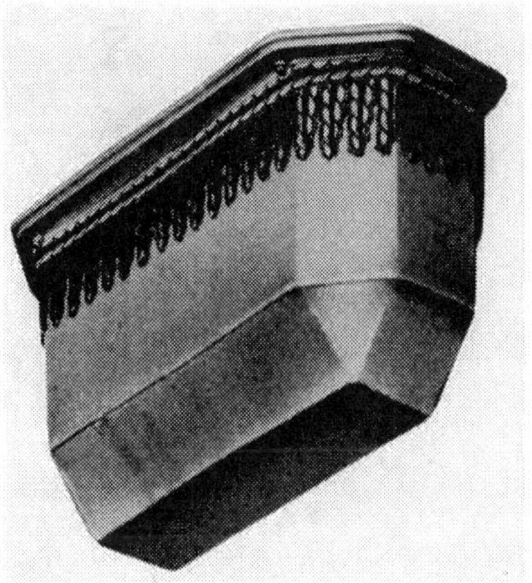

CEILING LIGHT, NO. 641-C

SILVERED WOOD

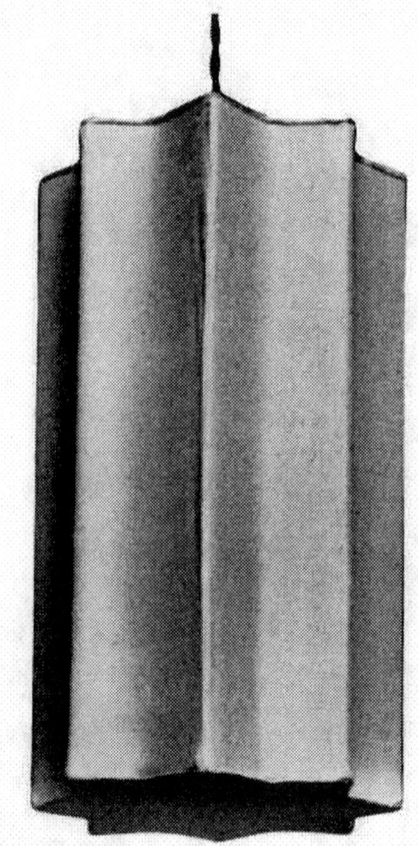

SILK LANTERN, NO. 638-C

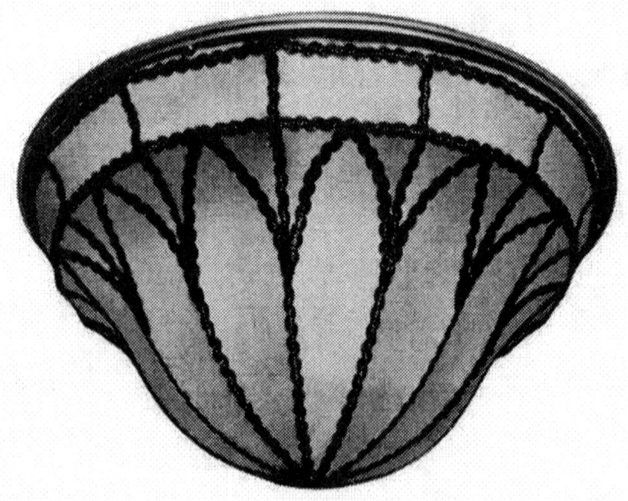

SILK CEILING BOWL LIGHT, NO. 632-C

BED LIGHT,
NO. 520-C
SILVERED
BRASS

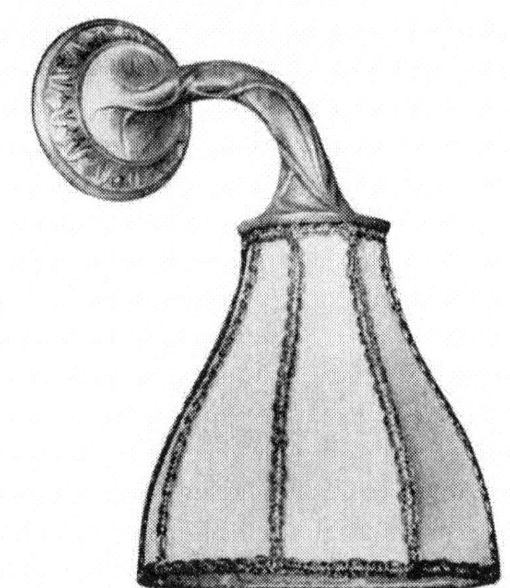

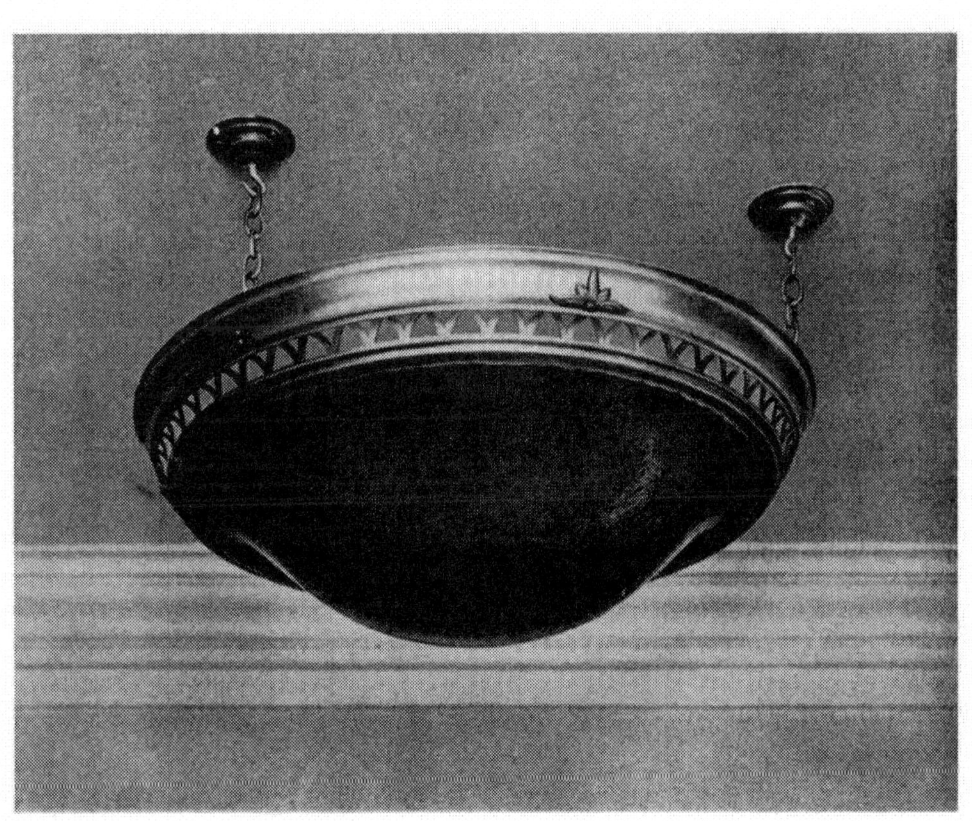

CEILING BOWL LIGHT, NO. 508-C
SILVERED BRASS

MAURICE ADAMS

# DETAILS OF ORNAMENT

FOLLOWING our policy of thoroughness we include examples of ornamental details designed in the style we have evolved and in the spirit of Maurice Adams' furniture. The illustrations show typical examples of Maurice Adams' ornament, and include a fireplace surround, pilaster caps, carved overdoors, carved "fans," ceiling ornament, etc.

The manner in which such details are employed is shown in the folding scale models, in which elevations of the various rooms are fully illustrated.

CARVED MAHOGANY DOOR HOOD

PILASTER CAPS IN MAHOGANY AND CARTON PIERRE
DESIGNED BY MAURICE ADAMS

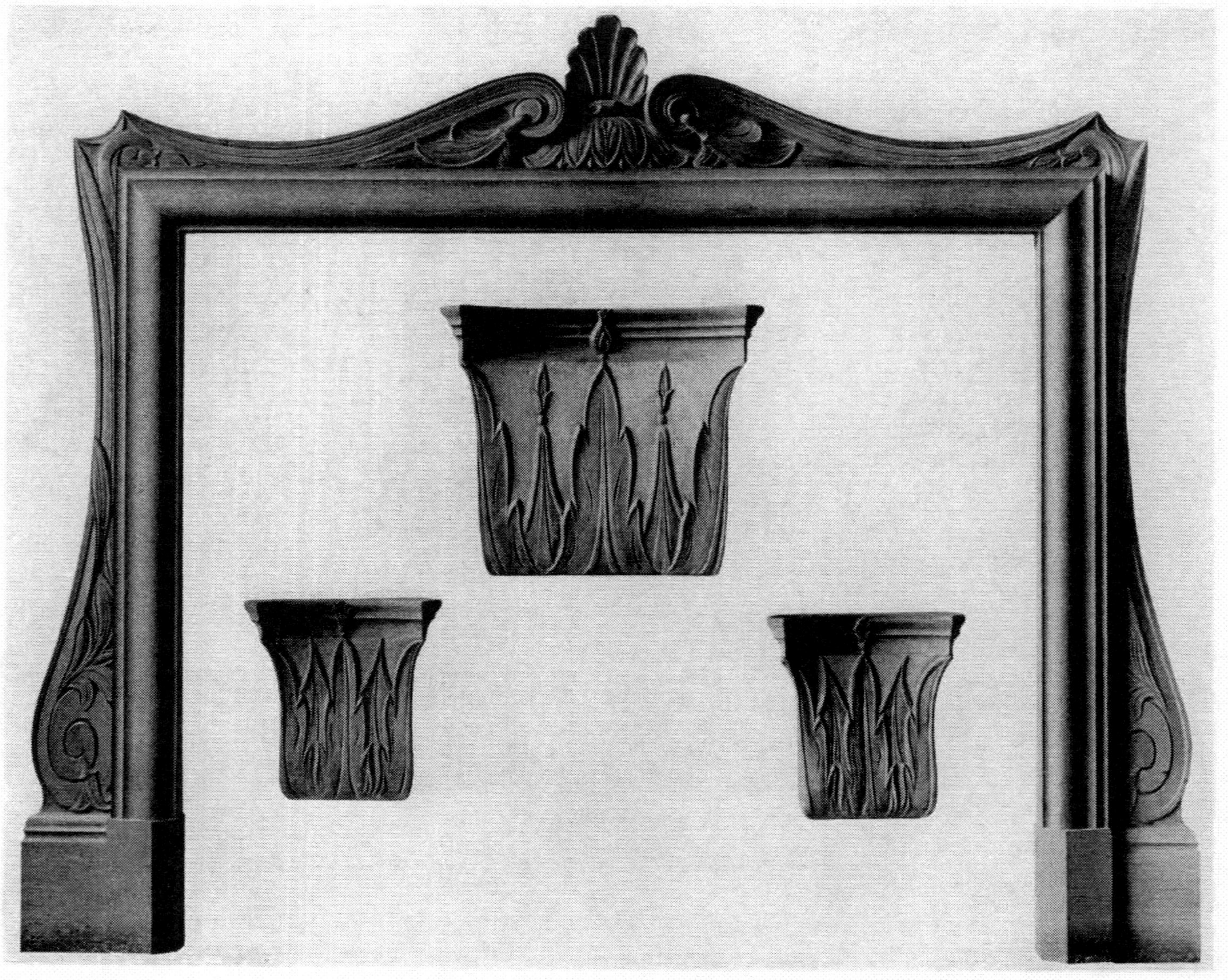

CARVED MAHOGANY MANTELPIECE DESIGNED BY MAURICE ADAMS

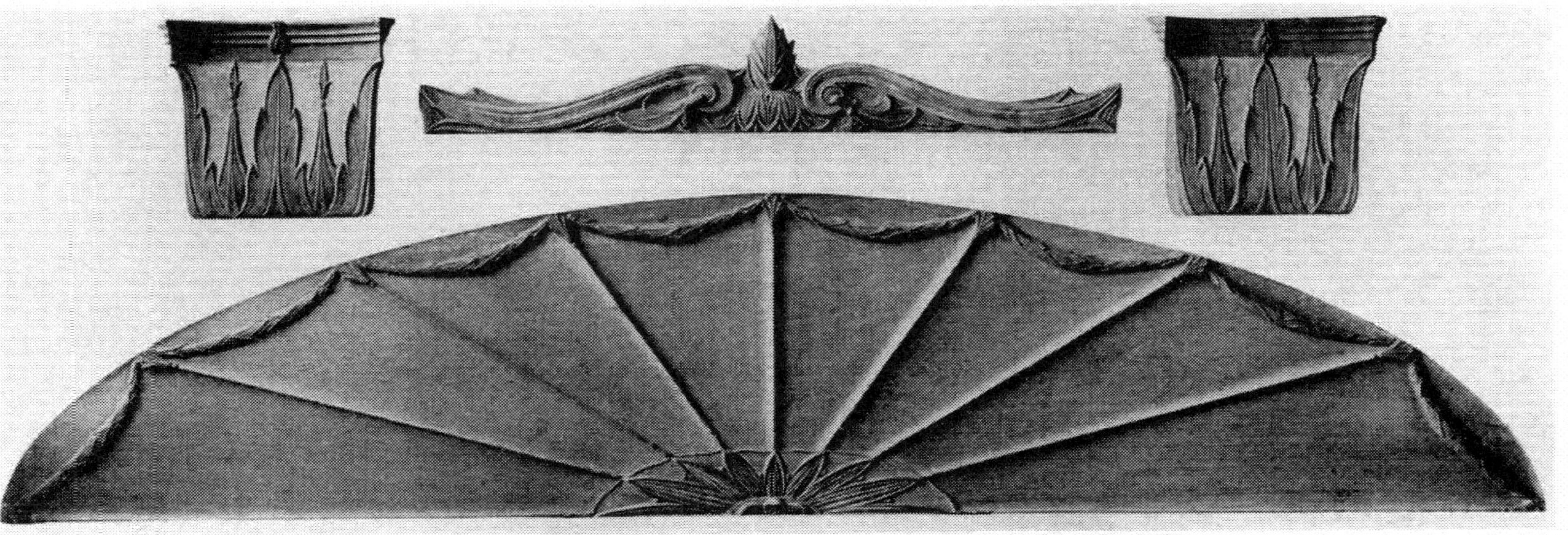

MAHOGANY AND CARTON PIERRE PILASTER CAPS.

CARVED MAHOGANY DOOR HOOD

MAHOGANY AND CARTON PIERRE "FAN"
DESIGNED BY MAURICE ADAMS

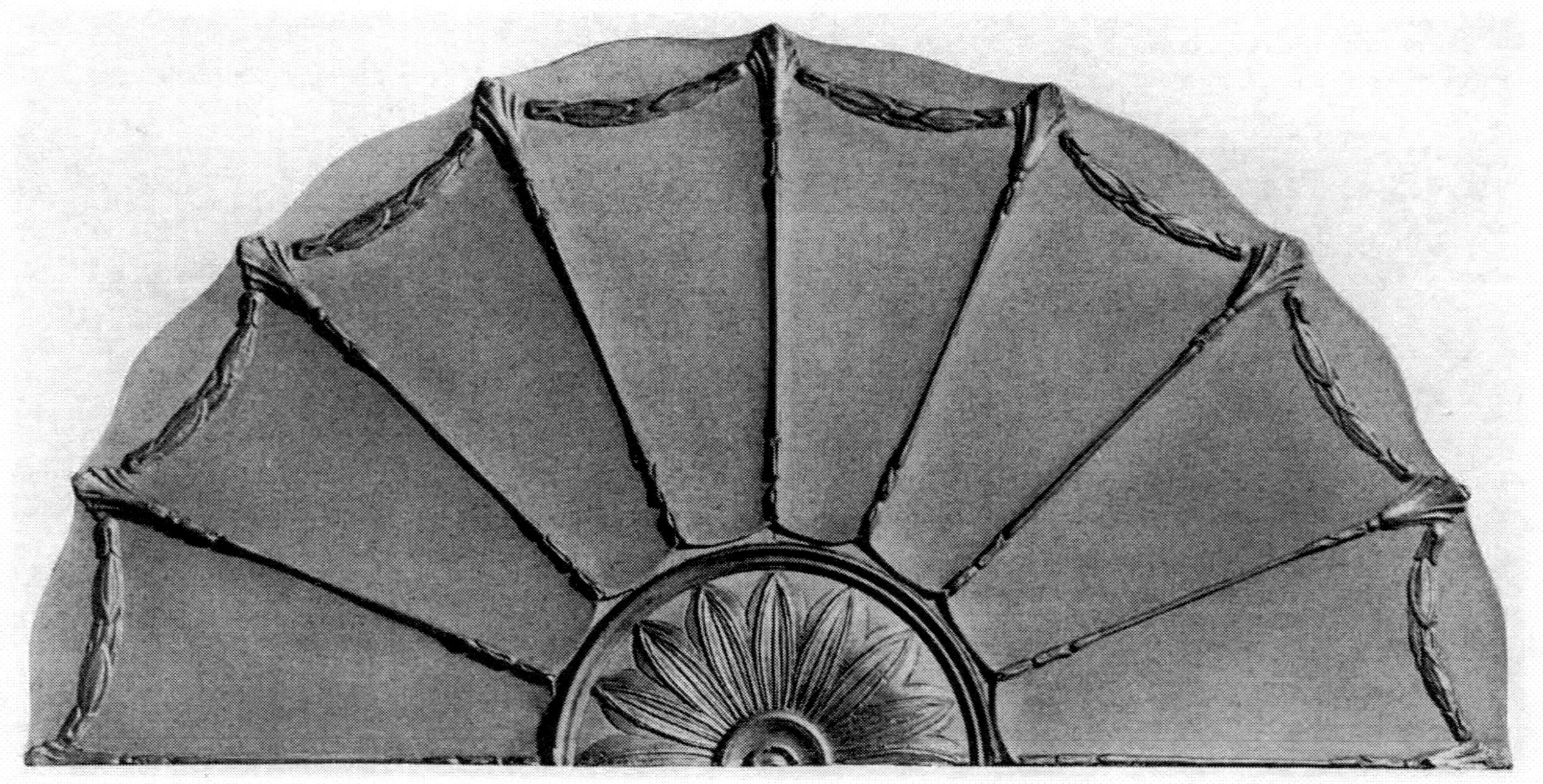

PILASTER "OVERDOOR" PAINTED GROUND AND SILVER ENRICHMENTS    DESIGNED BY MAURICE ADAMS

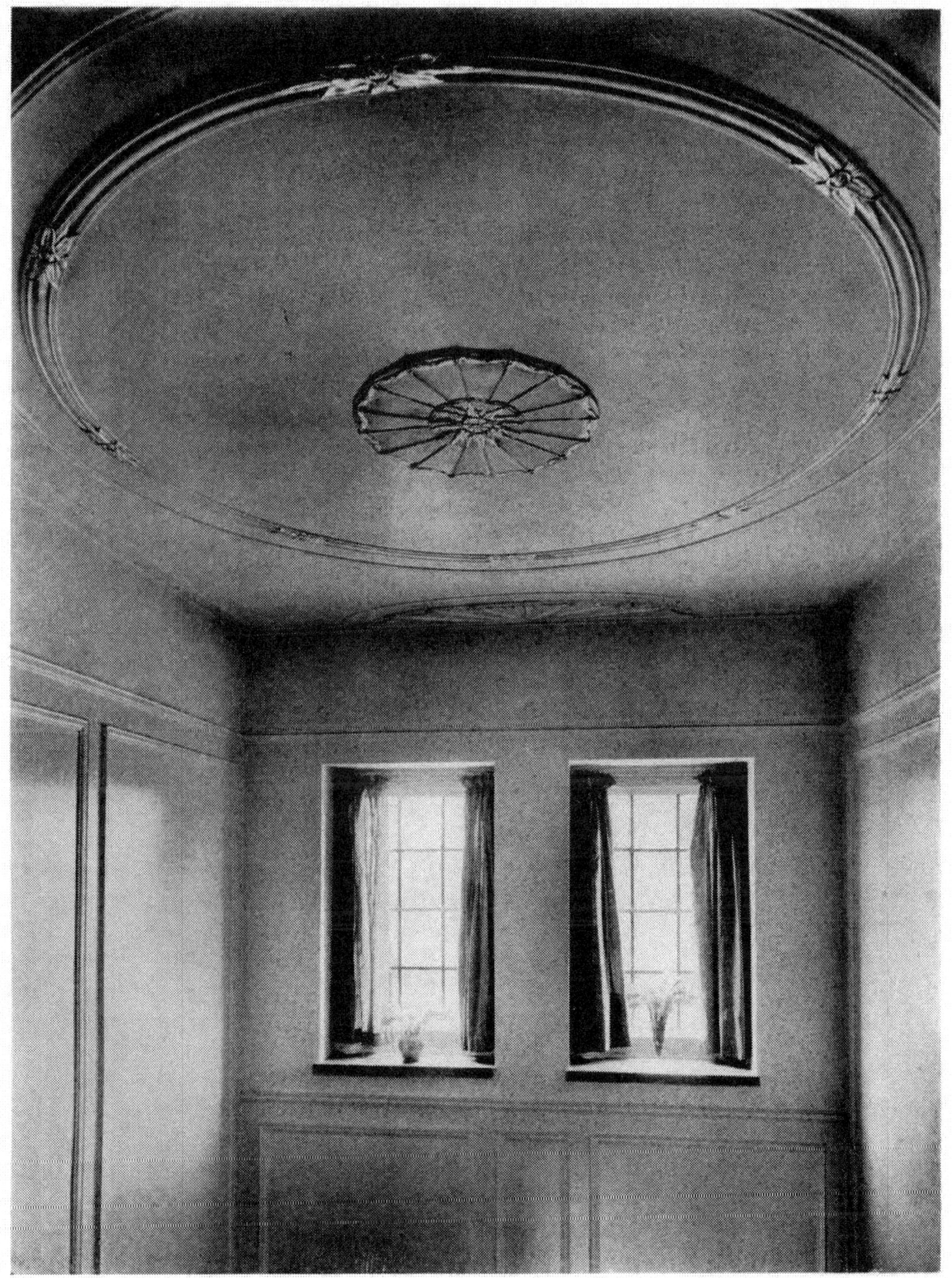

STAIRCASE CEILING WITH MAHOGANY AND CARTON PIERRE ENRICHMENTS — DESIGNED BY MAURICE ADAMS

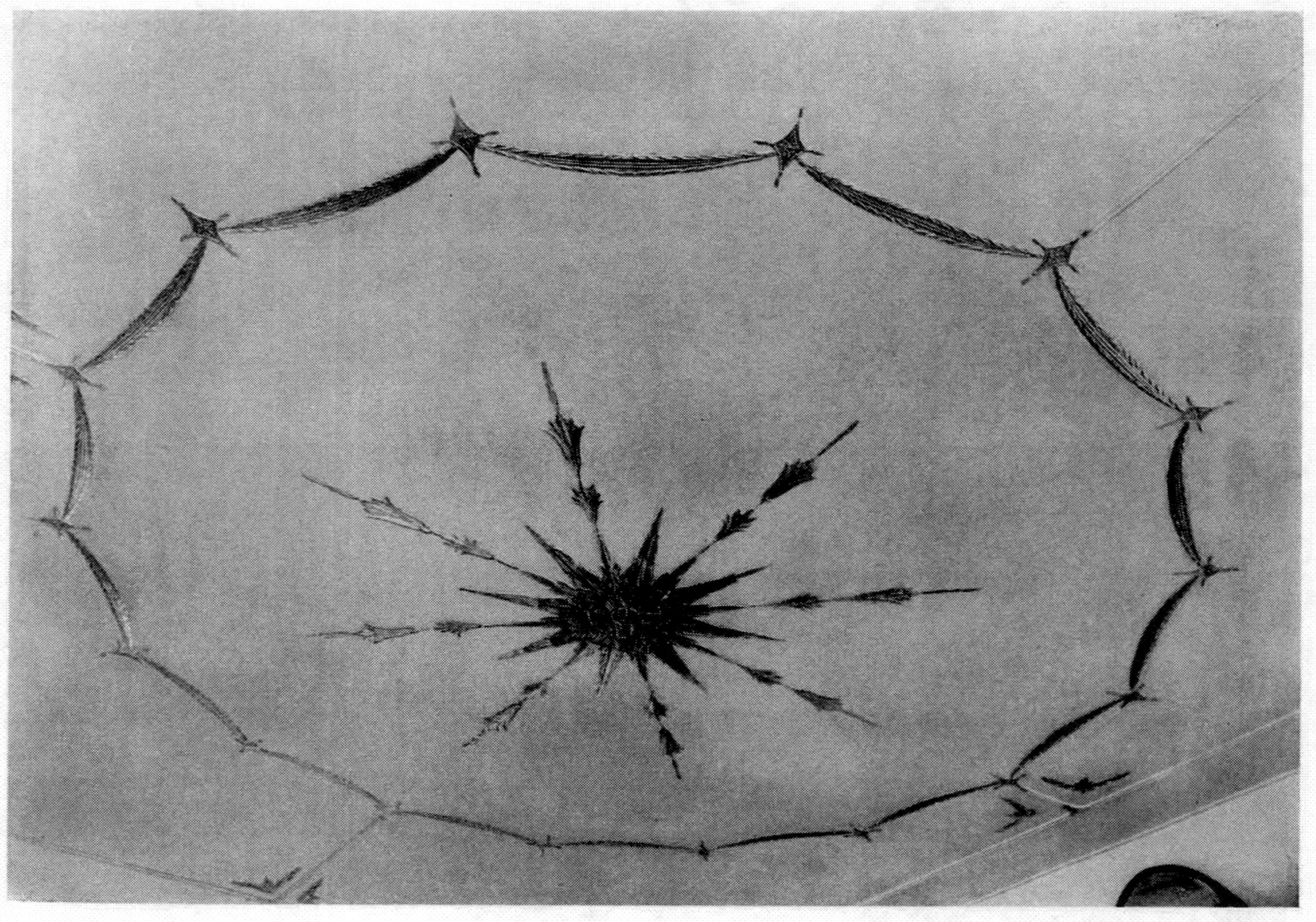

PLASTER CEILING WITH CARTON PIERRE AND MAHOGANY ENRICHMENTS

DESIGNED BY MAURICE ADAMS

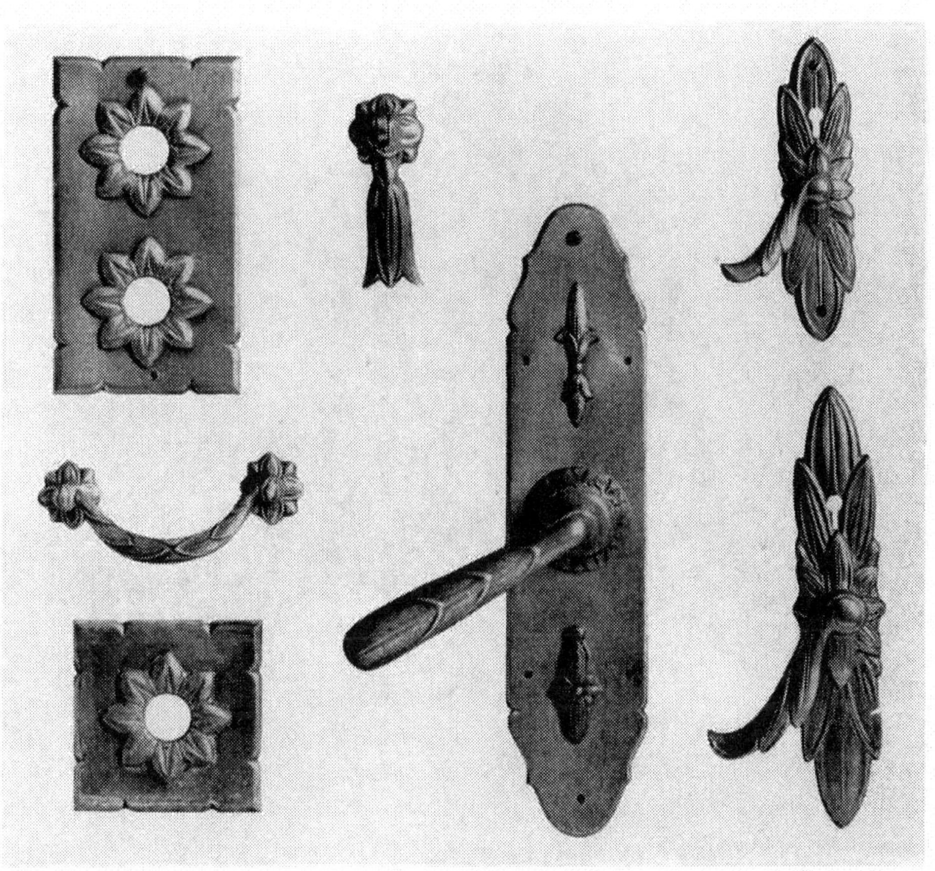

DOOR HANDLE, CABINET HANDLES AND SWITCH PLATES MAURICE ADAMS
SILVERED BRASS

PEDIMENT CARTOUCHE
CAST STONE

MAURICE ADAMS

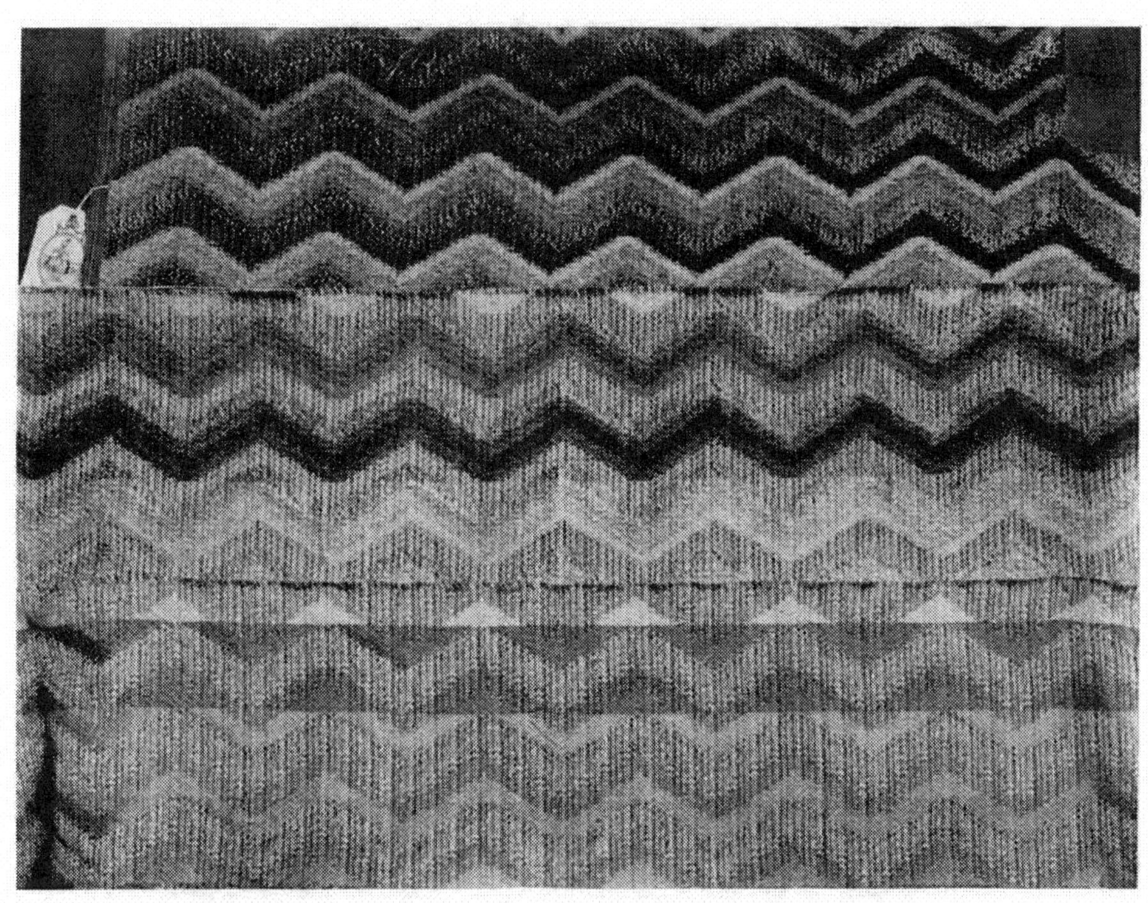

FURNISHING FABRICS

"FOLK" FABRICS.

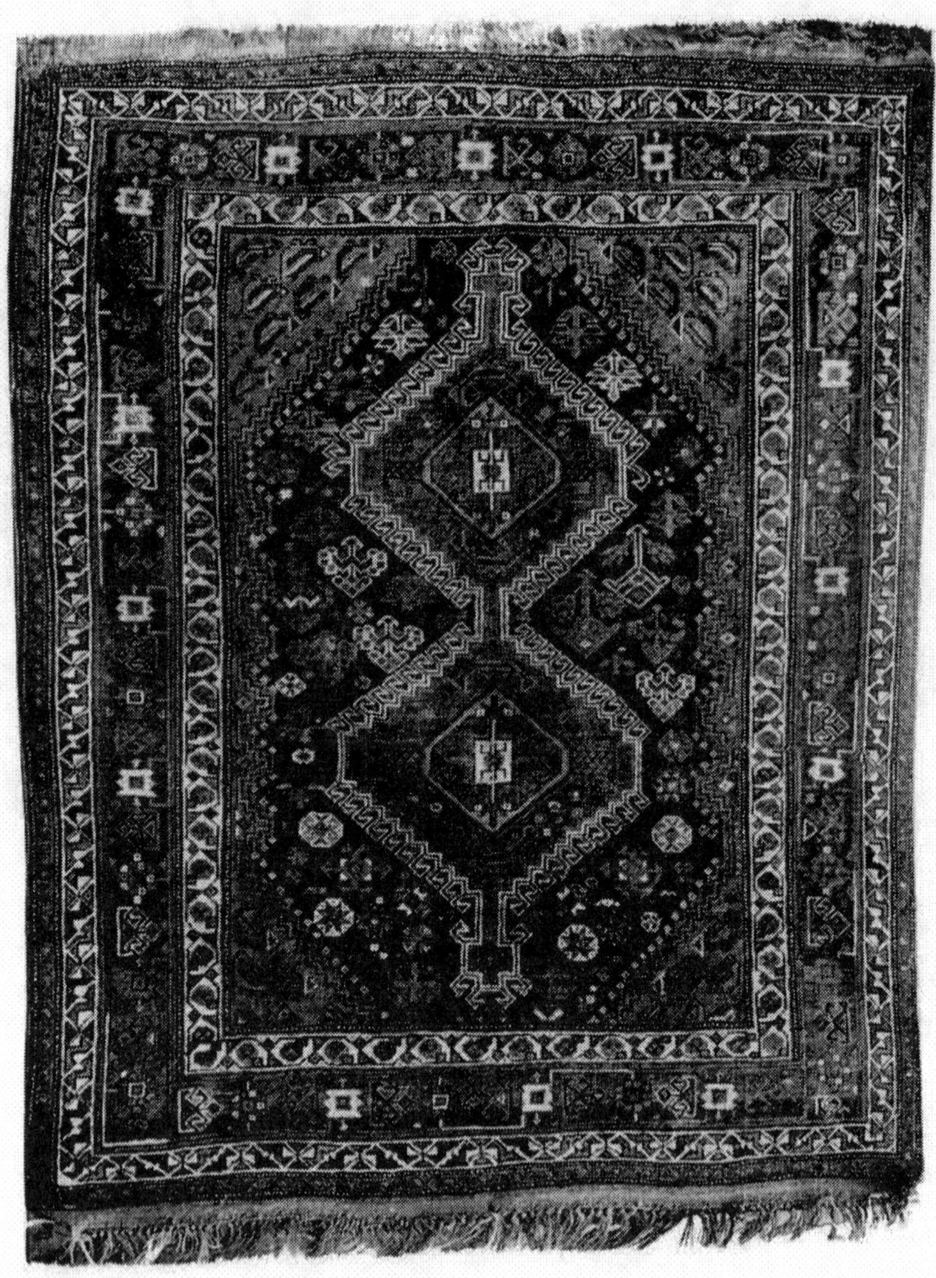

EXAMPLE OF PERSIAN HAND-MADE RUG
FLOOR COVERINGS

# THE "PALM" SERIES OF DESIGNS

# THE "PALM" SERIES OF DESIGNS

DESIGNERS and artists naturally try to improve their work. Consequently they are continually preparing further designs and trying out new ideas as these occur. During the preparation of this book I have created my new "Palm" series of designs. At time of publication this new furniture has yet to be made and cannot, therefore, be photographed for inclusion in these pages. It is, therefore, illustrated in this new series by means of sketches.

Naturally I am always keenest on my latest designs. It is fine work visualizing new conceptions and ideas, putting these down on paper and then waiting while craftsmen materialize these dreams at our workshops.

I believe that these new motifs here sketched show an artistic advance on my previous work. I have given much thought to the creation of the "Palm" leg. Considered artistically I believe this to be a thoroughly sound proposition.

The Pevensey dressing table has a small chest with slightly pointed front, a feature now introduced for the first time. This table is intended to be imposing without bulk. Most women favour wing mirrors and this is the first design where I have carried the side mirrors below the table top. This novel idea should work out well in execution. Full length side mirrors have an obvious advantage.

For some time past our Grosvenor dressing table has been perhaps our most universally admired table. Personally I like it and consider it to be one of our most successfully distinctive designs. After several attempts at improvement I have now produced the Atlantic dressing table. Probably I shall like this best of all.

In design this table is certainly more simple than the Grosvenor table, because the mirrors have plain curves only and their frames are shaped rather than moulded. The table is also much smaller in width. All these new designs have specially designed handles. The two side pedestals form part of the complete design but are quite detached. They provide an appreciable amount of additional drawer accommodation and table surface, besides the further advantage of adaptability to floor space. If desired they may be placed in advance of the dressing table to suit the individual convenience of the user This table may, of course, be used without the pedestals, which then make excellent bedside tables.

The 6-ft. Arundel wardrobe is intended for those requiring a simpler design than the Carlton wardrobe yet more elaborate than the Grosvenor wardrobe. It is provided with two open compartments above the two side shelf cupboards. Each of these has small jewel cupboard fitted with shelf. A large, deep hanging cupboard is provided in the centre. This piece will make an unusually fine wardrobe, distinctive and interesting.

The Pevensey wardrobe, 6 ft. wide, and the Sussex wardrobe, 4 ft. 6 ins. wide, are similar to the Arundel wardrobe but without the open compartments. The side shelf cupboards are accordingly of full height.

The Windsor writing table or bureau has been designed specially for use in bedrooms. It is quite unlike the usual type of bureau, my aim being to give marked individuality free from library or sitting room atmosphere.

The top of this table is level. The desk opens like a box revealing a sunk stationery compartment underneath. Pen and ink trays are provided within the sunk compartment so that all writing materials and odd papers are out of sight when the desk is closed. An ornamental rack or container for magazines, etc., is provided on top of the table as shown.

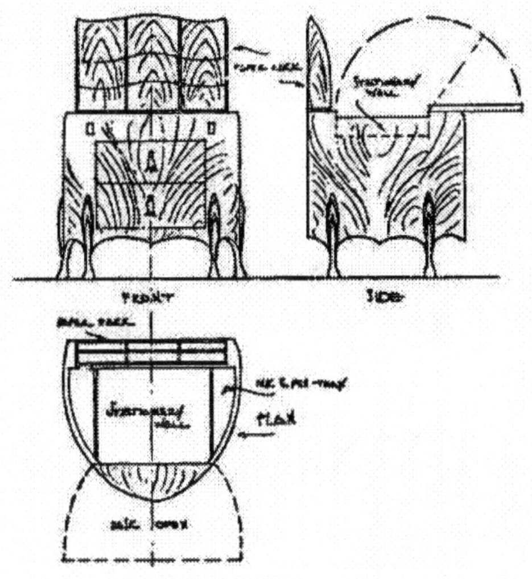


WINDSOR BUREAU, NO. 737-C. REGD.

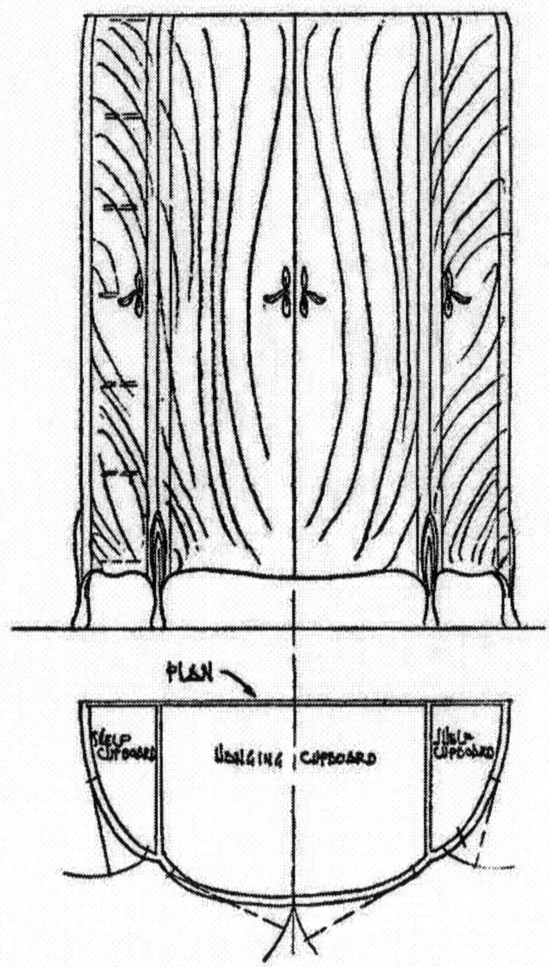


4 FT. 6 INS. SUSSEX WARDROBE, NO. 734-C. REGD.

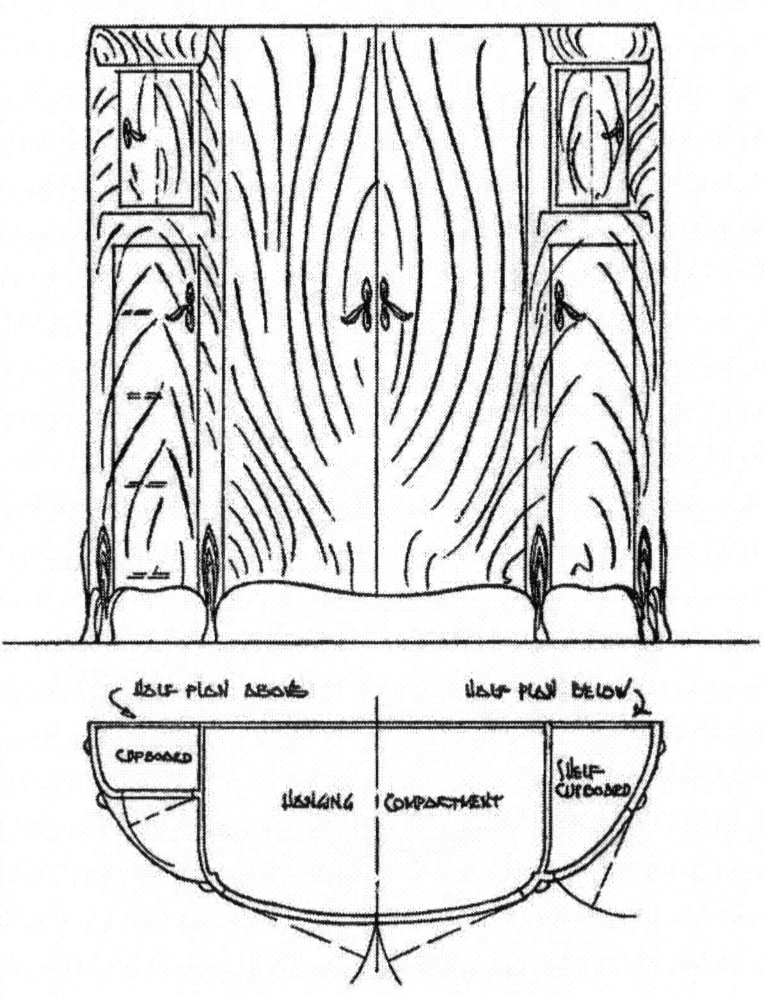


6 FT. ARUNDEL WARDROBE, NO. 736-C. REGD.

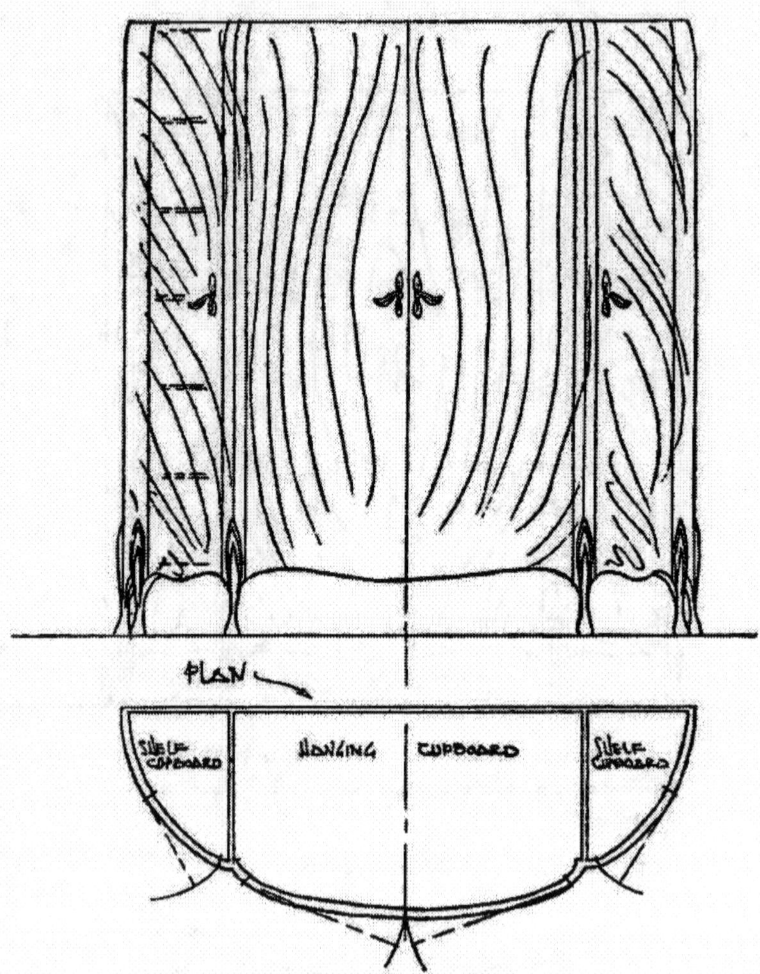


6 FT. PEVENSEY WARDROBE, NO. 738-C. REGD.

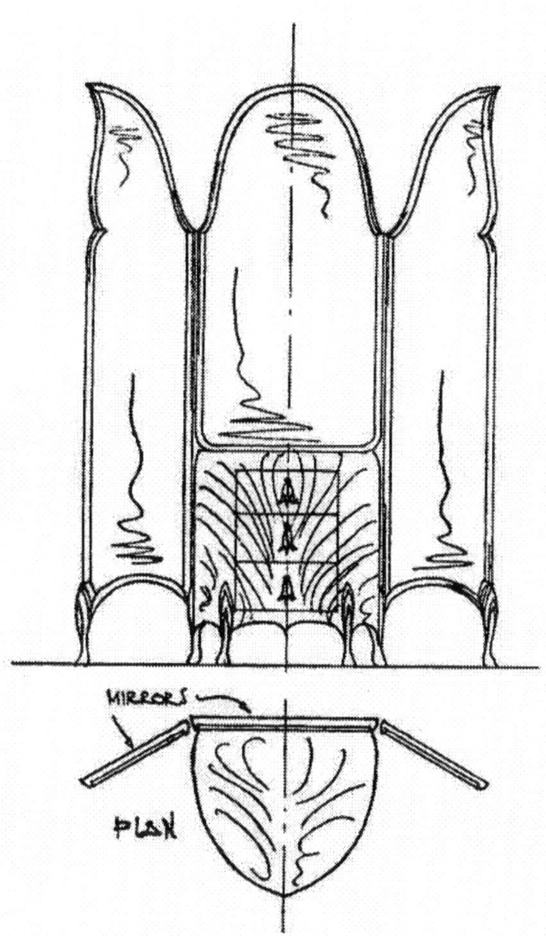


PEVENSEY DRESSING TABLE, NO. 733-C. REGD.

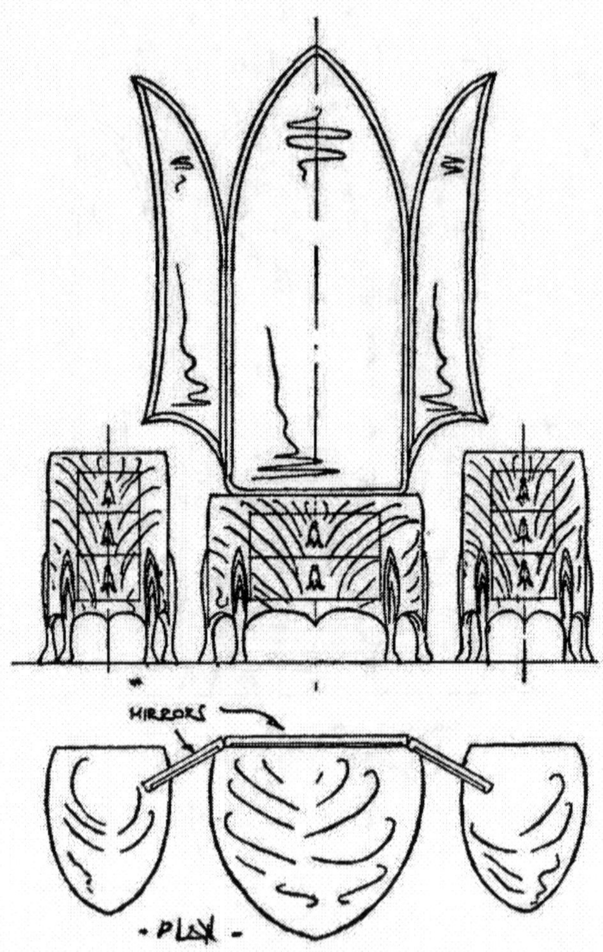


ATLANTIC DRESSING TABLE, NO. 735-C. REGD.

# ART AND NATURE

ART is but a natural interpretation of beautiful emotions—a natural harmony that creates a pleasant, æsthetic thrill. In nature there are no discords, for nature, ever striving towards beauty and unity, abhors disharmony. As Goethe says, "nature is an artist arriving at perfection without a trace of effort."

"A leaf of grass is no less than the journey-work of the stars—and the grain of sand—the egg of the wren, and the tree-toad is a chef d'œuvre for the highest. The running blackberry would adorn the parlours of heaven and a mouse is miracle enough to stagger sextillions of infidels." Creative art is alive; copied art is dead. A living creature is an adventure in self-expression. The supreme condition of maintaining life in nature is harmony. When art is made alive, the spirit within will survive after all else has perished. In art, as in nature, there can be no life without harmony.

It is a living spirit that gives charm to an artistically furnished room, where the creative thought of its designer is so obviously apparent. How else could be felt that complete sense of effortless rest; at once natural and satisfying.

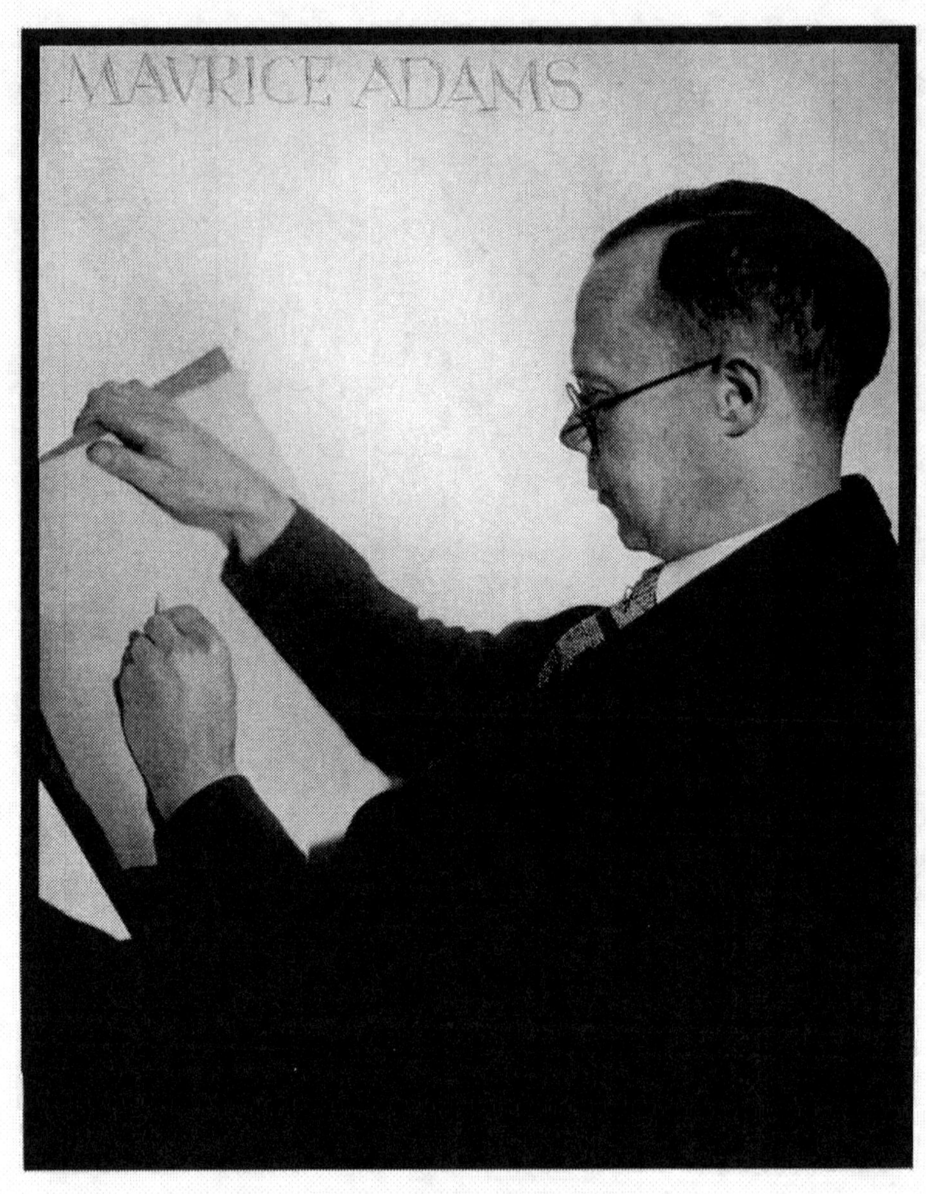


MAURICE S. R. ADAMS

MANAGING DIRECTOR, MAURICE ADAMS LTD.

FINAL EXAMINATION ROYAL INSTITUTE OF BRITISH ARCHITECTS

# THE EVOLUTION OF FURNITURE DESIGN

EARLIER in this book I emphasized the important part evolution should play in the creation of furniture designs, and described, step by step, how Maurice Adams' furniture was gradually evolved from designs based on eighteenth century furniture.

To clearly illustrate these stages of development, I have sketched the following three sheets of diagrams featuring (1) the leg, (2) table tops, (3) wardrobe tops. An examination of these diagrams will show the marked difference in initial appearance between the first and last stages of development. The intermediate diagrams, however, clearly trace development and establish relationship. The inclusion of these diagrams will, I hope, give additional interest to my subject.

*Sheet No. 1.—Leg details.*

Fig. 1. The typical cabriole leg, derived from a claw-footed animal, as used in eighteenth century furniture. Considered in design this leg is an attached member and not an integral part of the main design. It is joined on to the furniture it supports.

Fig. 2. The " King George V " leg allied to a hoof-footed rather than a claw-footed animal leg. The first stage of development.

Fig. 3. Here the leg no longer is purely an attached member as in Fig. 1. The structural lines of the leg develop direct from the supported furniture. Consequently the ears or side-pieces at the top of the leg show a break at their juncture. Observe also that the outer curve of the leg rises just above the base of super structure.

Fig. 4. The ears are now omitted, and the leg becomes more definitely a structural part of the main design. The curve of the leg is less " fat " and more upright.

Fig. 5. In this leg it will be seen that the supported furniture grows out of the sides of the leg, now structurally one with the main design.

Fig. 6. Carved foliage is now introduced changing the animal form into a plant form.

Fig. 7. The " Palm " leg. Here the central leaf is enlarged and carried up several inches above the bottom of the furniture, and the side leaves are omitted. This is the stage of development reached in April 1929, and thus employed in the more recent designs sketched in the following pages.

## THE EVOLUTION OF FURNITURE DESIGN

### Sheet No. 1. The Leg

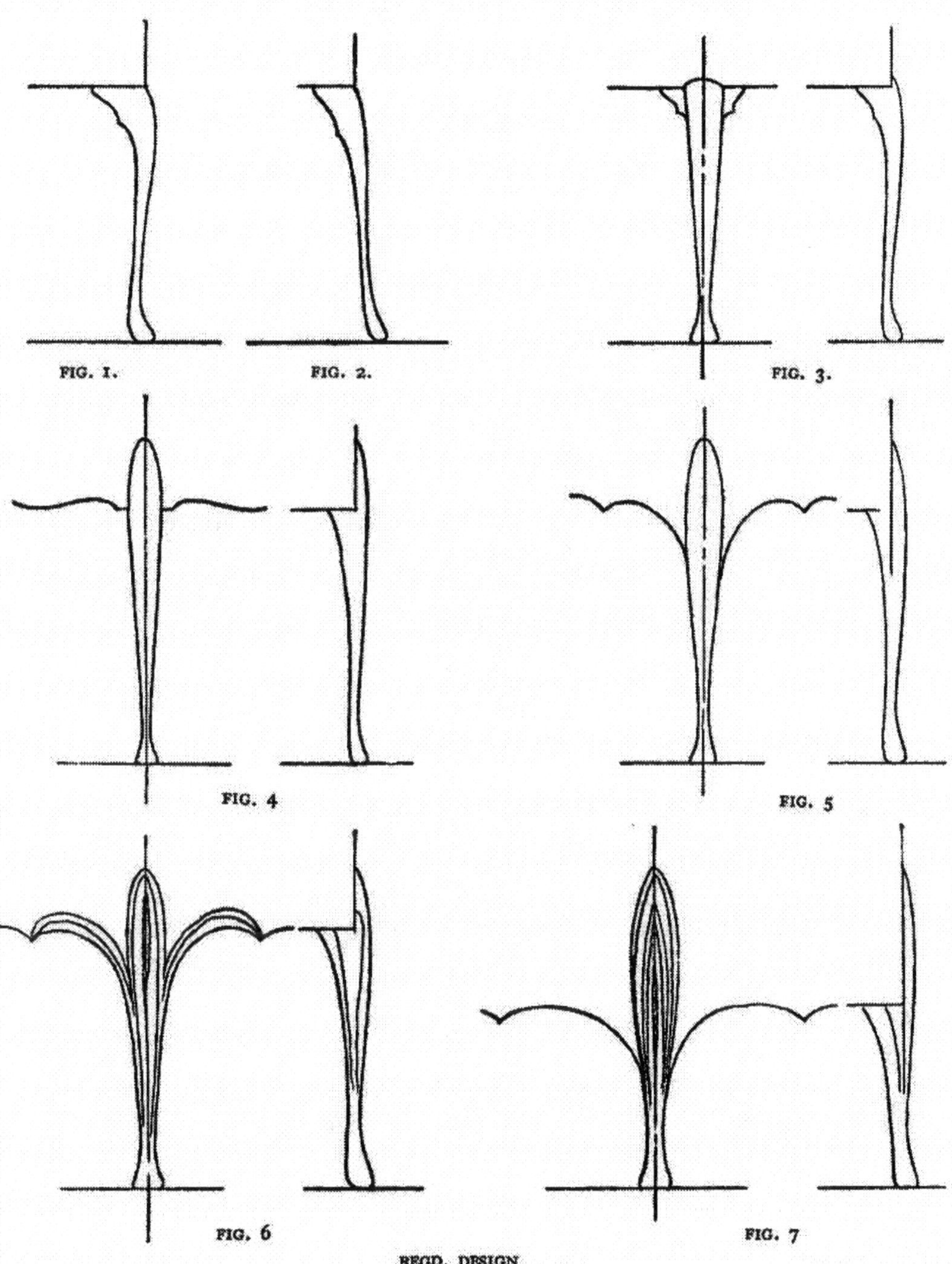


REGD. DESIGN

*Sheet No. 2.—Table top details.*

The character of the changes made in connection with table top design is similar to the changes already described. These modifications are concerned not only with design but with construction, and are brought about largely by reason of the introduction of laminated wood. The process consists of blending together and forming a single member, where previously there were two distinct features joined together.

FIG. 1. shows a " thumb " edged table top forming part of a chest. The top is a separate member serving as a cover or lid to the chest beyond which it projects about an inch all round the piece. The cross-banded margin and wide half-round beading around the drawer as shown in this sketch are typical of eighteenth century design. The cross-banding serves to mark the structural separation between the drawer and its case and to emphasize the structural nature of the chest top or lid.

FIG. 2. " King George V." design. The chest top no longer projects and is of reduced thickness. Cross-banding is omitted and the drawer beading is much smaller. The effect of these changes is to bring the drawer, its case and the case top into closer relationship.

FIG. 3. The top as a separate member has now disappeared and become an actual part of the drawer case. The drawer beading is also omitted. The nature of the drawer case is, however, marked by cross-banding.

FIG. 4. The blending between main surfaces of top, sides and front now begins. All cross-banding is omitted. The fronts are veneered as one surface without regard to any difference between the drawers and its case. The sharp breaks between main surfaces, by reason of the square corners in FIG. 3, give place to moulded corners along front edges and curved forms along side edges.

FIG. 5. Similar to FIG. 4 simplified.

FIG. 6. " Grosvenor " design. All mouldings are omitted. Front and sides blend by means of rounded corners. The top has the side detail of No. 5 used in front as well as at sides.

# THE EVOLUTION OF FURNITURE DESIGN

## Sheet No. 2. Table Tops

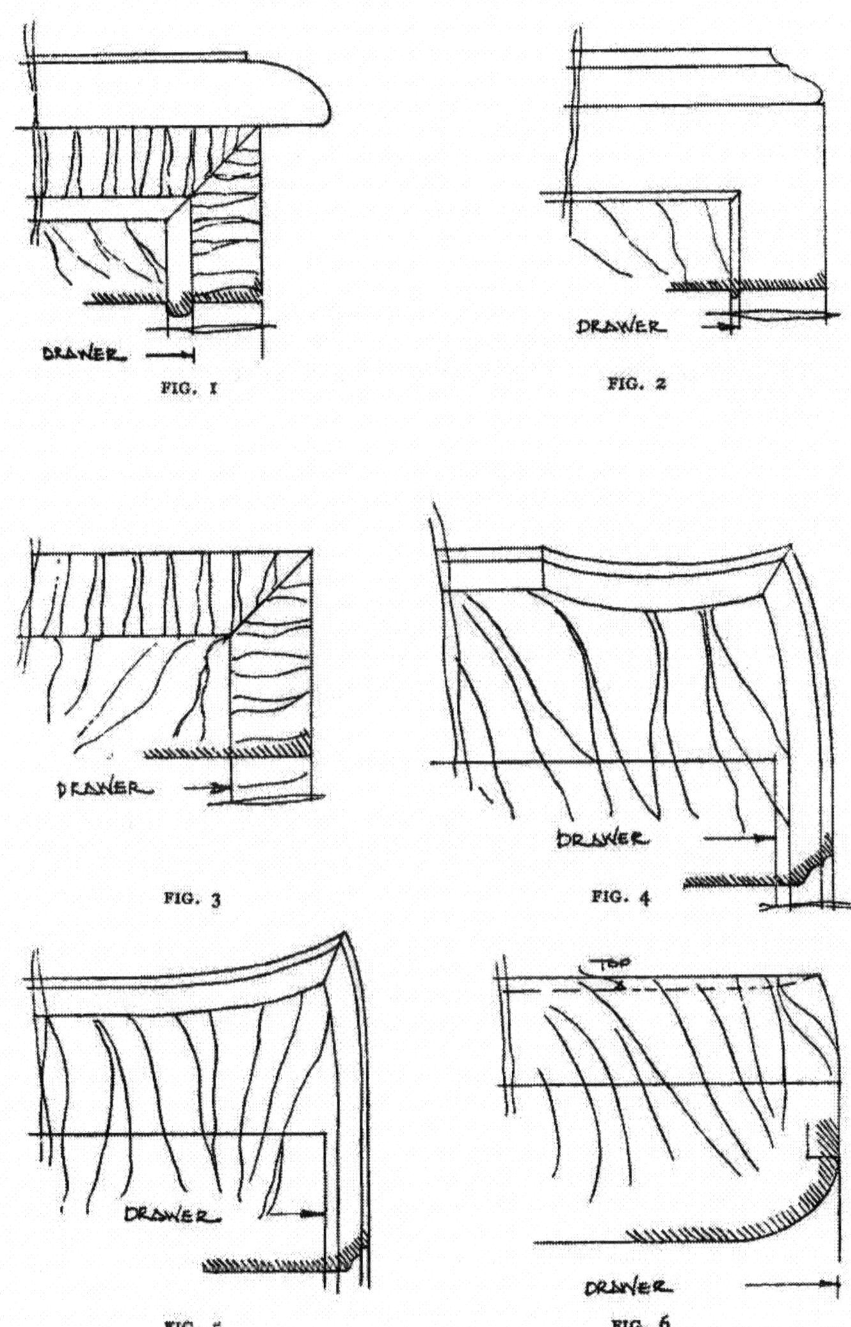


FIG. 1

FIG. 2

FIG. 3

FIG. 4

FIG. 5

FIG. 6

*Sheet No. 3.—Wardrobe top details.*

Fig. 1. shows historic design and construction. The door has stout frame carrying a panel. The junction between frame and panel is covered by means of an applied moulding. With this form of construction it is impossible to avoid shrinkage in the panel. The panel moulding hides this shrinkage and obscures any opened joint. Observe the door frame is cross-banded, thus marking its structural significance. The cornice is a separate member and not part of the main structure.

Fig. 2. "King George V." design. The cornice no longer projects. The door is constructed of laminated mahogany. The panel moulding no longer serves a structural purpose. The panel mould is smaller and the door has reduced margin.

Fig. 3. The cornice has disappeared together with door margins, door panel and panel mould. We observe the same character developing here as in the table top details, sheet No. 2.

Fig. 4. "Connaught" design. In Figs. 2 and 3 the changes simplify main surfaces without blending them together. In Fig. 4 we observe the commencement of changes which ultimately result in blending, as one unbroken surface, front, sides and top of the furniture.

Fig. 5. A further step in the simplifying of design as a whole.

Fig. 6. "Grosvenor" design. Surfaces blended. No sharp corners. No mouldings. Main surfaces have free flowing curves wherever possible.

## Sheet No. 3. Wardrobe Tops

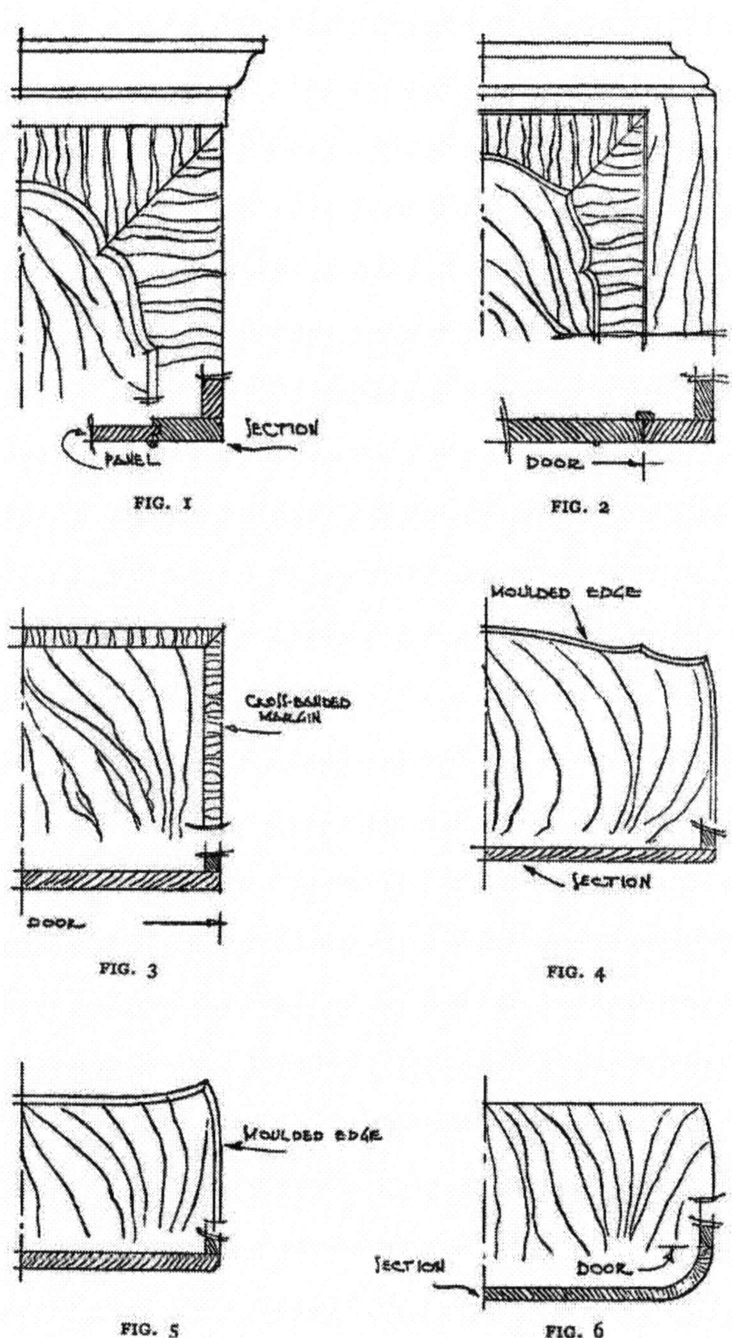


FIG. 1 FIG. 2 FIG. 3 FIG. 4 FIG. 5 FIG. 6

# YACHT FURNITURE

The yacht illustrated was decorated and furnished by us in a very complete manner. These rooms have a spacious appearance, seldom attained in rooms of similar size, due to the decorative treatment. All rooms have ornamented ceilings. The walls are panelled and painted. Detail photographs of the light fittings are given on pages 179, 180 and 182.

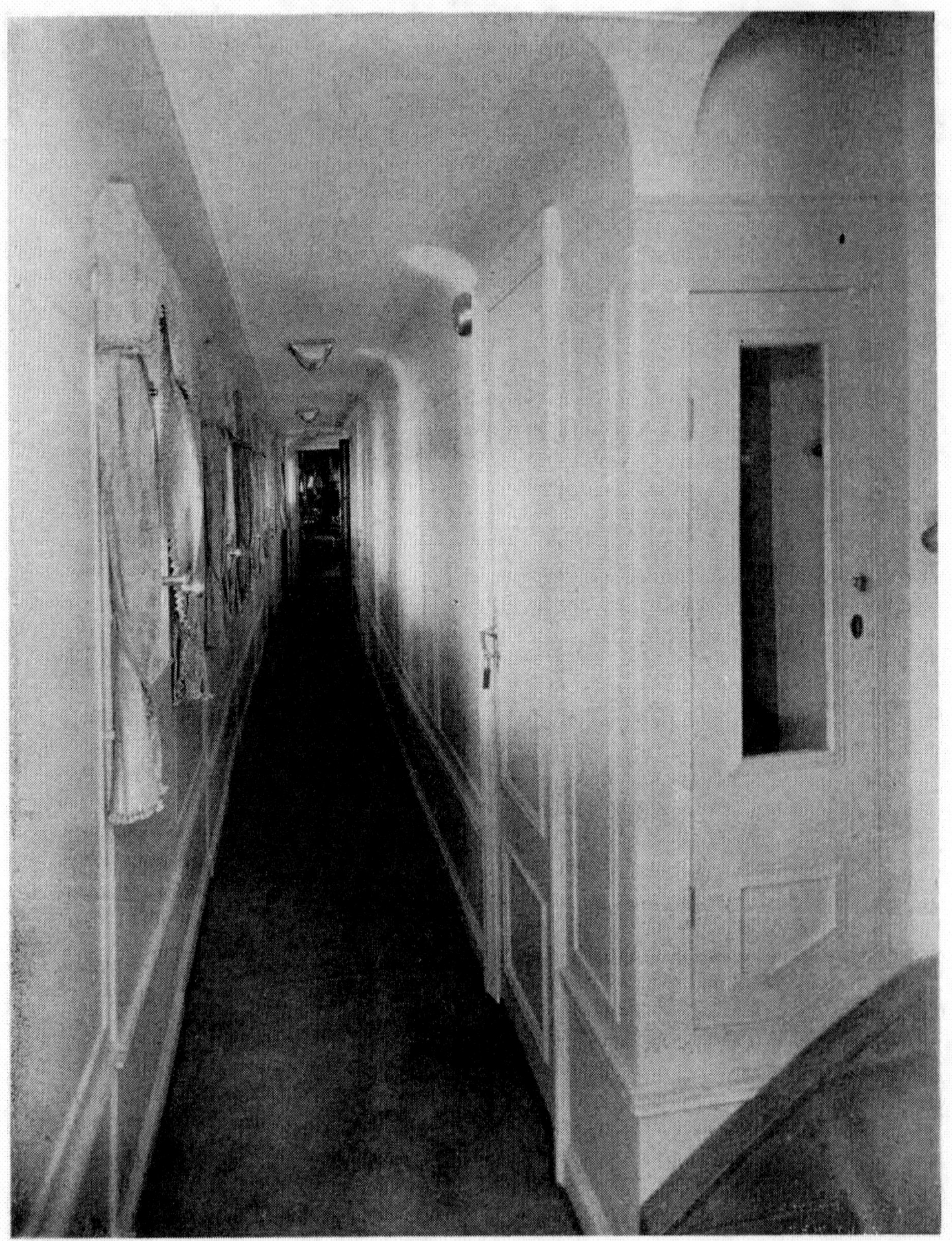

MAIN CORRIDOR ON YACHT — DESIGNED BY MAURICE ADAMS

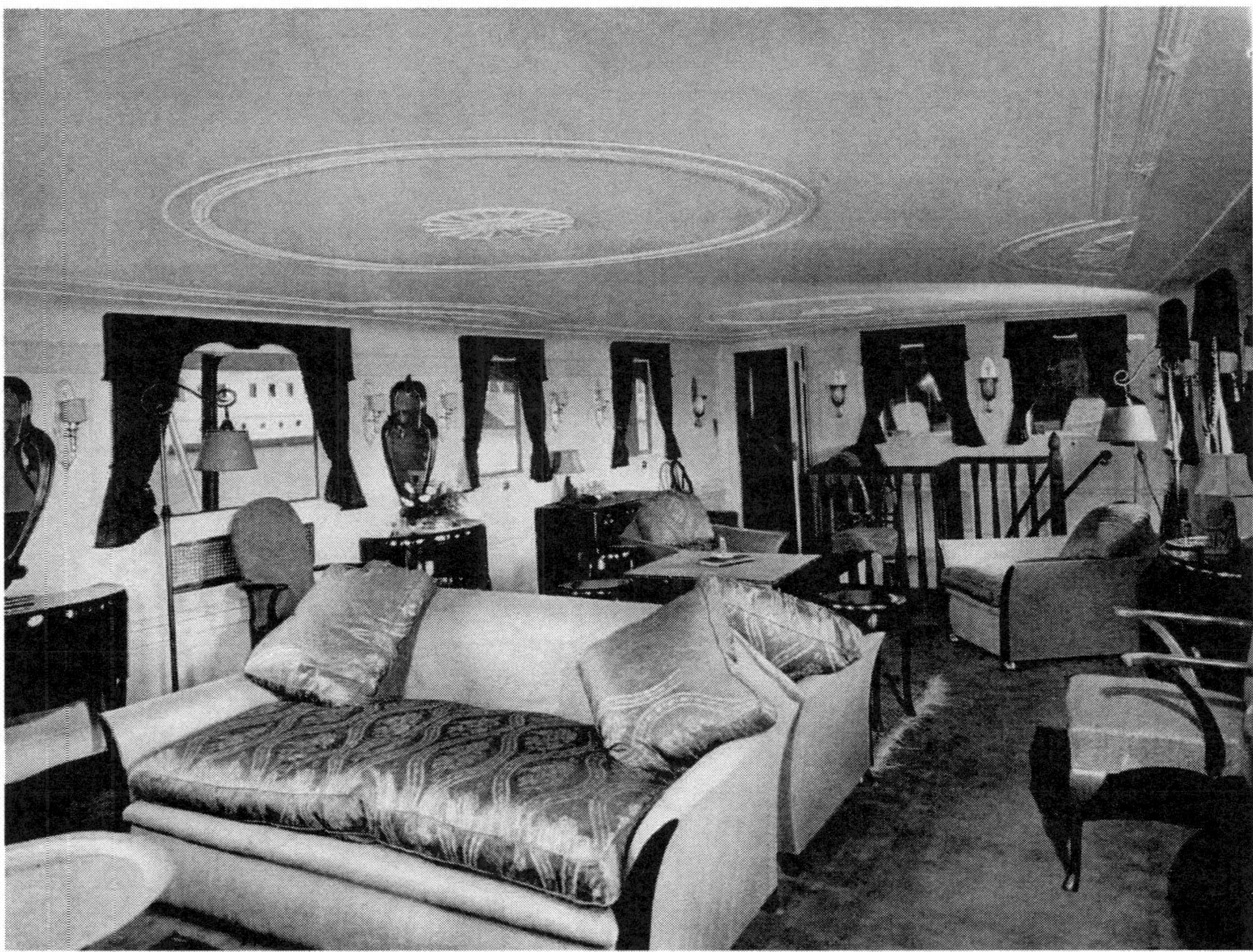

YACHT LIVING ROOM DESIGNED BY MAURICE ADAMS

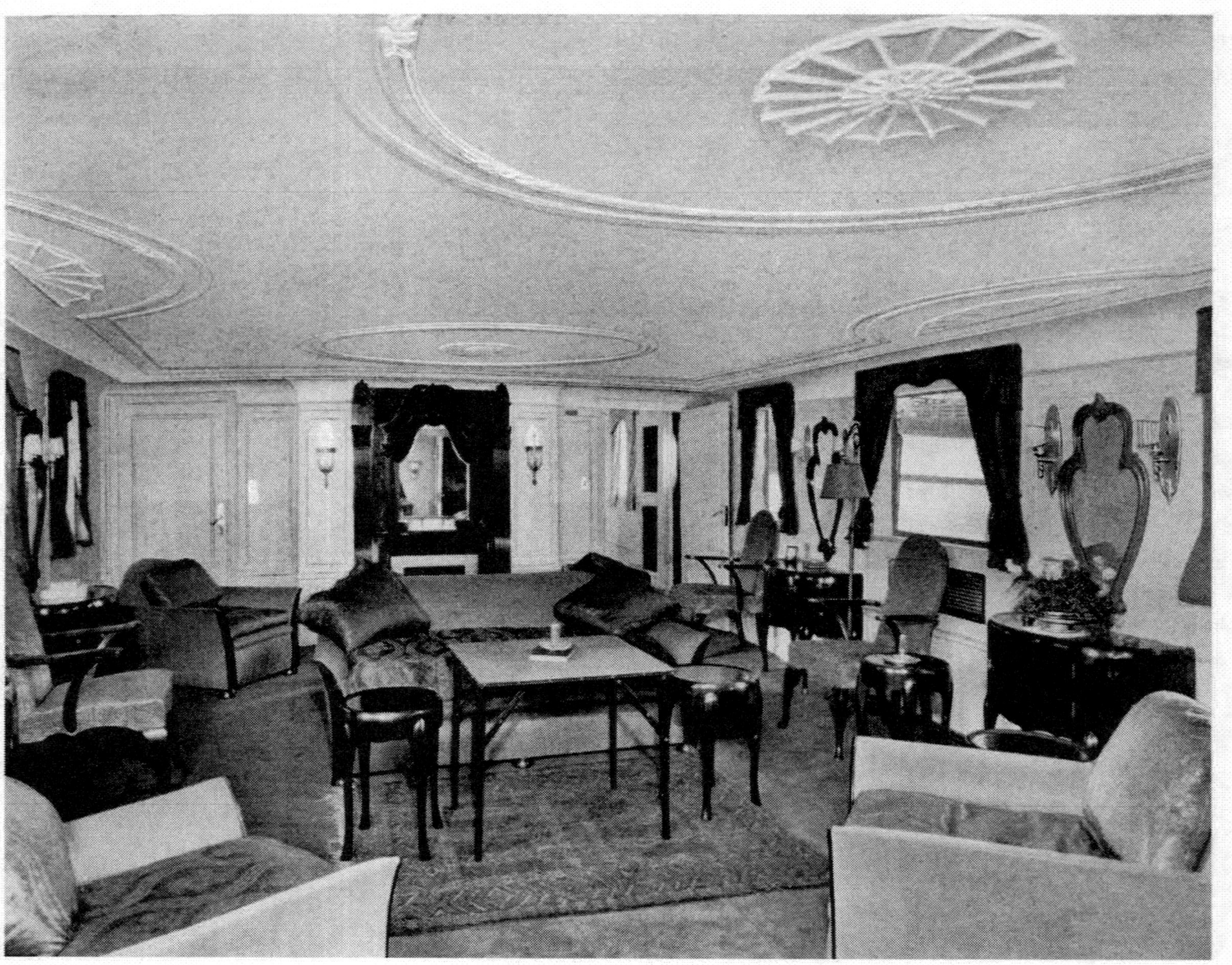

YACHT LIVING ROOM — DESIGNED BY MAURICE ADAMS

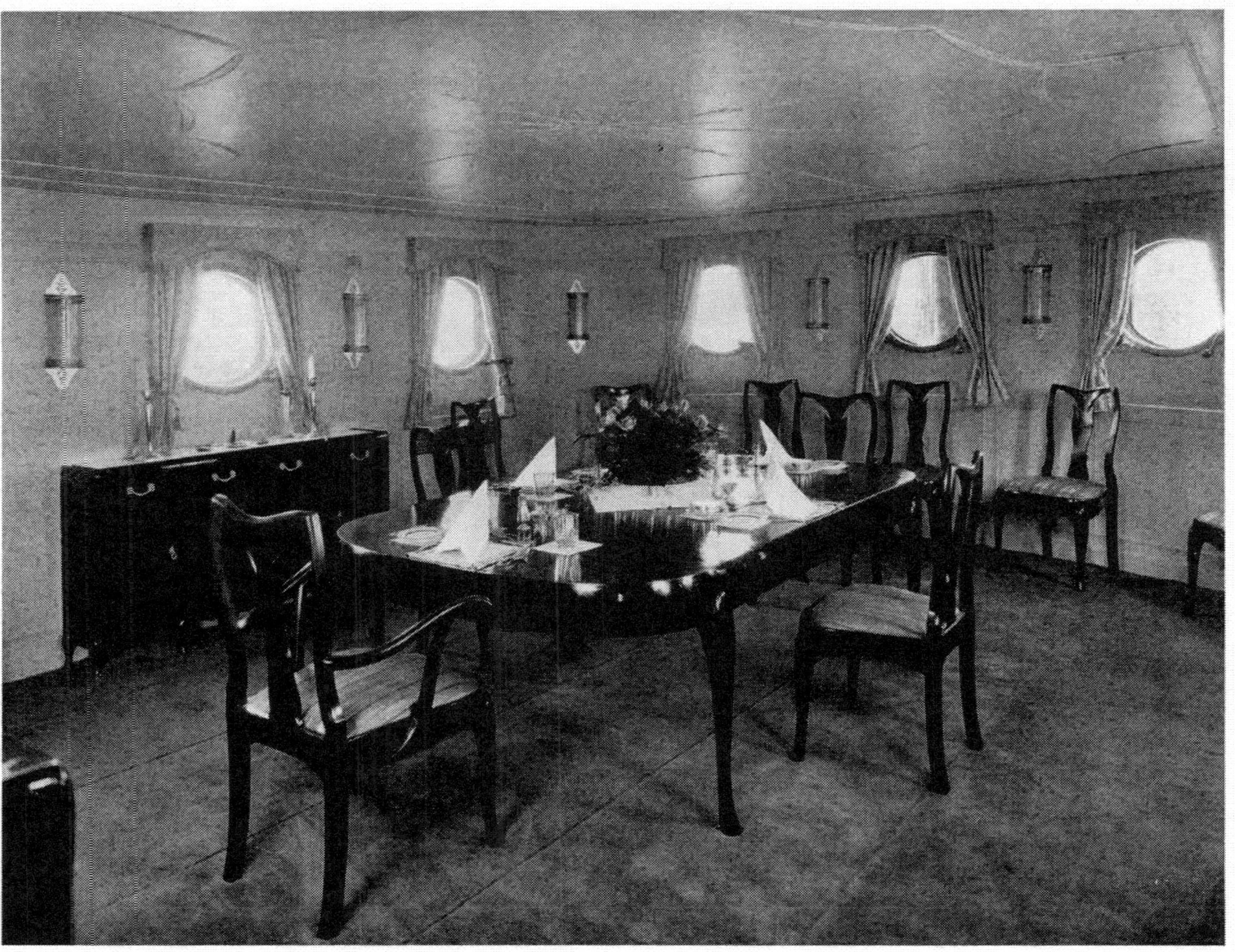

YACHT DINING ROOM DESIGNED BY MAURICE ADAMS

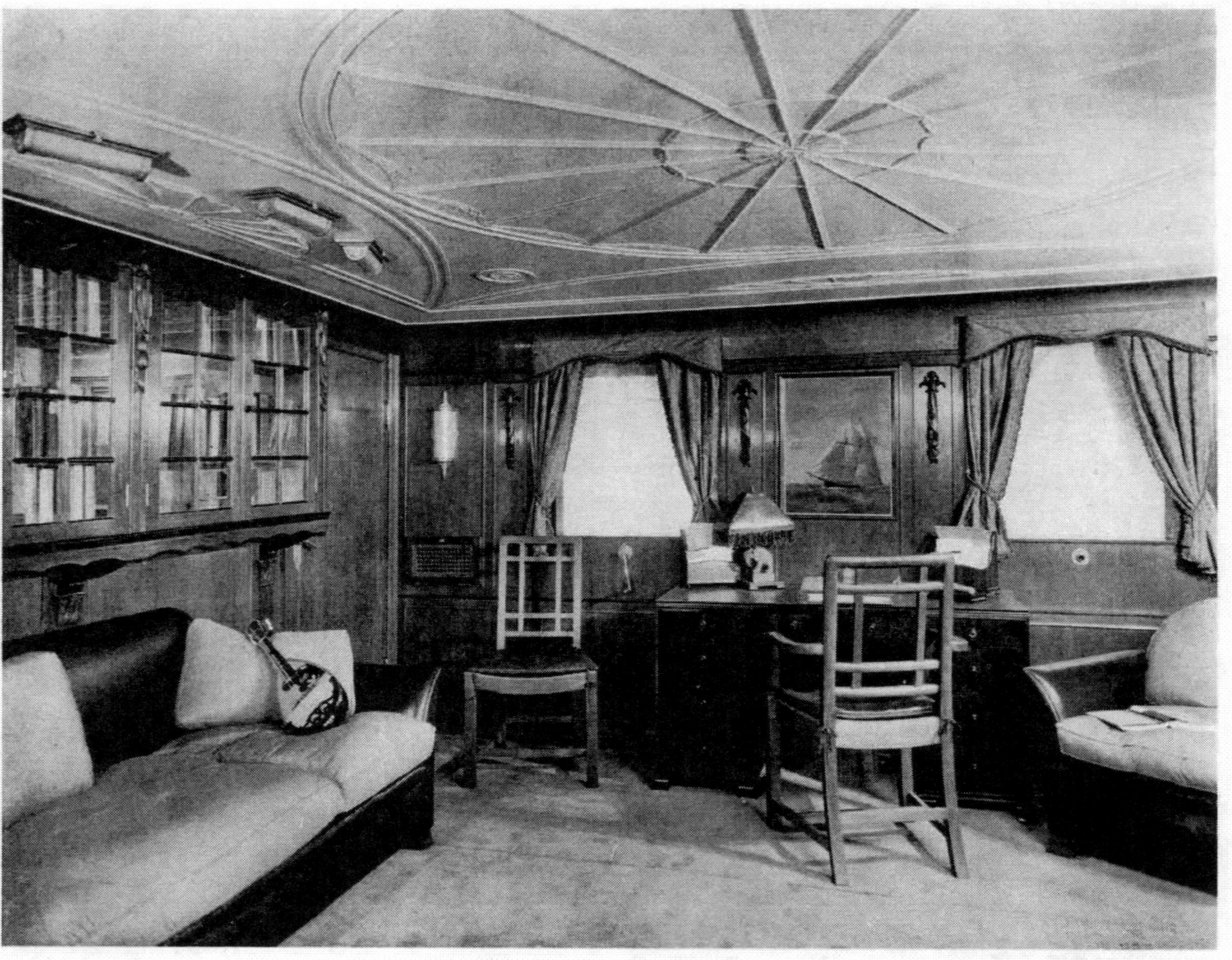

YACHT LIBRARY

DESIGNED BY MAURICE ADAMS

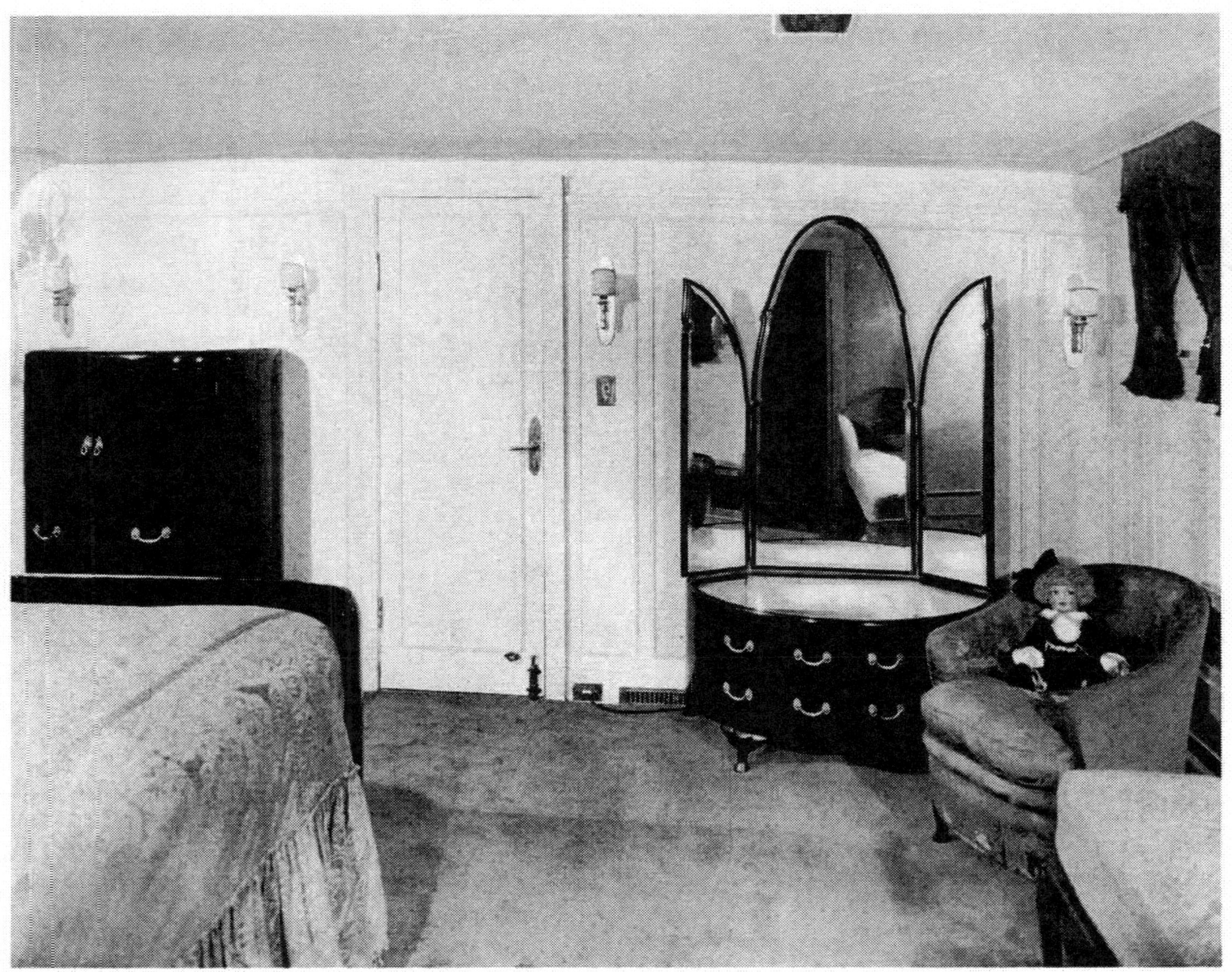

CHIEF STATE ROOM, YACHT " CORONET " DESIGNED BY MAURICE ADAMS

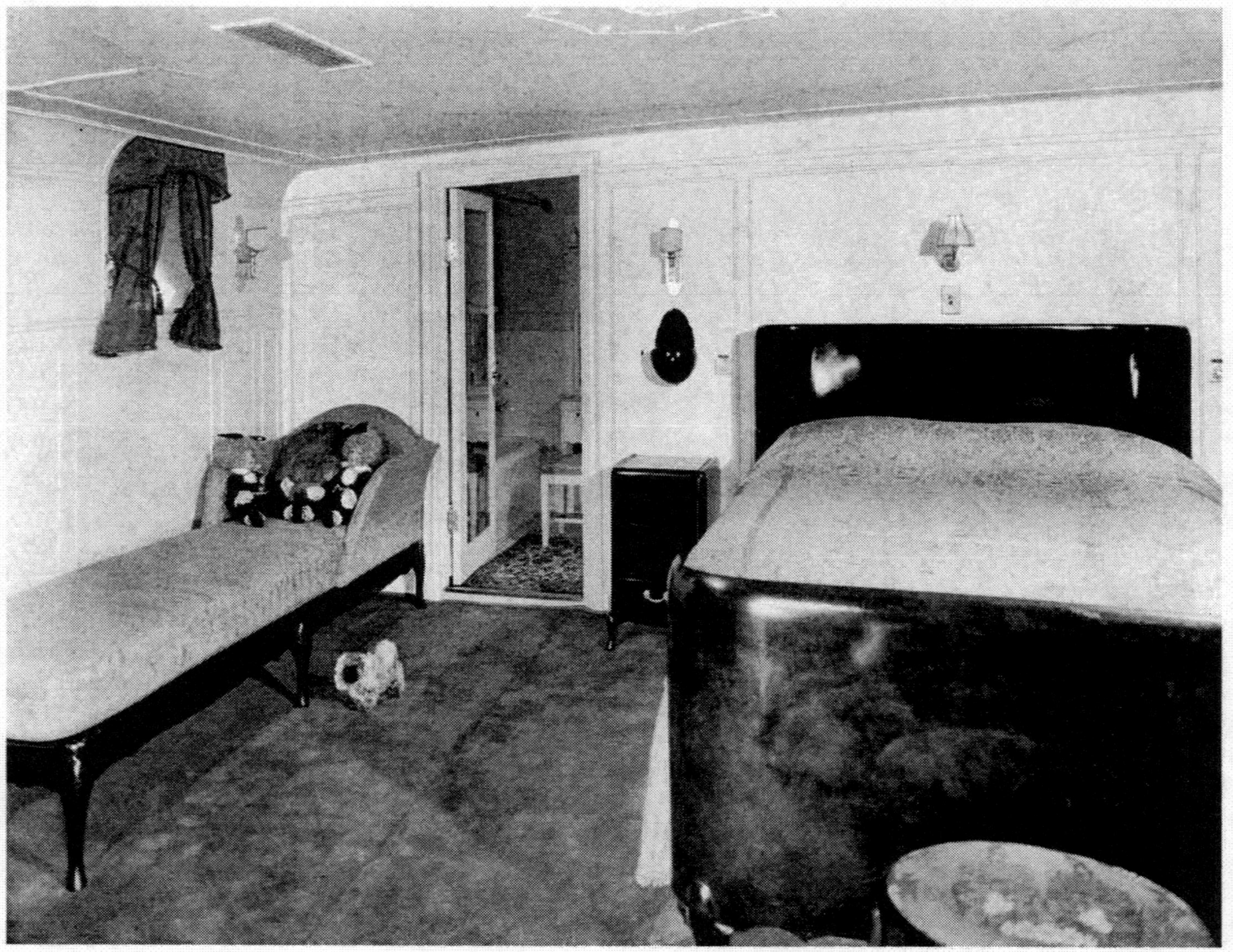

CHIEF STATE ROOM, YACHT "CORONET" DESIGNED BY MAURICE ADAMS

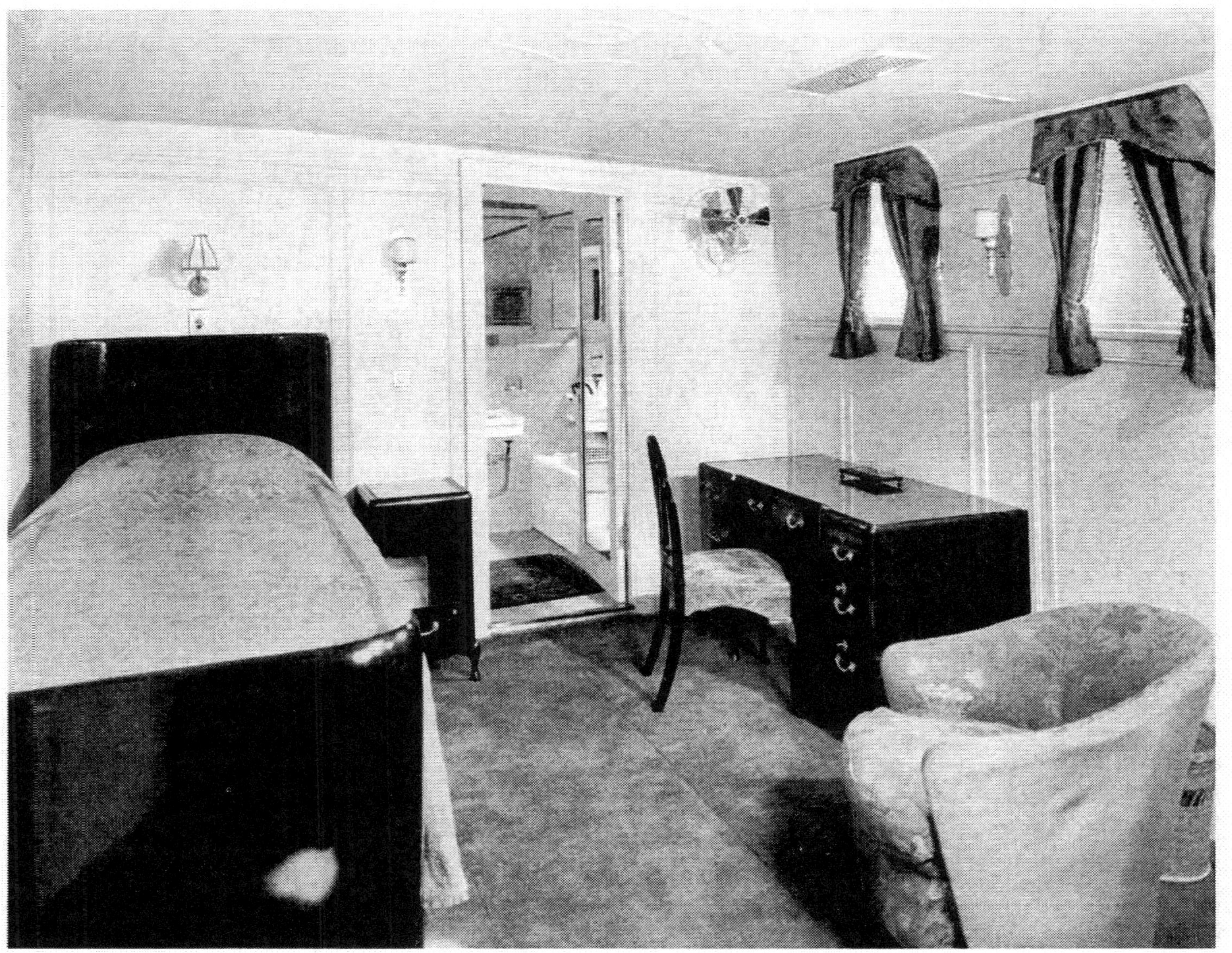

OWNER'S STATE ROOM, YACHT "CORONET"        DESIGNED BY MAURICE ADAMS

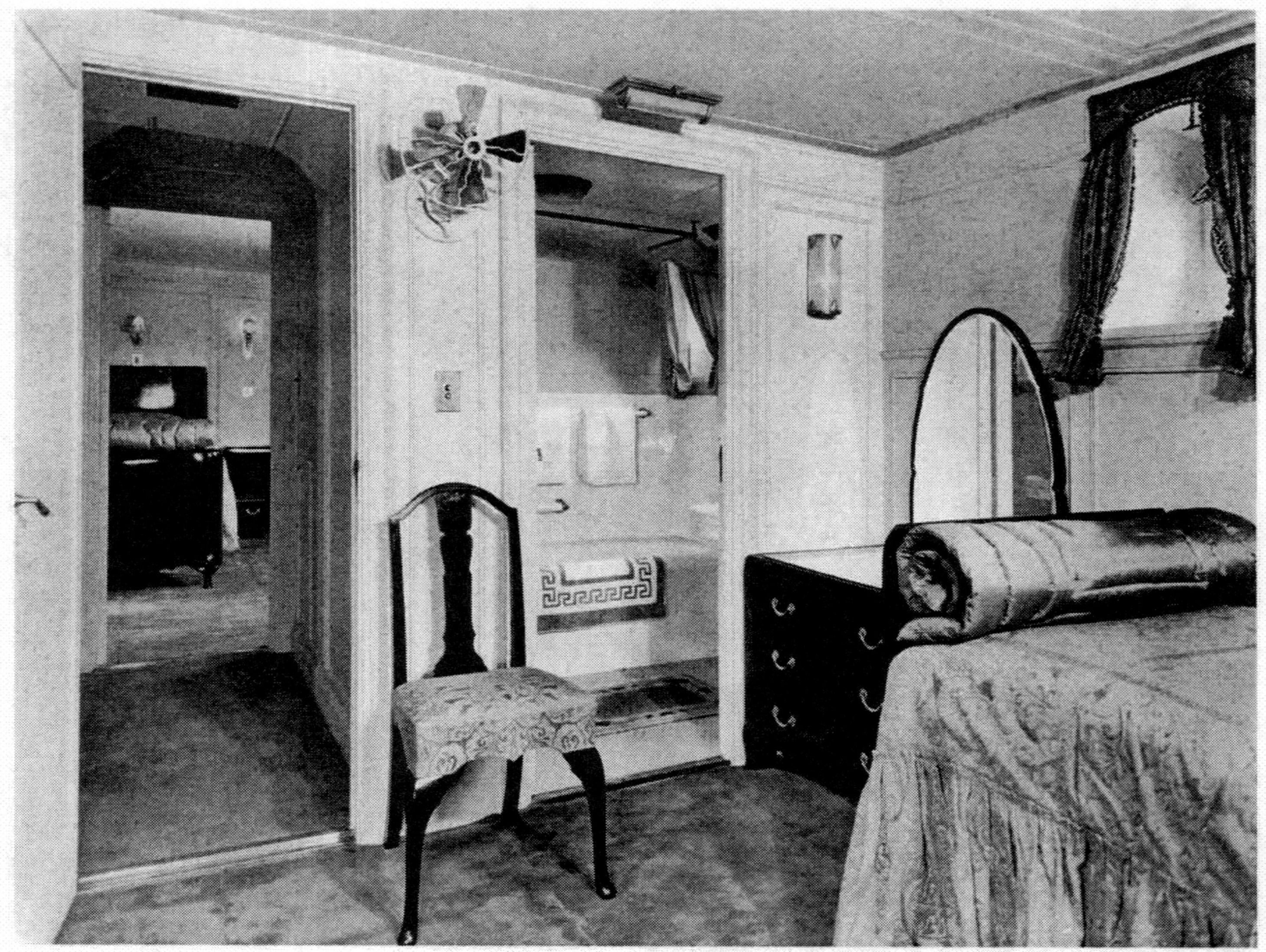

YACHT STATE ROOM DESIGNED BY MAURICE ADAMS

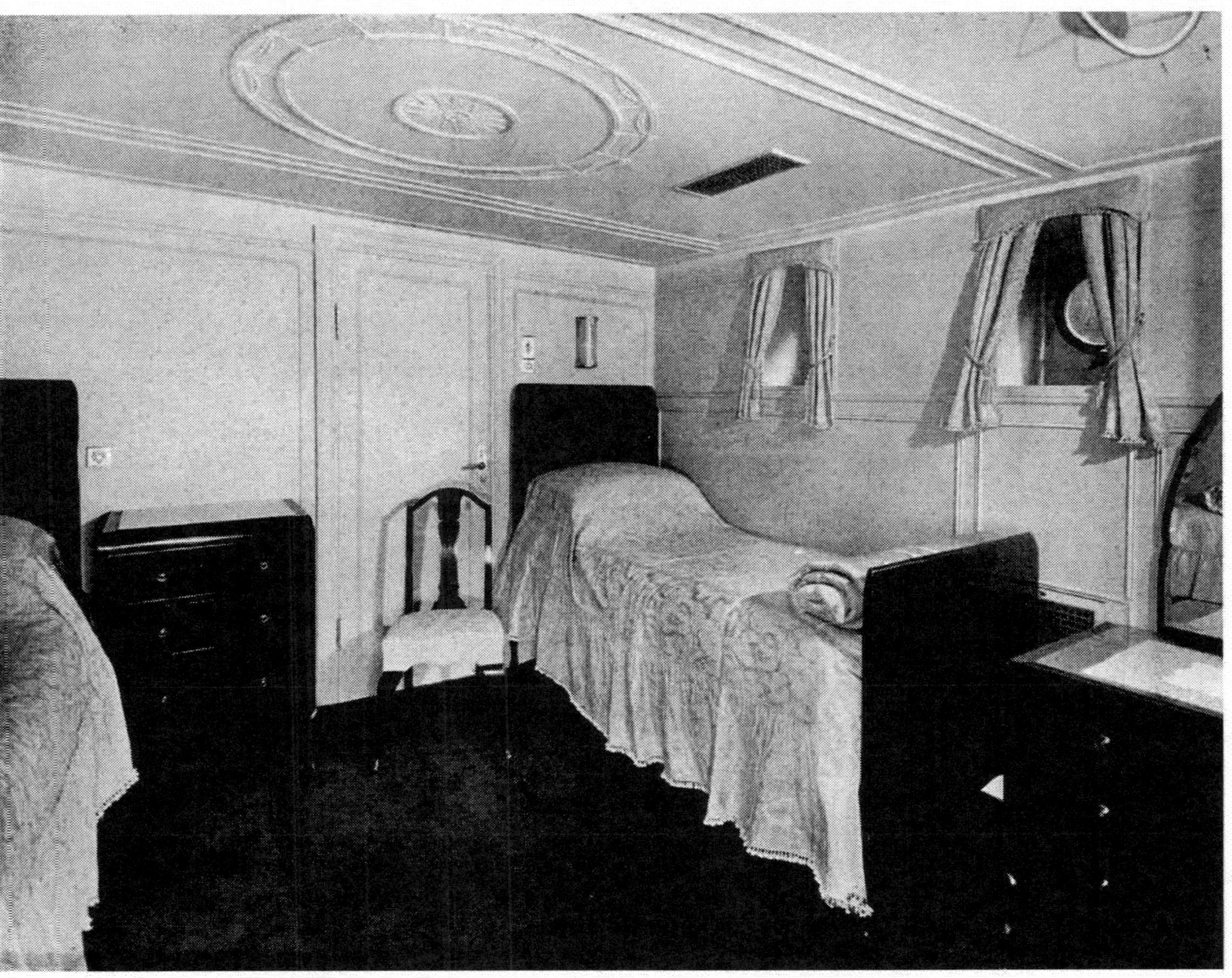

YACHT STATE ROOM DESIGNED BY MAURICE ADAMS

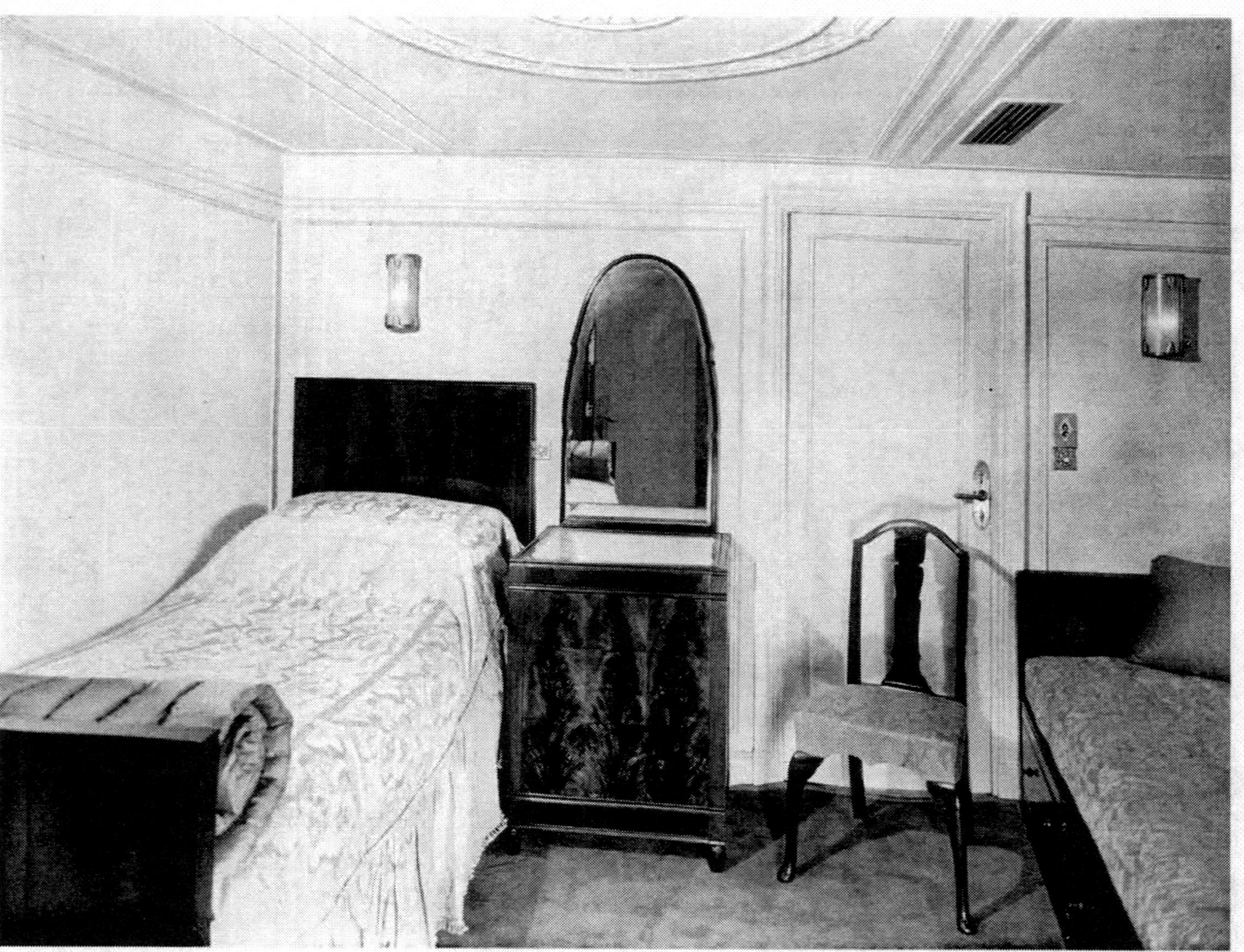

YACHT STATE ROOM

DESIGNED BY MAURICE ADAMS

# THE GARDEN

# THE GARDEN

EVERYONE loves a garden. Many wisely make gardening their hobby. Nevertheless it is almost exceptional to find a garden out of the ordinary. The reason for these conditions is partly want of imagination, and that more consideration is given to the cultivation of flowers than to the creation of gardens.

The point I wish to make is that the cultivation of flowers is one thing and the layout of gardens another.

Beautiful flowers, of course, are chief factors in any effective garden making. There are, however, many materials from which gardens are made. Flowers in themselves do not alone constitute a garden.

Most people who say they are fond of gardening, usually mean they are fond of cultivating flowers. Personally, I dislike " gardening," but thoroughly enjoy garden making.

The cost of gardens may be classified as, A—initial expenditure or cost of making the garden, and B—upkeep.

The conversion of an open and uncultivated piece of land into a garden is expensive, but the cost of a well-planned and properly-executed garden makes a very profitable investment. The cost of garden making should be reckoned as capital expenditure. When purchasing a house a definite amount of capital obviously has to be allocated for this purpose. Upkeep charges will depend, of course, primarily on the type of garden. For example, the principal factors (apart from flowers) in garden making, *i.e.*, grass, paving, trees and shrubs, cost very little to maintain, and gardens made from these materials only look almost as well in winter as in summer. If to these we add such flowers as roses (standard, climbing and dwarf), lily of the valley, bluebell, snowdrop, etc., and other perennials which flower abundantly year after year with little attention, our garden will cost little to maintain and will present an attractive appearance both summer and winter.

The cultivation of flowers generally entails much labour and corresponding expenditure. Where cost of upkeep is a main consideration, the proportion of flower beds should be such as will allow of their effective upkeep, since these will form the largest item in the annual expenditure. In this way one may have quality if not quantity. What can possibly be more beautiful than a well-kept lawn in which are arranged a few beds of profusely flowering bulbs, such as tulips, narcissus or daffodils? The same quantity scattered over a larger area are not nearly so effective as when closely bedded together.

Therefore, my advice to garden makers is first, carefully consider the proposed garden layout, and limit the size and number of flower beds as will allow of their effective upkeep. Properly planned and planted with grass, yew, box, cupressus, cedar, etc., a garden will entail a minimum upkeep charge. One cannot, however, have a beautiful garden for nothing, and the above-mentioned trees and shrubs are expensive. Once planted, however, their value increases year by year. They cost little to keep in good condition and provide an ample return on their cost.

Of course, amenities are important, but size has little to do with the beauty of a garden. Large gardens are not always beautiful, and it should be possible to make even the tiniest garden attractive and interesting. At the time I am writing a small "picture" garden, approximately 20-ft. square, is featured in an Oxford Street window.

In planning a garden, careful attention should be given to actual conditions, features and circumstances; since the best lay-out will be determined by taking these factors into consideration. A plan, carefully drawn to scale, should always be made of the site. Upon this drawing will be indicated the house and adjoining roads, boundaries, existing trees, paths and other features. If the garden is large, or where there are big differences in level, these differences should also be indicated on the site plan. Without such a plan it is quite impossible to devise a really effective and interesting scheme for the layout. To prepare such a plan it is necessary to have professional assistance. Nothing elaborate is necessary, because absolute accuracy is not required. Such a plan may, therefore, be prepared quickly and at slight cost. Obviously it is a waste of time and money to do other than one's best under any given circumstances. To spend money planting a garden, forming paths, etc., to a bad plan is more than foolish. It costs no more to put a little interest and intelligent thought into one's garden plan, but on the other hand, in the absence of the necessary skill, it is impossible for the garden to be made an artistic success.

There are two main types of garden plan, the irregular and the formal. Formal lay-outs require a fairly level site, because symmetry of arrangement is not possible on an irregularly sloping site. This difficulty may be partly overcome by the creation of terraces and sinkings. Such methods, however, are prohibitive except to the wealthy. Where the site is irregular and uneven as regards level, it will be best not to attempt a formal treatment, but to determine the layout as dictated by natural features of the site without regard to symmetry of arrangement.

I do not propose more than to touch on the subject of garden plans in these pages, my main purpose being to illustrate and describe the garden I have designed at Moor Park, Rickmansworth, as this typifies my own idea of what an ideal garden should be.

This garden has exceptional advantages as regards amenities. Formerly it was a part of Moor Park, over which it now looks, commanding extensive views over park land well studded with centuries-old timber. The garden itself has a unique specimen of an oak tree several hundred years old. This is situated close to the front of the house. In the back garden is a magnificent fully-matured chestnut tree.

Although the house stands upon a hill, midst undulating country, the garden itself is practically level throughout. This circumstance, added to the symmetrical design of the house, left me in no doubt as to the most suitable form for the garden layout.

If the reader will now refer to the garden plan at the end of this book, it will be observed that I have built a garage at the left side of the front garden. The garage is designed something on the lines of a small orangery. The side elevation is symmetrical. It has central door glazed in small squares right to the floor.

It will be observed that the front garden layout is determined by three main axial lines corresponding with the elevation of house and one main axial line cutting these at right angles corresponding with garage elevation.

This arrangement provides main centre path to the house, and two rectangular enclosures on either side. The main lines of the layout are marked by crazy paving. The two enclosures just mentioned are divided into four flower beds each surrounded by stone paths and enclosed with dwarf-cut box hedges.

At the right side of the house is an enclosed rose arbour. Through this arbour an axial line runs right from the front of the front garden to the back of the back garden. On this line the formal lily pond with enclosing beds, paths and hedges is arranged in the back garden. Beyond the lily pond enclosure extends a further small enclosed garden.

From the side of the lily pond radiate three main stone paths or walks. Between these radiating paths beds are formed in the grass in the form of flower sprays. These beds are planted with dwarf box representing the foliage and small flowers representing the buds.

These radiating paths are bordered with standard roses, alternating with cupressus allumii. To the left of house, between the front and back gardens, is a further pattern garden, enclosed with yew hedges and planted with dwarf roses in the diamond-shaped beds cut in the grass.

Stone paths and garden sculpture are almost essential in a formal garden, but here a word of warning is advisable. Garden ornaments require selection with the greatest possible care. Firstly, each ornament must be artistically attractive. Secondly, each must have a suitable setting. Cheap garden ornaments are an abomination. They are not beautiful and can only spoil the effect desired. Ornaments at first attractive lose their charm when seen too often. Some ornaments are good of their kind, but being mass produced and sold at low prices destroys their interest.

It is a good plan never to select garden ornaments until the garden is actually formed. The garden layout should be arranged to provide a definite setting for the ornaments. Ornaments cannot be placed anywhere or they will look superfluous and out of place. The ornaments should provide the final climax and touch of interest to the garden as a whole.

The front garden at Moor Park was planned to provide a setting for five garden ornaments. These are essential to the appearance of the scheme.

Without the ornaments there is a blank look about the garden. The layout is so devised that the eye travels instinctively to the ornaments whose delightful charm reacts over the entire garden. In the middle of the entrance path is placed a solid-looking " abbey " sundial. This is of attractive design and pleasing outline. The heavy appearance, placed as it is, in the very centre of a symmetrical garden, gives just that touch of " weight " where a lighter design would appear trifling and out of place.

Placed in its own specially contrived setting, like a little god in a garden of its very own, is a set of four charming child figures—Peter Pan, Bluebell, Blossom and Harebell, each seated on a small tree trunk. During the summer months, when the beds surrounding these figures are in full blossom, and seen in conjunction with the crazy paths, and close-cut enclosing box edging and yew trees, the effect is perfectly delightful. Even without the flowers, as seen in winter, the effect is charming.

The back garden also has its sculpture. Chief of these is the " water-carrier " fountain—a charming little boy figure in the centre of the lily pond. The crazy stone paths around the pool are planned to pattern. Either side of the pool, on the paving, is a baby and shell bird bath.

Looking across the pool, at the end of the further enclosed garden (Pixie garden it is called) we see a delightful little boy fawn figure seated on a round pedestal and marking the hour with a stick upon a stone mushroom. This little figure is the obvious lord of his yew-enclosed flower garden.

Let us now stand to the right of the lily pool where the eye may travel uninterrupted across the pool down the three radiating rose-flanked walks. At the far end of the path on the right we see a boy fawn playing his pipe, sitting at the edge of a circular pool. His form stands out clear against the dark yew hedge which partly encircles his pool.

At the corresponding end of the middle rose walk is a girl figure seated on the ground amid a circular bed of flowers. She also has her partly encircling back-ground of yew hedge.

At the end of the third rose walk, or path on the left we see the diamond-pattern rose garden. This path leads to the front garden and also to the garage.

While we thus stand at the side of the lily pond there is much to please and charm the eye, for between the radiating paths will be observed the " flower-spray " beds of box and flowers formed in the turf.

One of the best views in this garden is seen by standing at the side of the boy fawn looking down the " Pixie " garden across the lily pool with its boy fountain—through the rose arbour to the little seated figures in the front garden. Thus seen from end to end the eye is charmed by the figures, paths, water, flowers and enclosing cut yew hedges.

In planning this garden my aim was to create as much charm and interest as possible. To make the most effective use of well-cut yew and box trees. It was desired to create a very beautiful picture garden which would look well all the year round, and which could be kept in order at a moderate annual expenditure. The garden is enclosed on all boundaries with rhododendrons.

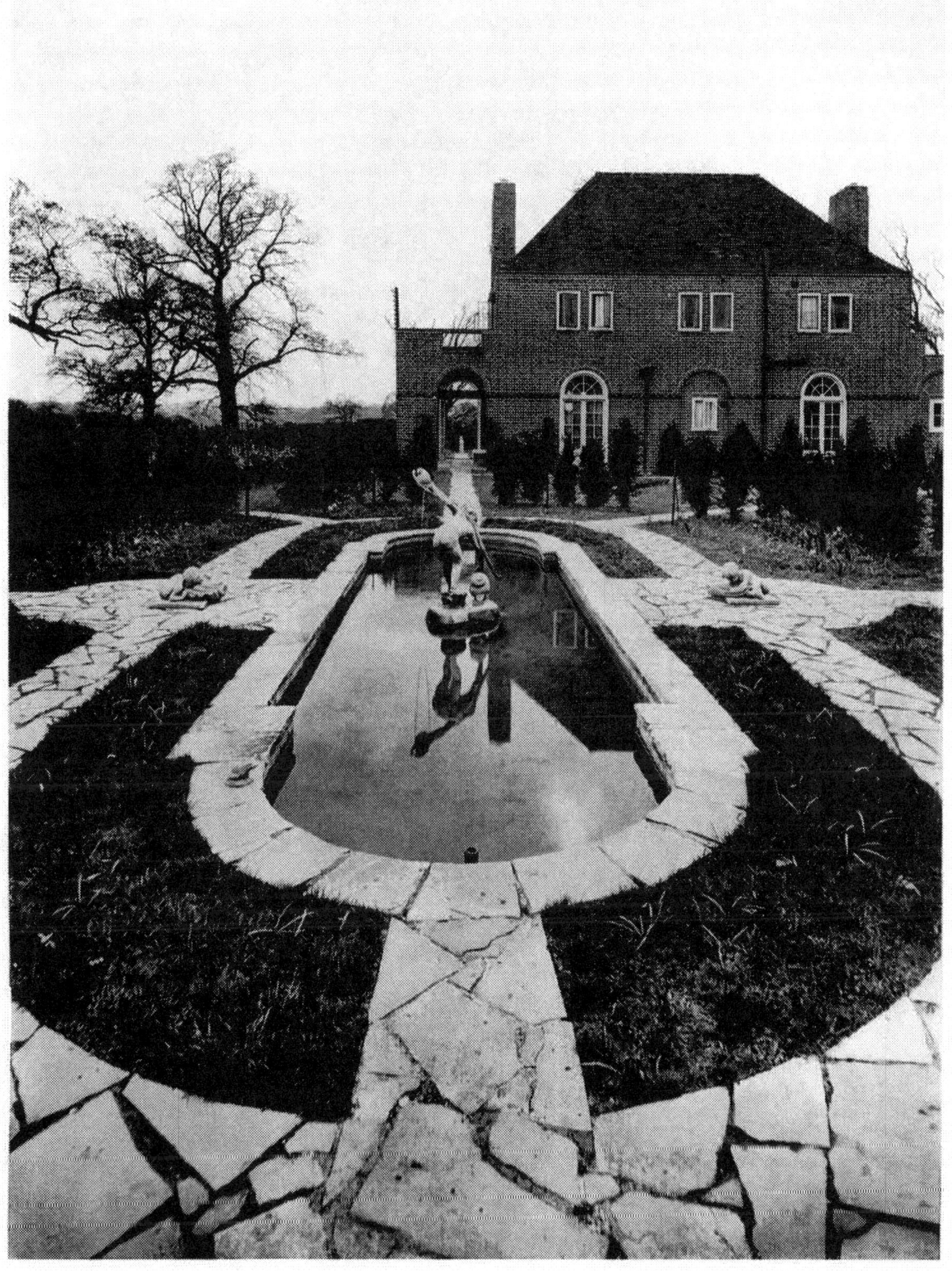

LILY POOL, MOOR PARK MAURICE ADAMS

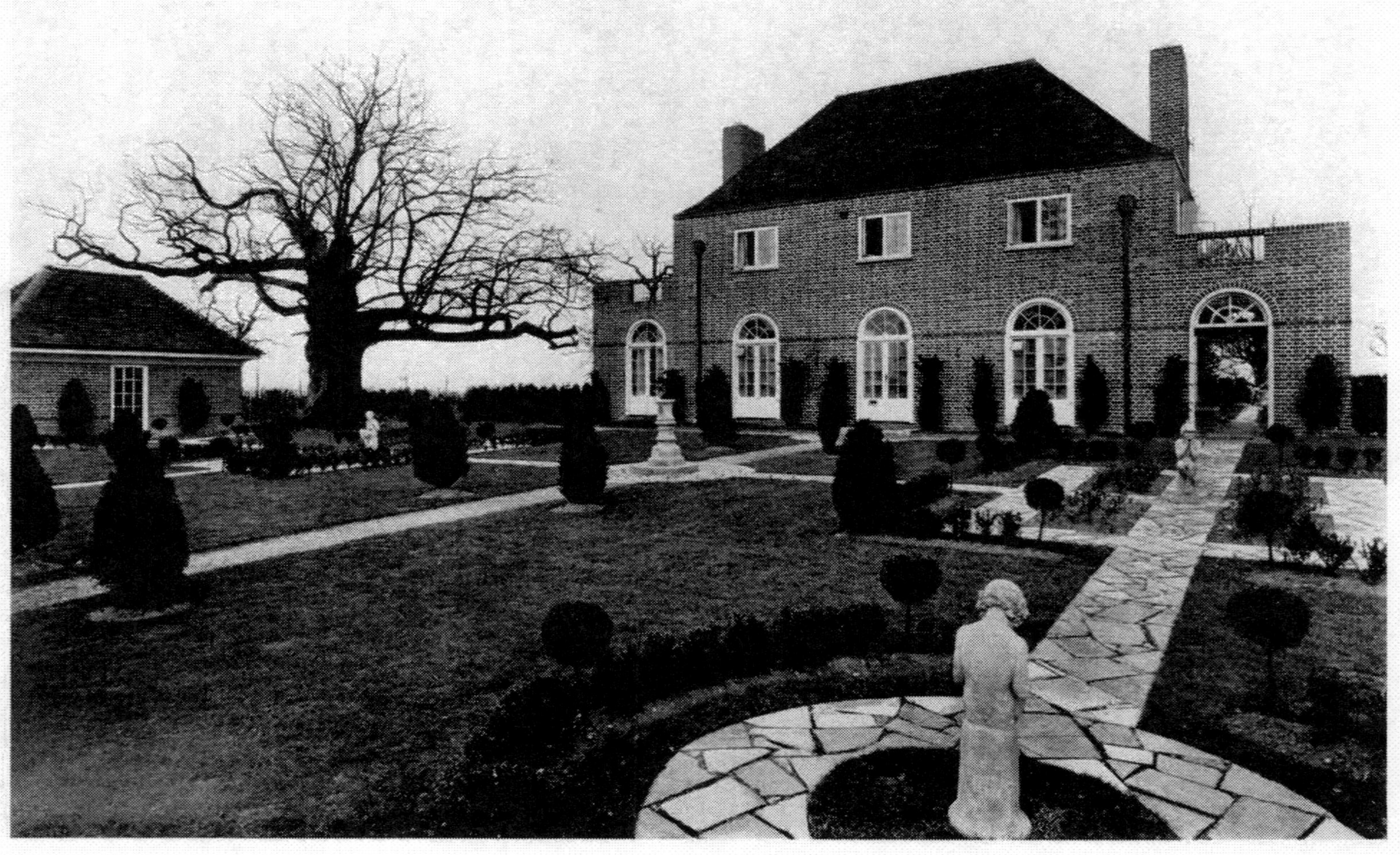

FRONT GARDEN, ADAMS HOUSE, MOOR PARK — MAURICE ADAMS

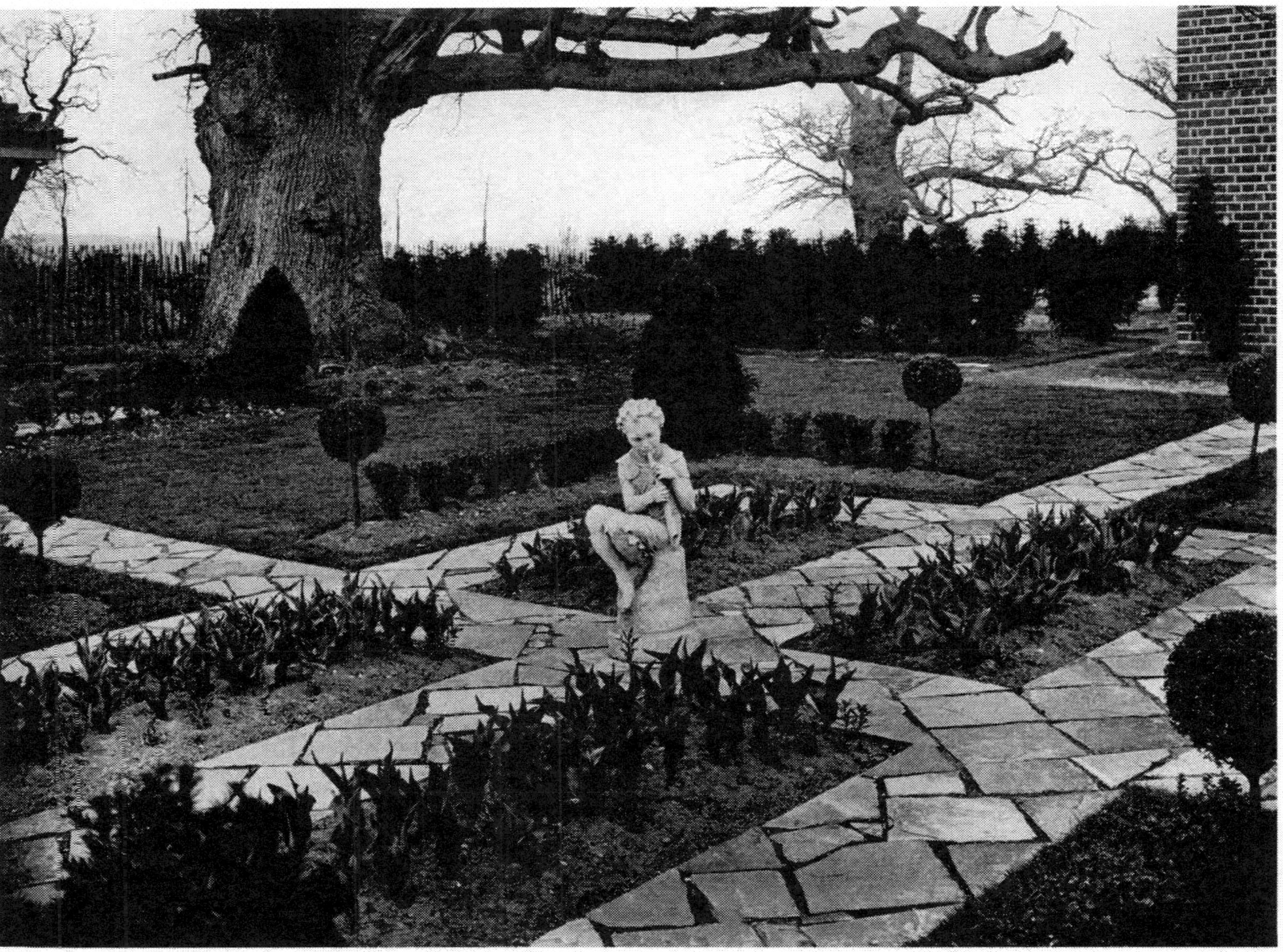

"PETER PAN," ADAMS HOUSE, MOOR PARK

MAURICE ADAMS

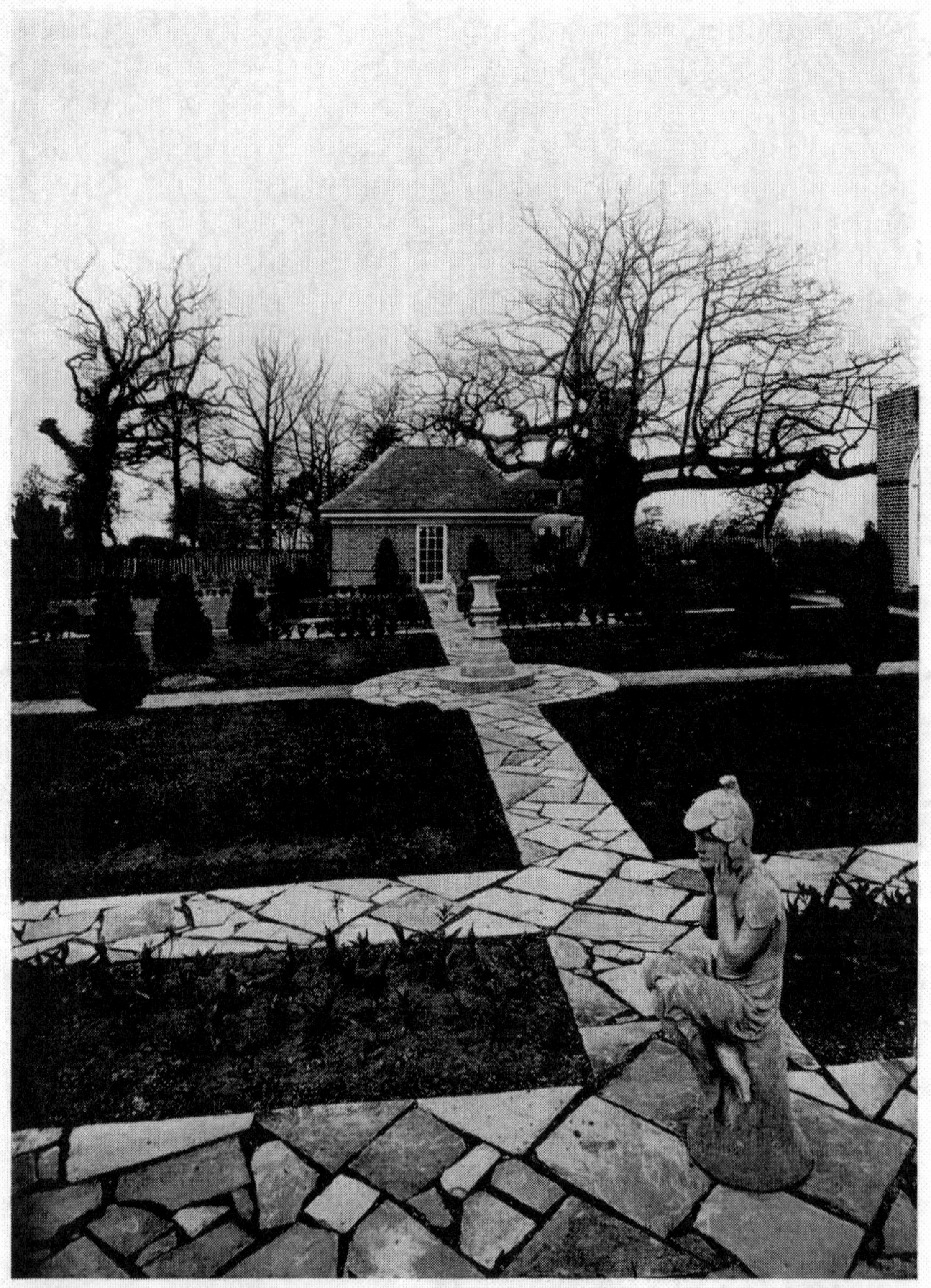

FRONT GARDEN AND GARAGE, ADAMS HOUSE, MOOR PARK MAURICE ADAMS

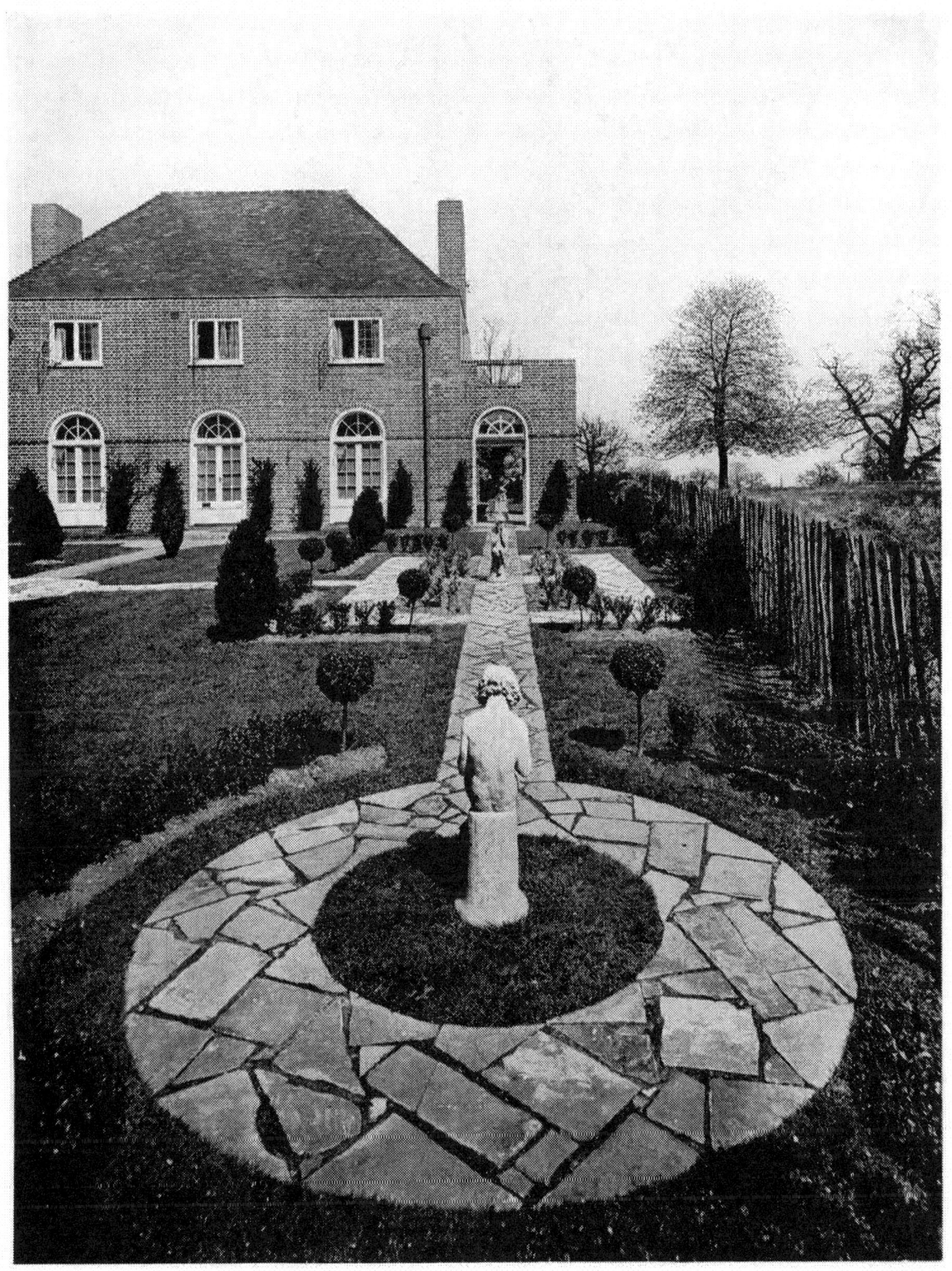

FRONT GARDEN, ADAMS HOUSE, MOOR PARK MAURICE ADAMS

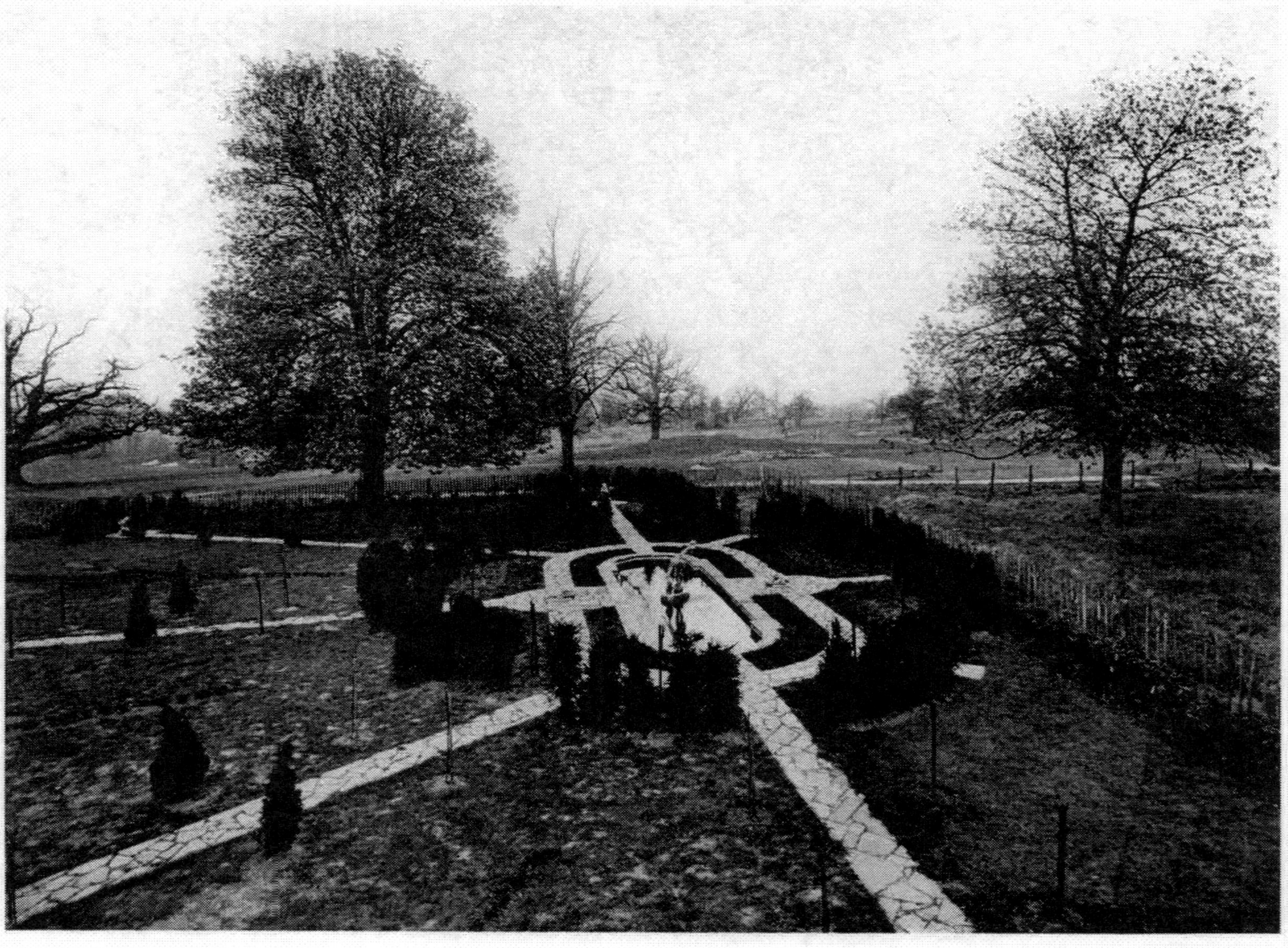

POOL ENCLOSURE, ADAMS HOUSE, MOOR PARK

MAURICE ADAMS

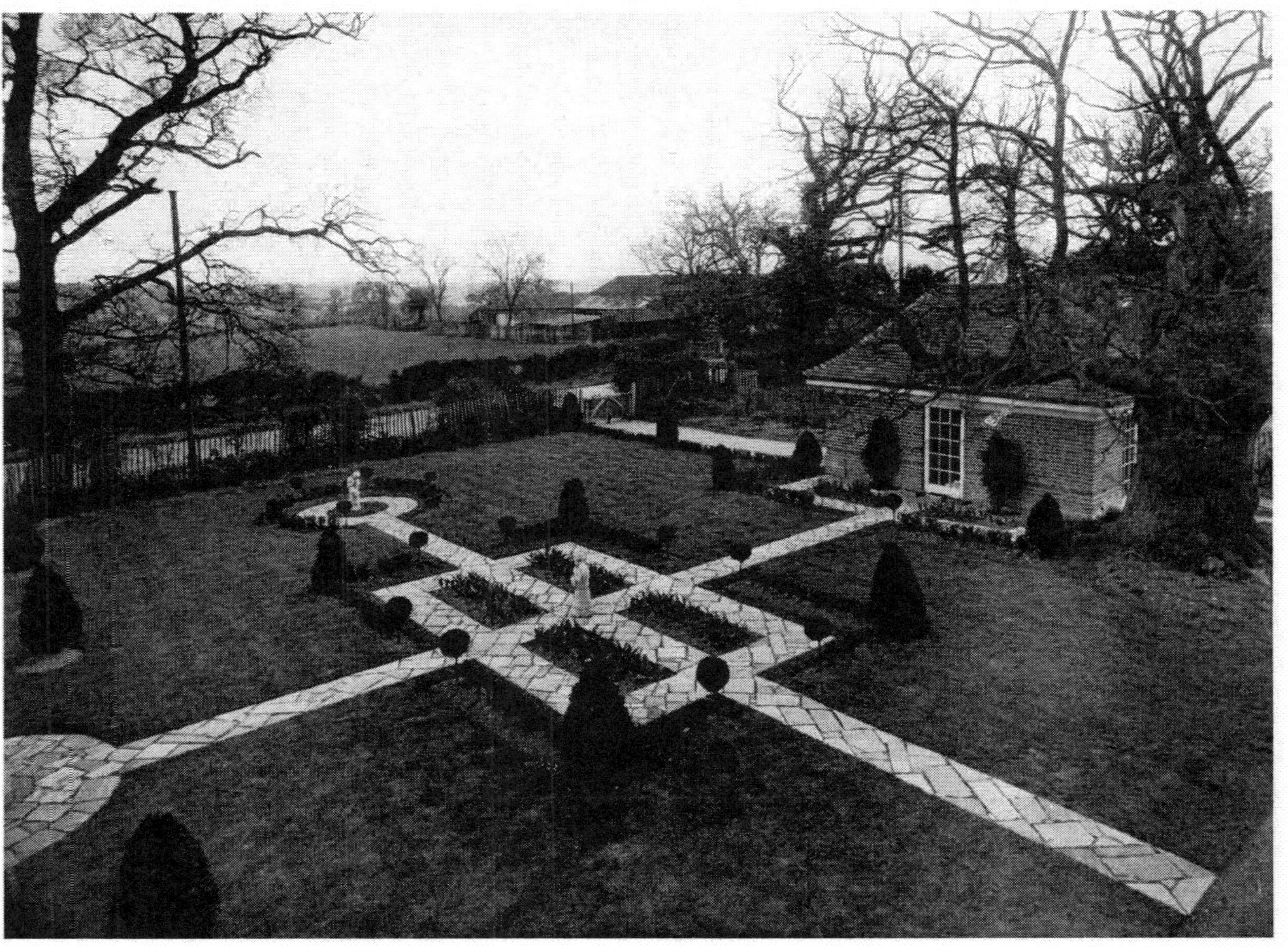

FRONT GARDEN AND GARAGE, ADAMS HOUSE, MOOR PARK

MAURICE ADAMS

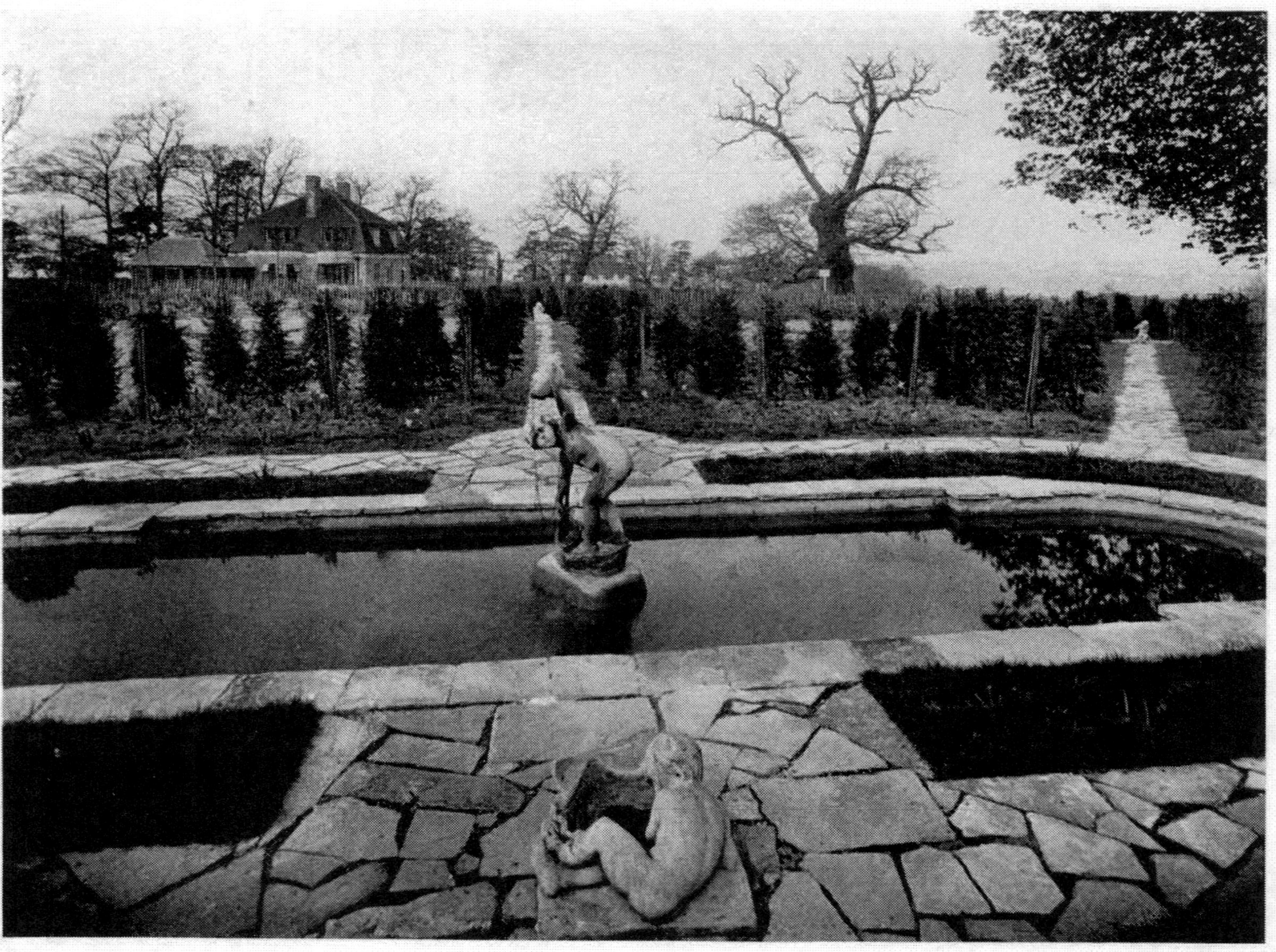

LILY POOL, ADAMS HOUSE, MOOR PARK

MAURICE ADAMS

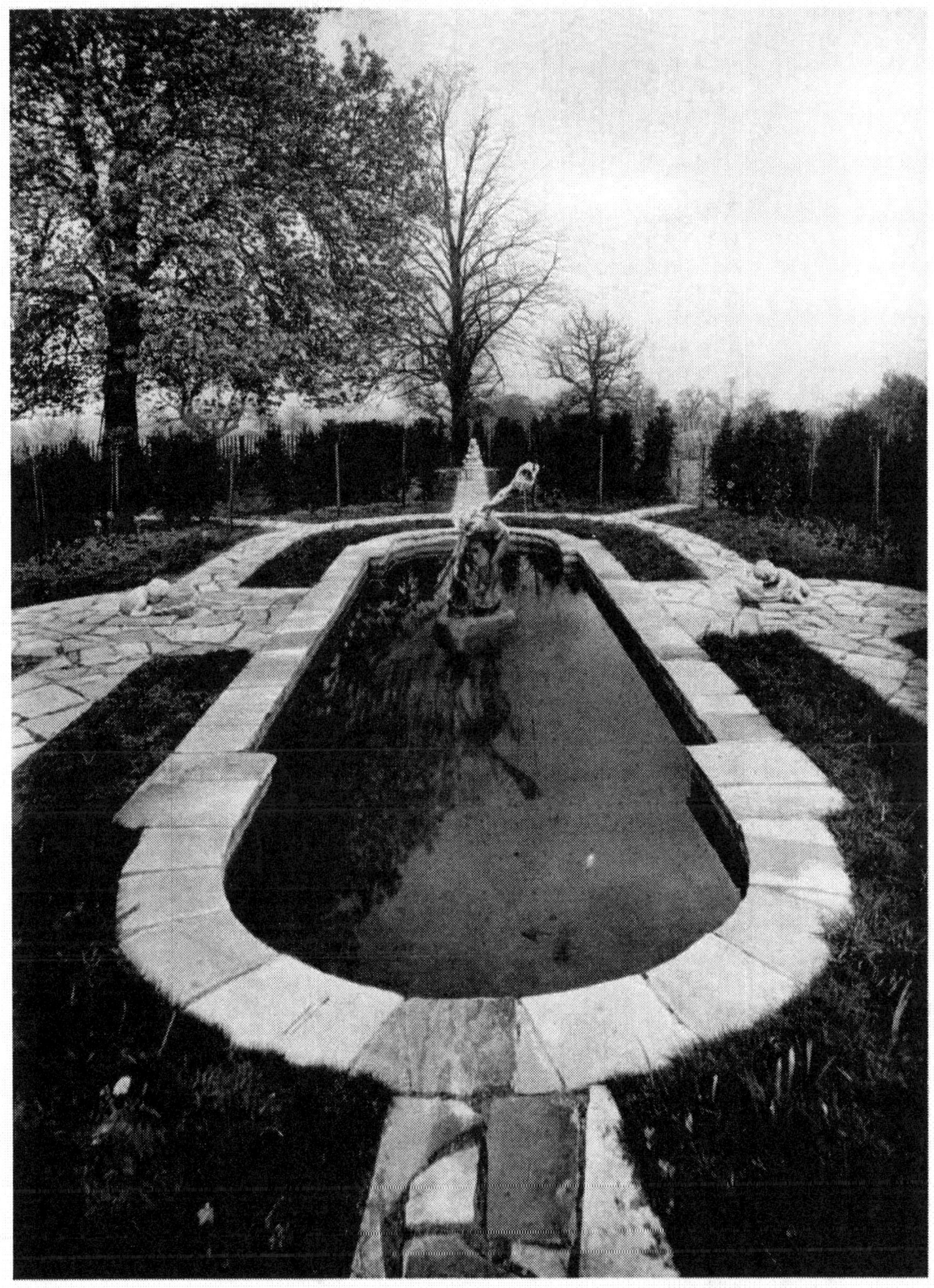

LILY POOL, ADAMS HOUSE, MOOR PARK

MAURICE ADAMS

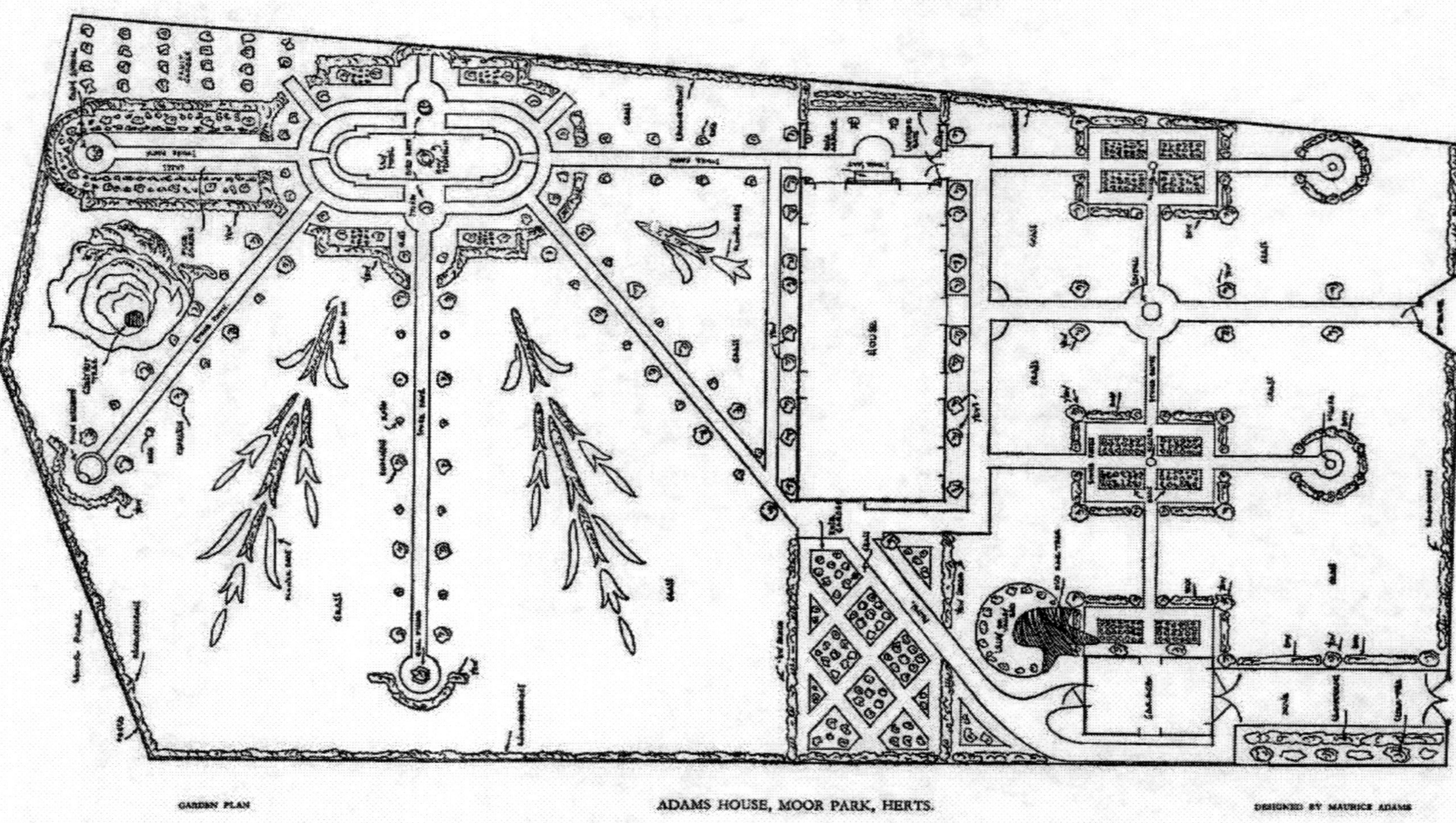


GARDEN PLAN

ADAMS HOUSE, MOOR PARK, HERTS.

DESIGNED BY MAURICE ADAMS

www.ingramcontent.com/pod-product-compliance
Lightning Source LLC
LaVergne TN
LVHW080309110826
845155LV00023B/102

* 9 7 8 1 9 0 5 2 1 7 6 3 2 *